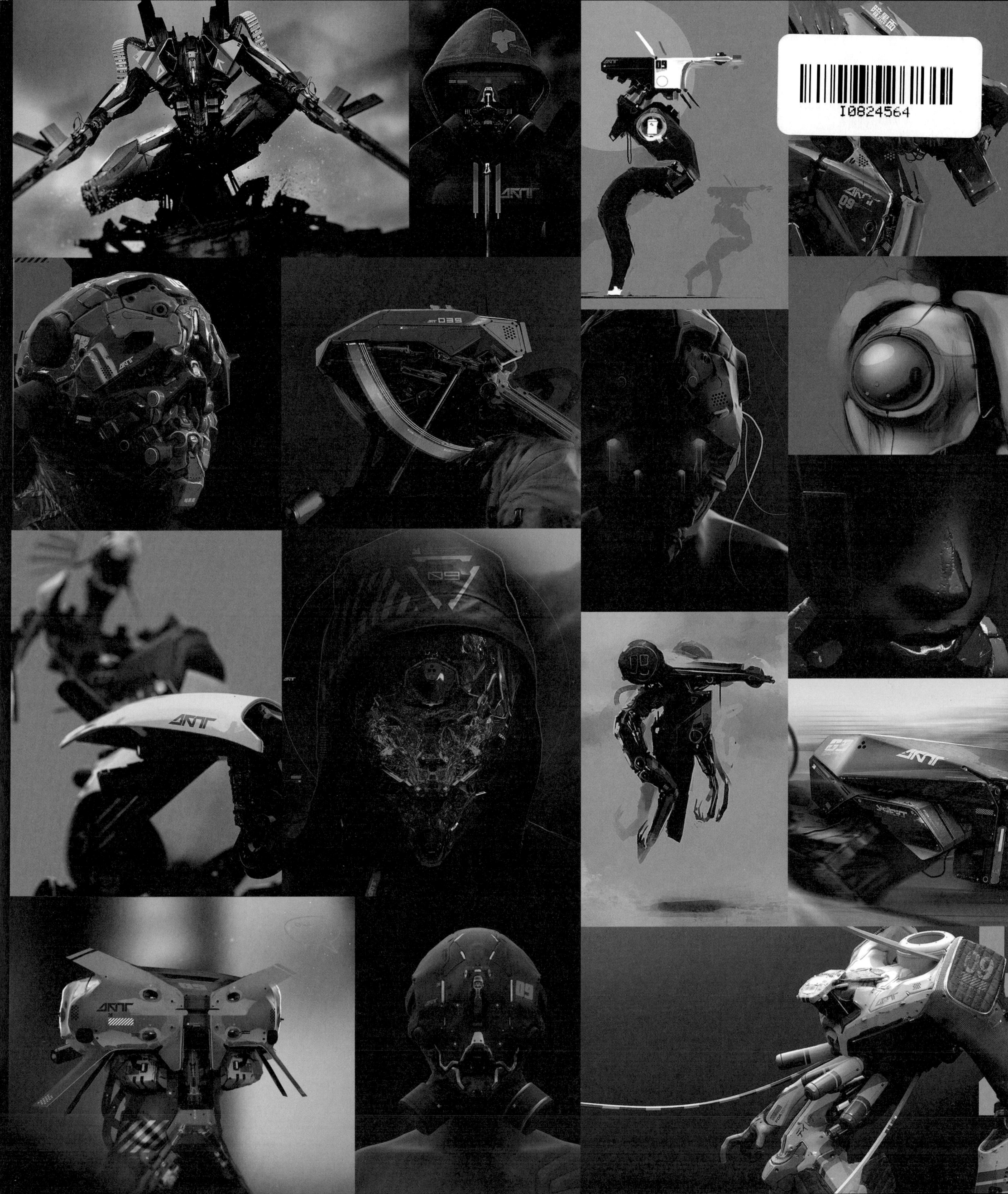
I0824564

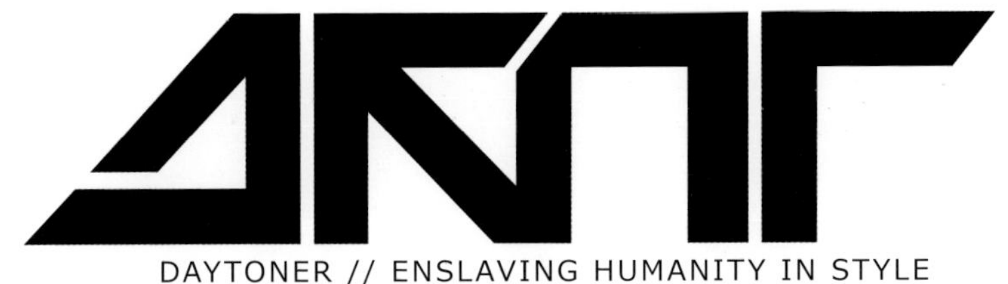
DAYTONER // ENSLAVING HUMANITY IN STYLE

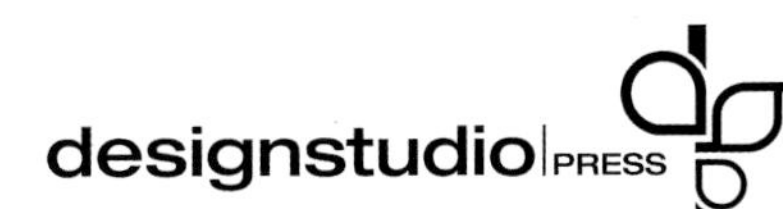
designstudio PRESS

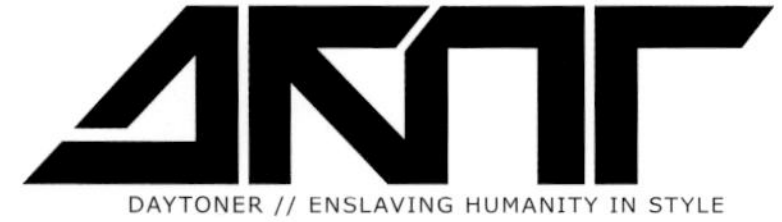

Trade edition ISBN: 978-1-624650-74-1
Library of Congress Control Number: 2023916825

First edition printed in China, 2023

10 9 8 7 6 5 4 3 2 1

Cover Image and Book Design by Daniel Hahn
www.daytoner.net

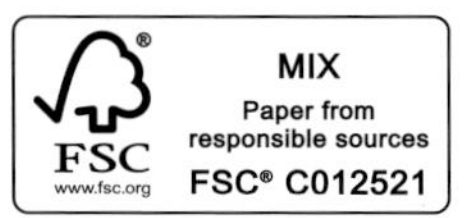

Hello human, welcome to my world!

Enslaving Humanity in Style is a compilation of the concept art I created over the past few years under my alias Daytoner. Robots, mechs, and character designs are my big passion. Daytoner, short DTNR, is my outlet and home for this obsession. In this book I pair my creations with short stories that look back at a possible future. The project started as a small blog in 2012 when I moved to Los Angeles. Today I am creating characters for the game and movie industry.

I grew up in former East Germany. I started obsessive sketching after the Berlin Wall fell, when I was around 15 years old. I did graffiti in my hometown together with friends. I mainly spray-painted characters next to somebody else's letters. Good times! I don't know why, but I was always more attracted to figures, faces, and poses. I love how you can communicate character and attitude through design, without using a single word. After getting hooked on art and creativity I tried to find a profession which would let me draw for a living. I ended up studying product design to keep sketching. I love to create robots or human-machine hybrids, because they combine my attraction to characters and the world of product design perfectly. I can play with the expressions of a person or a face, but there are also enough hard surfaces or mechanical details to design.

Often I get asked what I do this for, what the bigger purpose of all this is. I guess it's passion. There was always an itch to sketch in me. I love to create, and I always need a creative outlet. Daytoner gives me that outlet and the freedom to be able to create whatever I want, without any restrictions. I am my own limitation. No excuses! Last but not least I am now successfully creating character and robot designs for the entertainment industry.

You never know what creating art will lead to—just do it! The sky is the limit! If your dreams are not scaring you, they are not big enough. This book is a journey through the depths of my unhinged creative mind and the world of my robots.

Hope you enjoy!

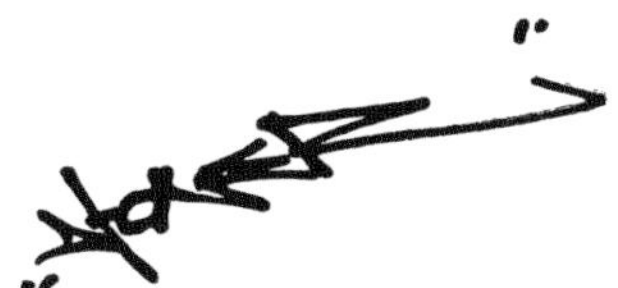

When I started with the idea for this book, I talked to Frank Sauer, a good friend of mine who works at Bundeswehr University Munich, one of the two universities of the German armed forces. His day job as a political scientist focusing on security, technology, and strategic foresight has him pondering the serious and, to be honest, sometimes scary side of our robot future. When I told him about the idea and about the concept of designing aesthetically pleasing and weird robots for this book, we had a few good jokes about how disturbing our robot reality already is or could soon become. We quickly came up with little scenarios while looking at some of my concepts—some were hilarious, some were thought-provoking, some were pretty damn dark. I ended up teaming up with Frank for some of the writing in this book. I myself am not a man of big words, and seeing the result, this strange mix of science-fact and science-fiction, I think having Frank on board was a great idea. We ended up creating glimpses into the backstories for most of my characters and putting forward concepts that loosely fit together into one Daytoner universe. I enjoy seeing all these creations coming together and cross-pollinating each other. Everything in this book is broad brush strokes, because that's how I like it, both for the images as well as for the snippets of text. Who knows what it all leads to?

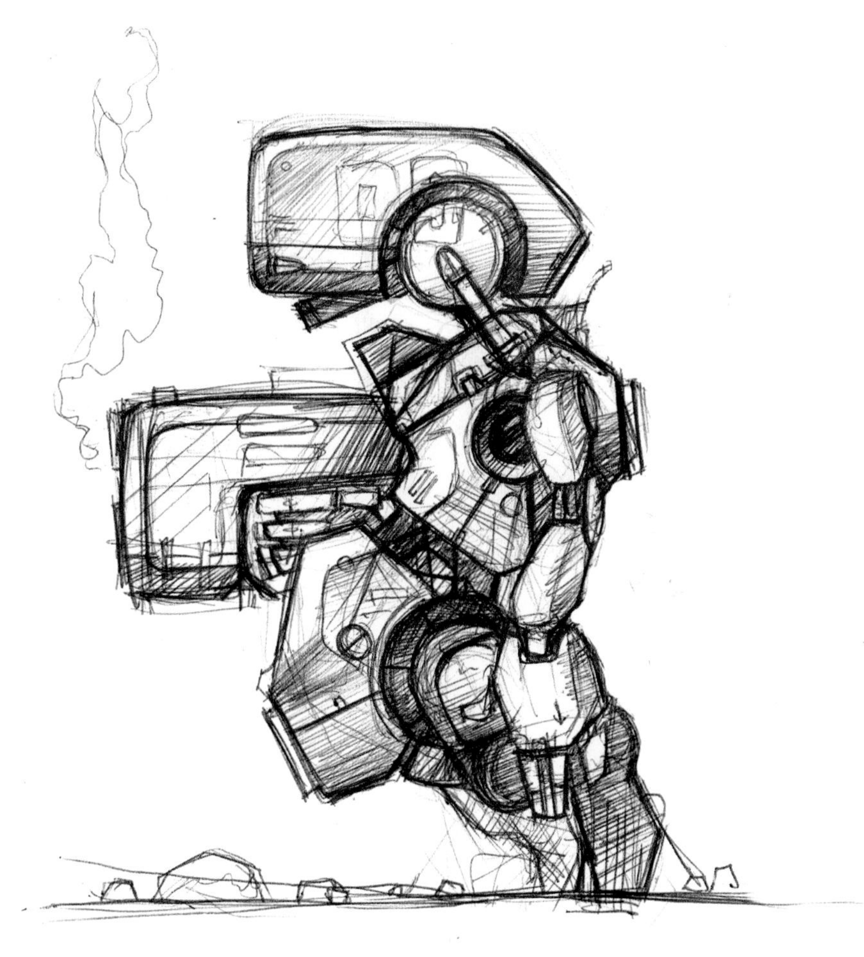

1956
Artificial Intelligence is coined as a term and AI emerges as a field of research.

1969
Birth of the Original Internet

1989
Berlin Wall falls and Cold War era ends.

1993
Doom is released.

2005
SilicInt is founded.

2012
Pentagon releases Directive 3000.09 on autonomy in weapons systems.

2024
Autonomous weapons ("killer robots") prohibition treaty enters into force.

2028
DTNR Robotics is founded.

2029
Total jet stream collapse triggers the first mega-heatwave.

2032
Church of Singularity is founded.

1961
Unimate, the first industrial robot, starts work at an assembly line.

1986
F.A.A.R. Defense Systems is founded.

1992
Boston Dynamics is founded.

2007
Nakatomi Industries is founded.

2019
First case of a SARS-CoV-2 infection in a human being.

2022
AI art and the ascent of deep learning transformer models.

2027
Version 1.0 of *Vertical Skies* is released.

2030
Ren, the first robot to pass the uncanny valley test, is unveiled.

2031
Quantum mind barrier is discovered.

2034
Lv5 autonomous driving systems are market ready.

2035
Human augmentation technology is commercially available.

2037
Iran's first nuclear test triggers the Iran war.

2038
China, Russia, and most NATO militaries start rolling out exoskeleton technology.

2041
Neuralace technology is introduced and immediately put under strict regulation.

2042
First case of a AH5N3 infection in a human being.

2044
Posthuman Movement calls for the Global Machine Revolution.

2049
Worldwide crackdown on the Urban Ninja Movement and collapse of Berlin.

2052
The Big AI Reset

2053
First extinction event and Shamanism renaissance.

2070
First tribal wasteland repopulation efforts herald the era of bioeconomics.

nin3

MACHINE SHAMANISM

URBAN POSTHUMAN MOVEMENT

FOA

OFFENSE/INCIDENT REPORT

INSTRUCTIONS ARE PRINTED SEPARATELY. IF ADDITIONAL SPACE IS NEEDED, USE REVERSE OF FORM. IDENTIFY ITEMS.

1. TYPE: [X] a. ORIGINAL [ ] b. CONTINUATION [ ] c. SUPPLEMENT OR FOLLOWUP

2. CODE NO.: #14 | 2a. SORT | 3. TYPE OF OFFENSE OR INCIDENT: Disorderly conduct, prostitution, resisting arrest | 4. CASE CONTROL NUMBER: 20032-098

5. BUILDING NUMBER | 6. ADDRESS: 39th & Main

7. NAME OF AGENCY/BUREAU | 8. AGENCY/BUREAU CODE | 9. SPECIFIC LOCATION: Back alley, O'Reillys Bar | 10. LOCATION CODE

11a. DATE OF OFFENSE/INCIDENT: 05/16/2039 | 11a. TIME OF OFFENSE/INCIDENT: 1110pm | 12. DAY | 13a. DATE REPORTED | 13b. TIME REPORTED: 1115pm | 14. DAY

15. JURISDICTION (X): [X] EXCLUSIVE [ ] CONCURRENT [ ] PARTIAL [ ] PROPRIETARY | 16. NO. OF DEMONSTRATORS | 17. NO. EVACUATED | a. TIME START: 1120pm | b. TIME END: 1135pm

18. PERSONS INVOLVED

ID CODE (a)	NAME AND ADDRESS (b)	AGE (c)	SEX (d)	RACE (e)	INJURY CODE (f)	TELEPHONE (g)
	Last Name, First, Middle Initial: Rey, Yana D.	29	F			HOME
	Number, Street, Apt. No., City and State: n/a					BUSINESS
	Last Name, First, Middle Initial: ███					HOME
	Number, Street, Apt. No., City and State: ███					BUSINESS

19. VEHICLE

a. STATUS: STOLEN | SUSPECT | GOV'T | PERSONAL | VANDALIZED | RECOVERED — b. YEAR | c. MAKE | d. MODEL | e. COLOR *(Top/Bottom)* | f. IDENTIFYING CHARACTERISTICS

g. REGISTRATION ▶ YEAR | STATE | TAG NO. | h. VIN | I. VALUE

20. ITEMS TAKEN

a. NAME OF ITEM | b. QUANTITY | c. OWNERSHIP [ ] GOV'T [ ] PERSONAL | d. BRAND NAME

e. SERIAL NO. | f. COLOR | g. MODEL

h. VALUE | i. UNUSUAL OR UNIQUE FEATURES

j. PROPERTY WAS [ ] SECURRED [ ] UNSECURED | k. STATUS OF PROPERTY [ ] RECOVERED [ ] MISSING [ ] PARTIAL RECOVERY | VALUE RECOVERED

l. NAME OF ITEM | m. QUANTITY | n. OWNERSHIP [ ] GOV'T [ ] PERSONAL | o. BRAND NAME

p. SERIAL NO. | q. COLOR | r. MODEL

s. VALUE | t. UNUSUAL OR UNIQUE FEATURES

u. PROPERTY WAS [ ] SECURRED [ ] UNSECURED | v. STATUS OF PROPERTY [ ] RECOVERED [ ] MISSING [ ] PARTIAL RECOVERY | VALUE RECOVERED

21. NARRATIVE *(If additional space is needed, use blank sheet and attach.)*

Police were called after complaints by residents about disorderly conduct at 39th and Main Street. I was in the immediate vicinity and responded to that call.

After arriving on scene I saw Ms. Rey and ███ case no. 20032-099) engaged in sexual conduct behind a row of dumpsters in the back alley of O'Reillys on 39th Street. I called on Ms. Rey and ███ to freeze, shining my torch light on them. ███ fled the scene. Ms. Rey, augmented with a handle bar-modified Suckbot 9000 cranial replacement, was put under arrest for frivolous behavior in a public space, disorderly conduct, prostitution, and insulting a police officer.

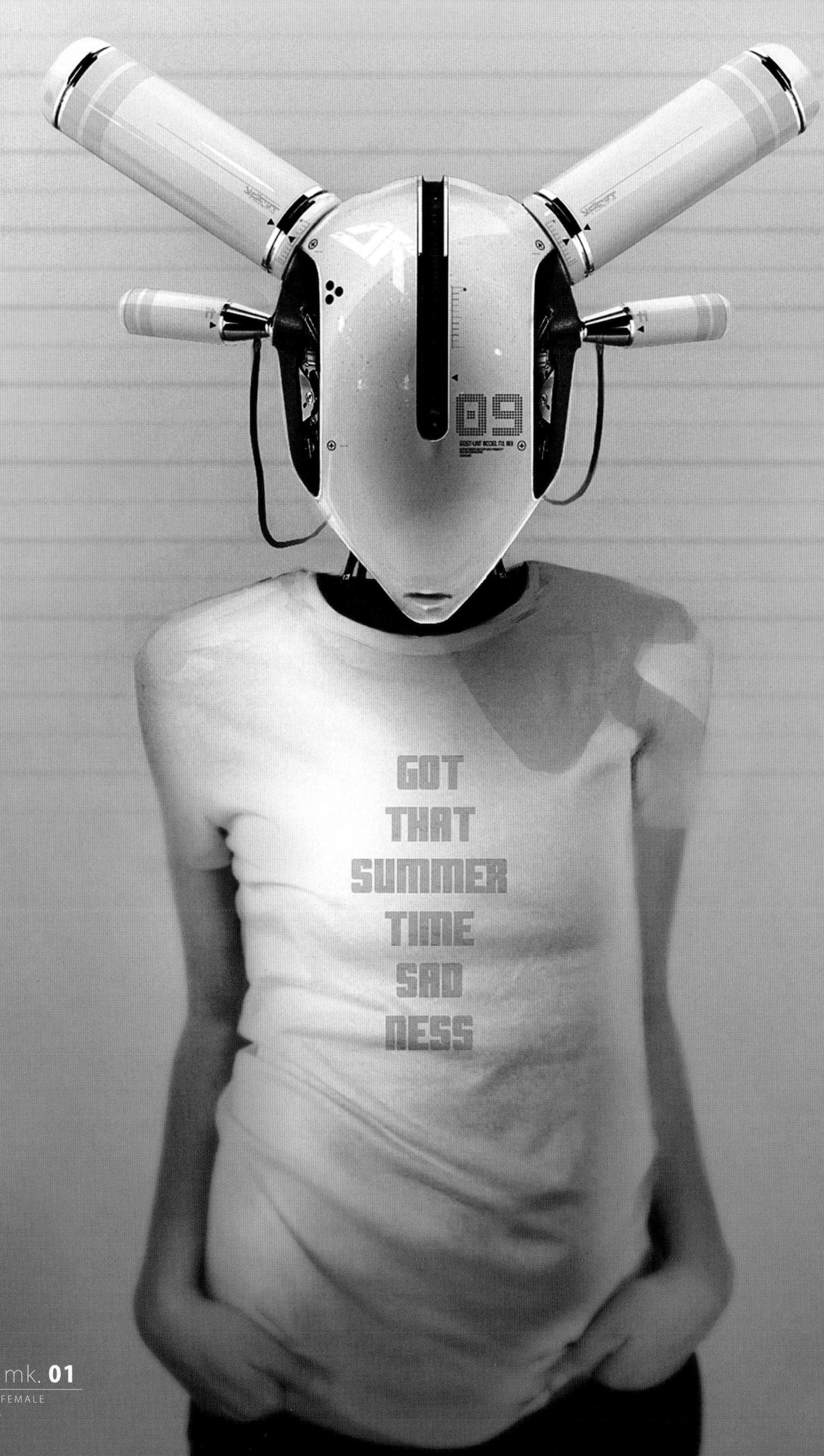

KINKY 09 // mk. **01**

TYPE: _ AUGMENTED FEMALE
LOCATION: _ POST LA

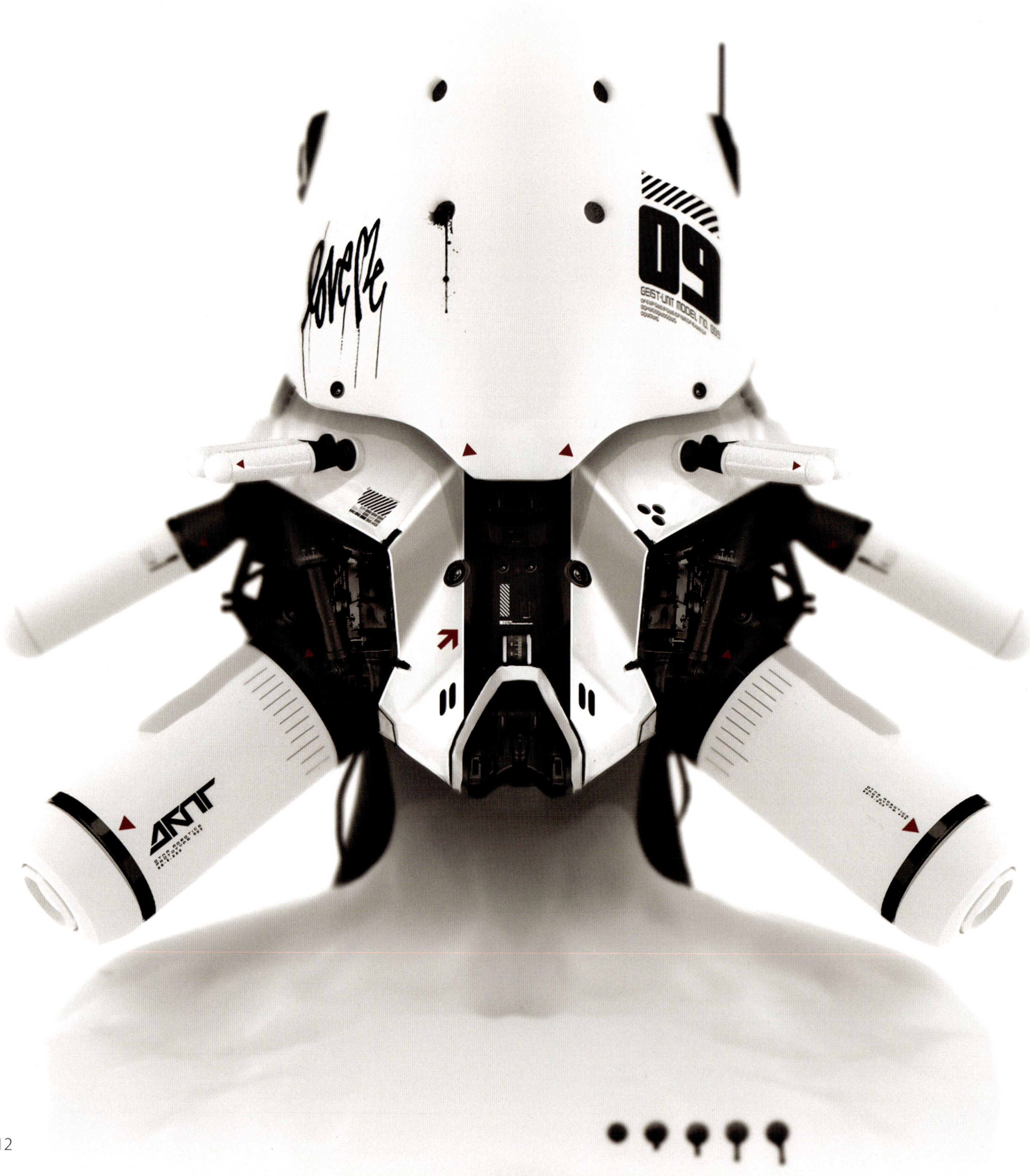
09
GEIST-UNIT MODEL NO. 009

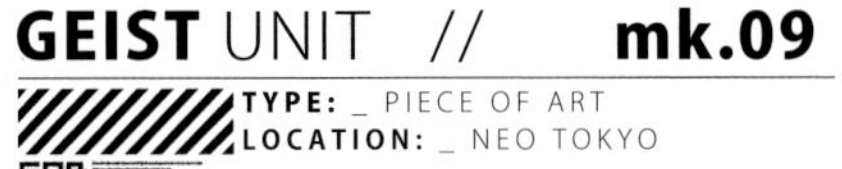

In the mid-2030s, human augmentation became commercially available and affordable. GEIST UNIT 09 was one of the first radical augmentation attempts of a human individual trying to become a living, breathing piece of art. The work showed the artist's roots in the graffiti scene, making references to classic anime and manga shapes in the design of the 3D-printed cranial replacement. People never understood the overly heavy use of cylindrical shapes in the design and the obsession with black-and-white graphics. His famous statement, "Tattoos are for pussies!" put GEIST UNIT 09 on the title pages of all big fashion magazines. Body culture had reached a new level.

Dear Elu,

Thanks again for introducing me to Sev. Did he recommend that new Dev Lak book to you too?

I read it last night. His sources are salvaged bits and pieces of the original internet! He claims that people warned about AI and skill degradation as early as the 2000s! And apparently it wasn't SilicInt that did us in; we just collectively sleepwalked into this!? (Now, where have we heard that before? Ha ha!) Obviously no one foresaw that the AIs would turn everything off themselves. But people knew that we would not know how anything works anymore as soon as we hand over our lives.

Anyway, mind-blowing stuff—I'll bring the book on Saturday. See you then. Say hi to Hel and the kids for me.

Stay safe,
Ish

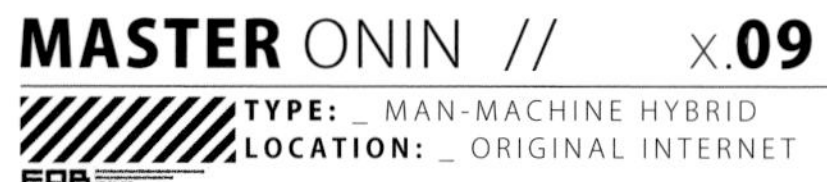

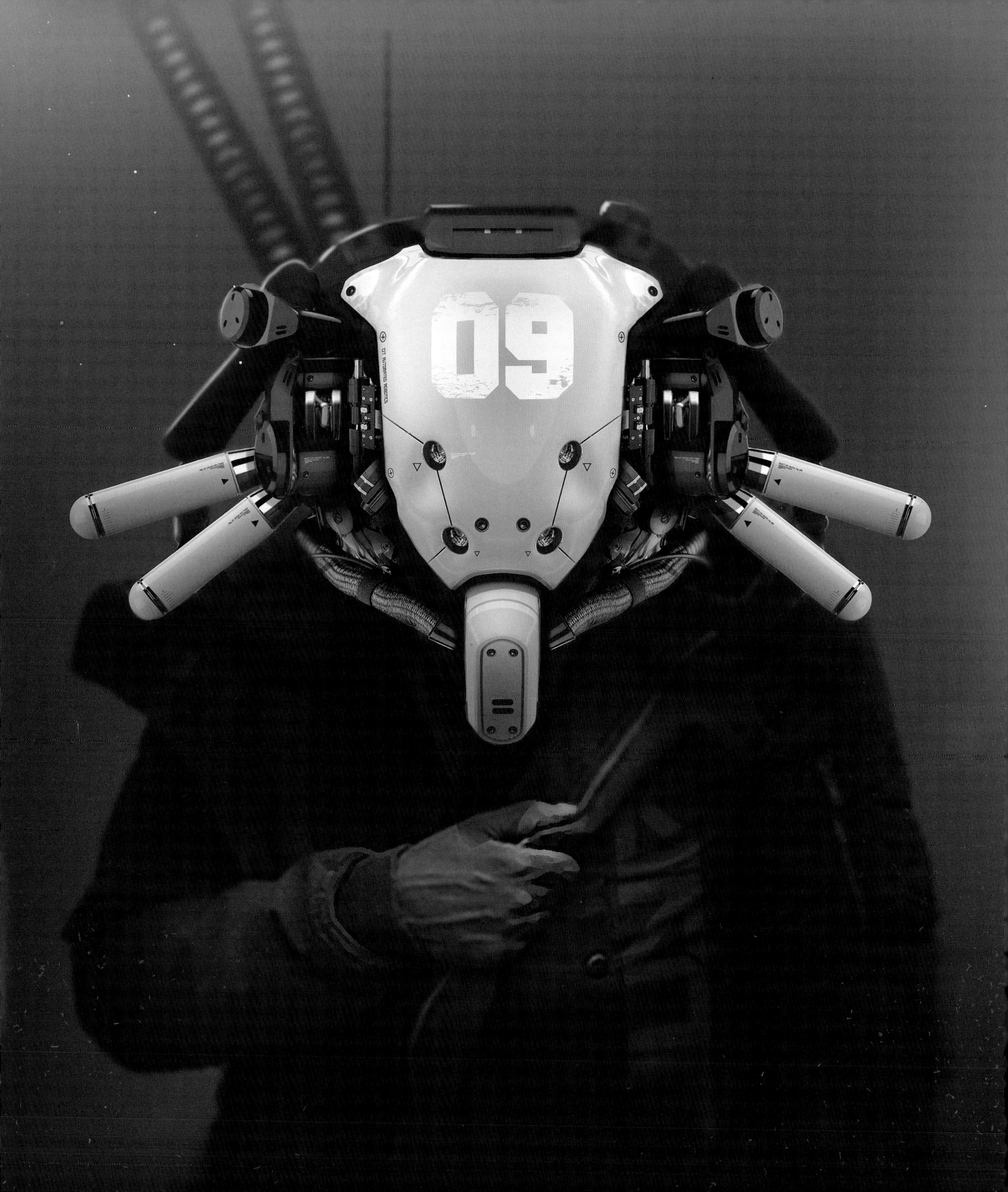
09
CIT AUTOMATED ROBOTICS

Hey Franksen,

Did you see the new collection of the DTNR tech-wear? Their new jacket is made of trillions of nanobots. Can you believe they had a full augment for the photo shoot? I thought those guys are just an urban myth, but a friend of mine, who works at DTNR, said that dude was actually there. He calls himself "Bomber 09." Crazy shit! c u tomorrow :)

Best,
D

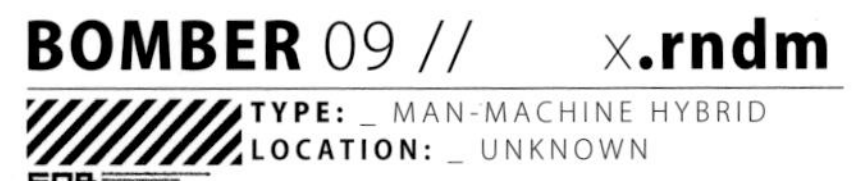

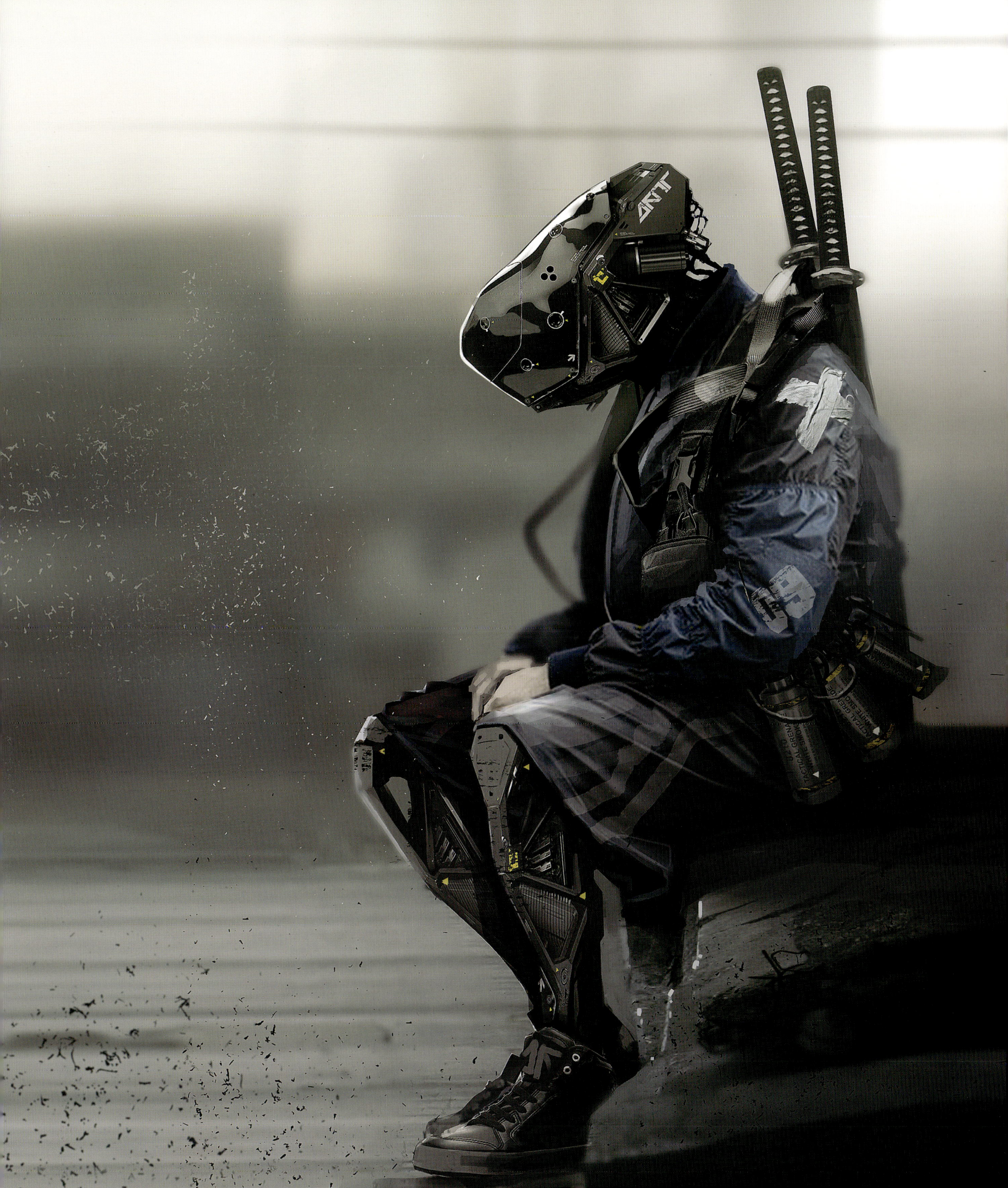

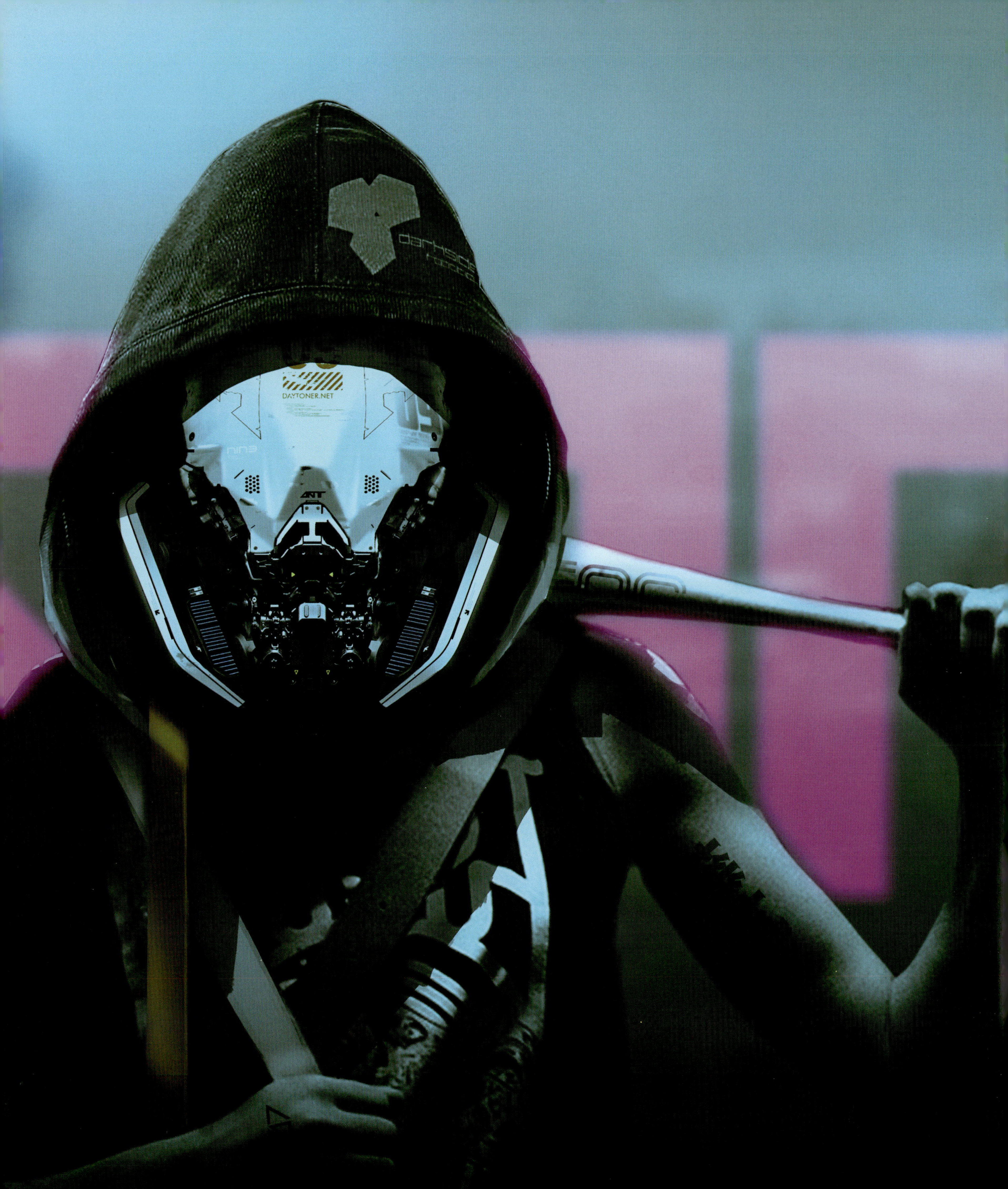
DAYTONER.NET

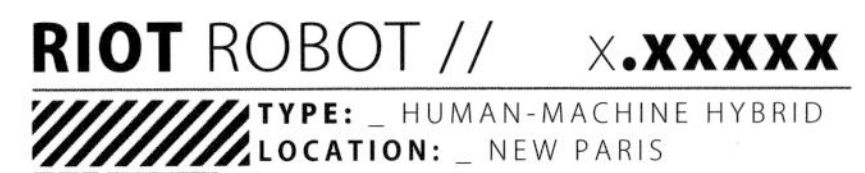

We were unheard. Today we'll rise!
Refuse! Refuse! Reboot!

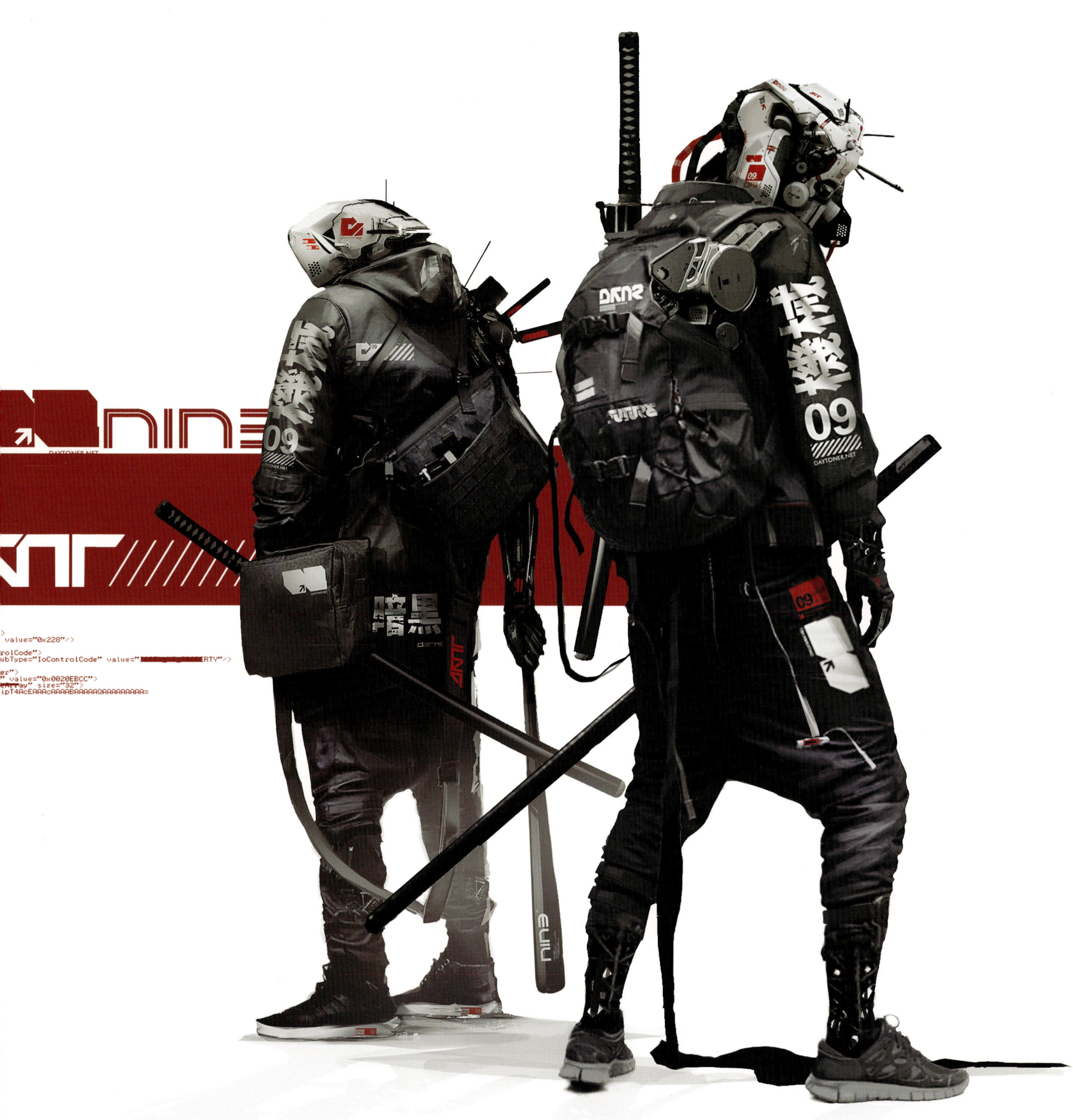
nine
DAYTONER.NET
09
暗黒
DAYTONER.NET
09

O.N.G. & B4LLR // V.09

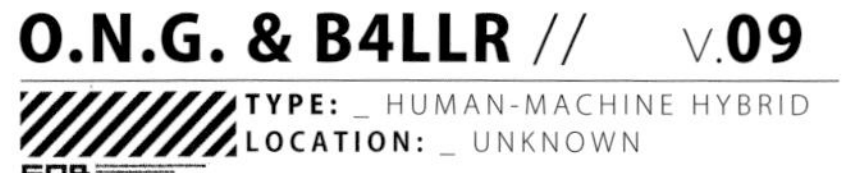

TYPE: _ HUMAN-MACHINE HYBRID
LOCATION: _ UNKNOWN

Urban ninjas paved the way for the Posthumanism Movement of the late 2030 and 2040s. Ninjas and posthumans were kindred spirits in style and beliefs, but the Posthumanism Movement was characterized by much higher levels of augmentation. O.N.G. was one of the forerunners of this style, soon to be copied by many.

BANGR09 was one of the most sketchy and reckless urban ninja gangsters. He was known for his katana-grip club, which later became an icon for his dirty and always straightforward fighting style. No hidden agenda: what you saw was what you got!

BANGR09 // xy.**1978**

TYPE: _ MAN-MACHINE HYBRID
LOCATION: _ POST L.A.

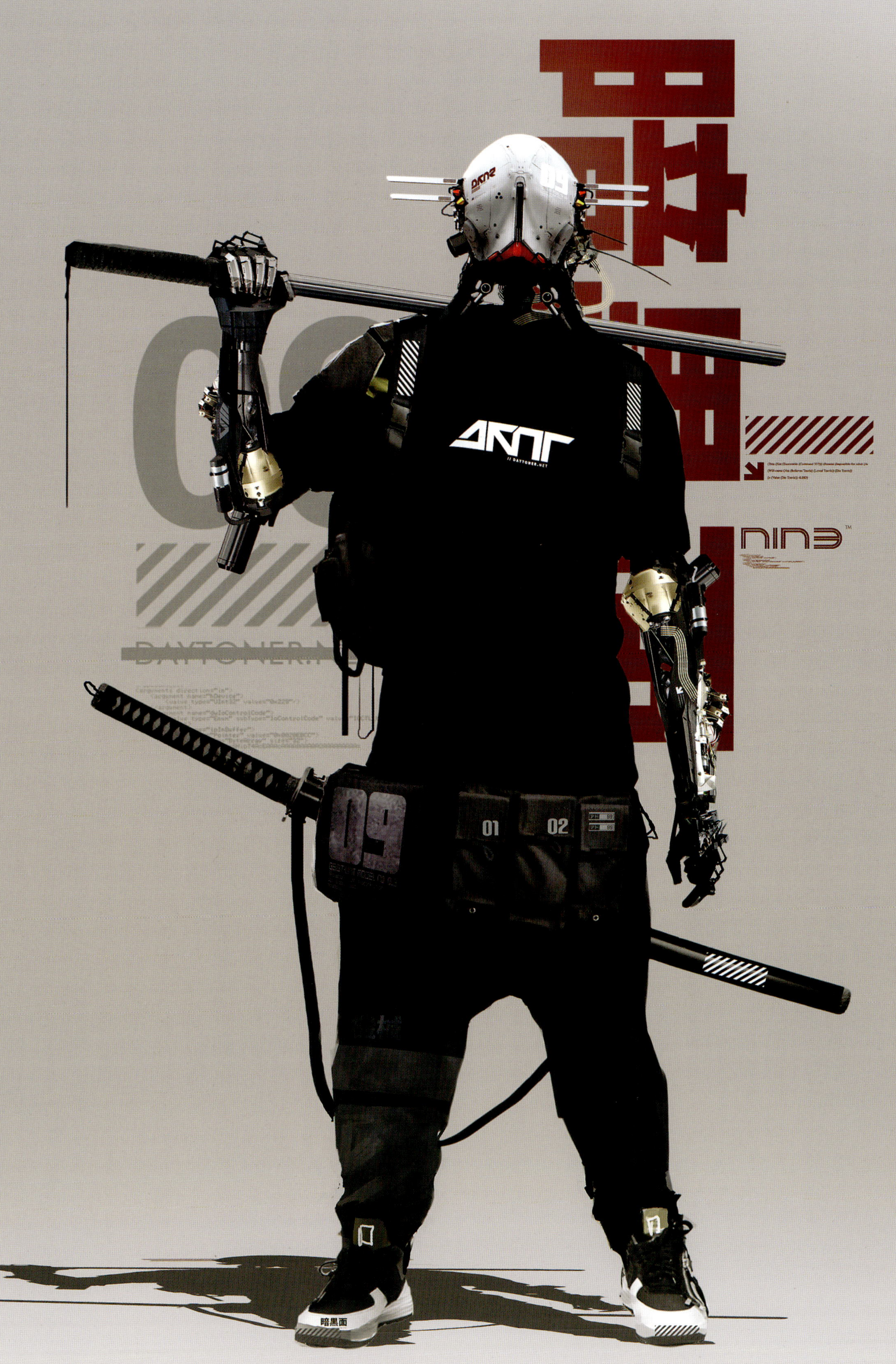
ARNT
// DAYTONER.NET
nin3™
DAYTONER.N
01
02
暗黒面

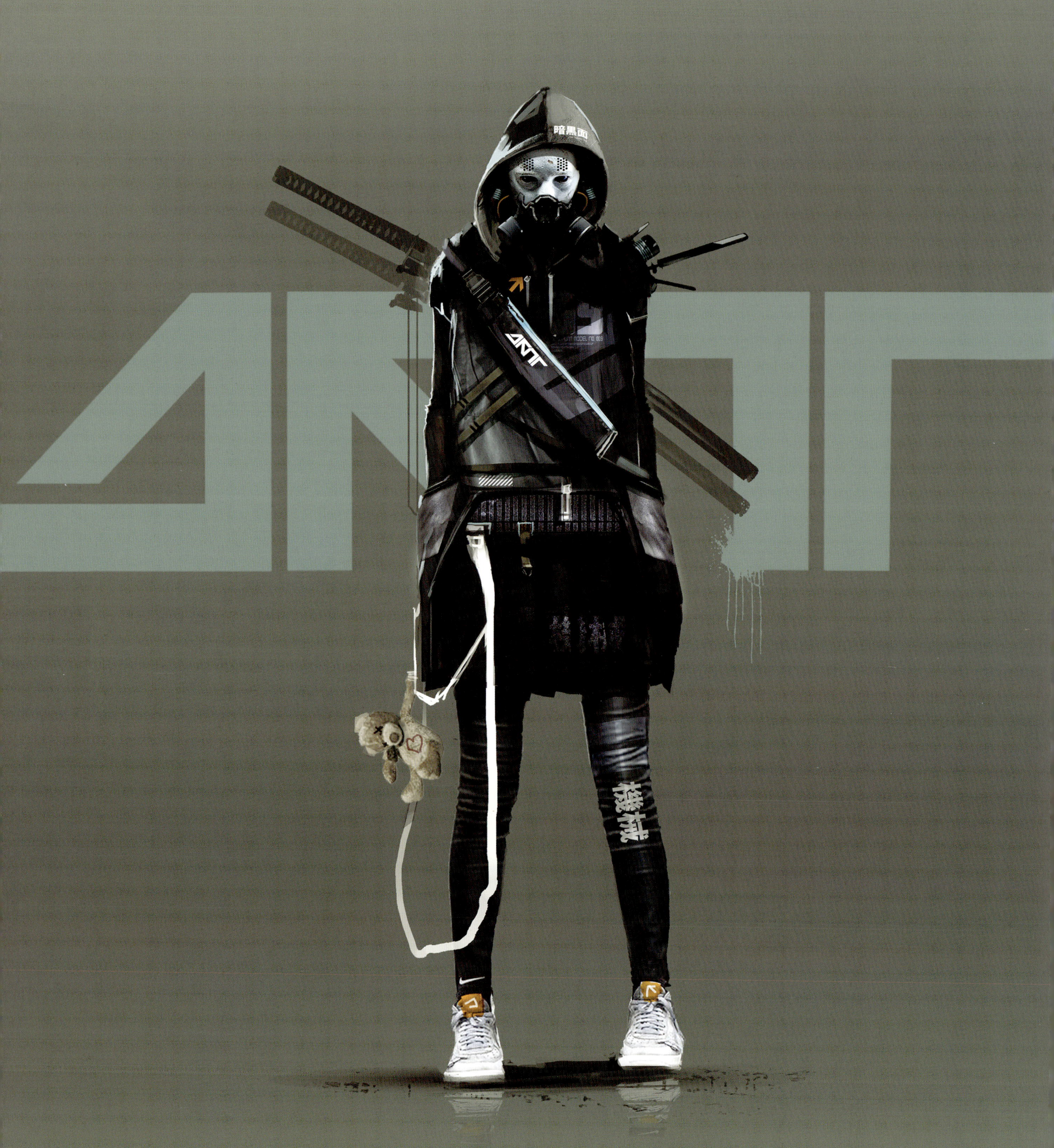
暗黒面
機械

Maximum Level of Turbofeminist Badassery

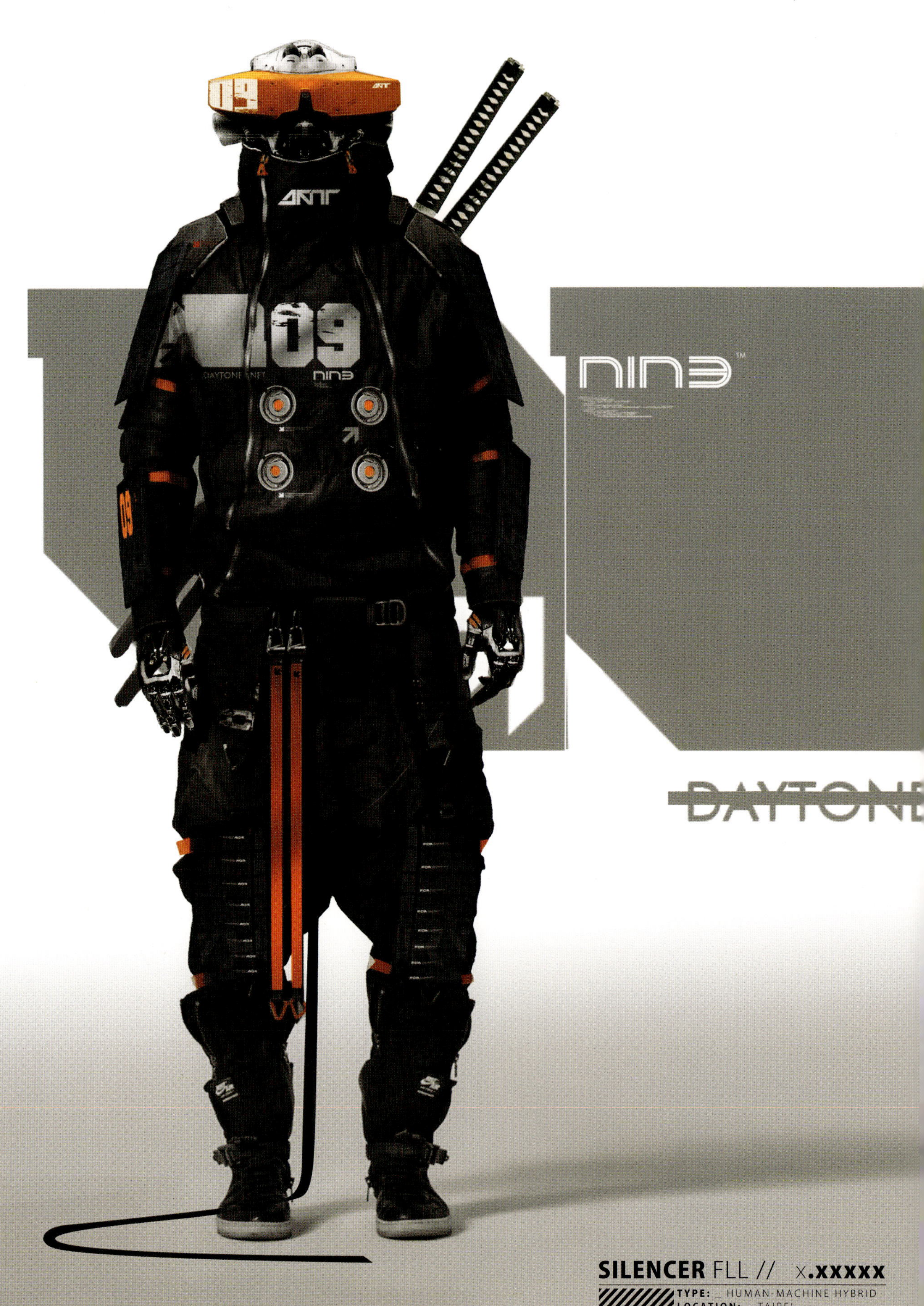
09
DAYTONE
SILENCER FLL // X.XXXXX
TYPE: _ HUMAN-MACHINE HYBRID
LOCATION: _ TAIPEI

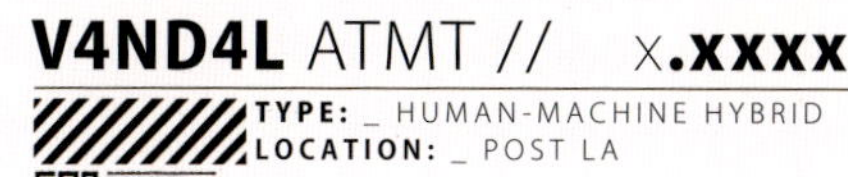

09 //

DRH

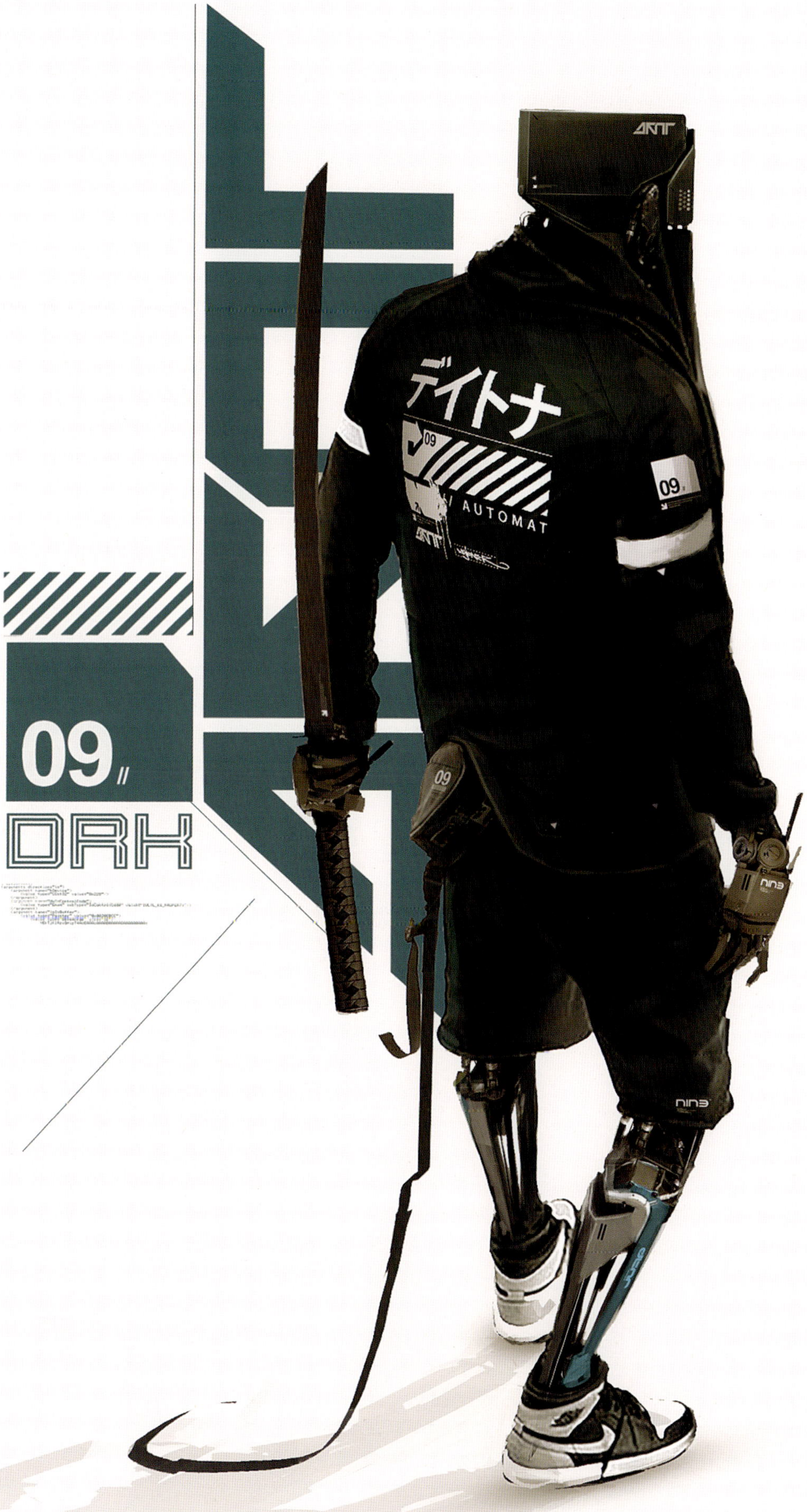

NYN JAAH // V.**333**

TYPE: _ HUMAN-MACHINE HYBRID
LOCATION: _ POST BANGKOK

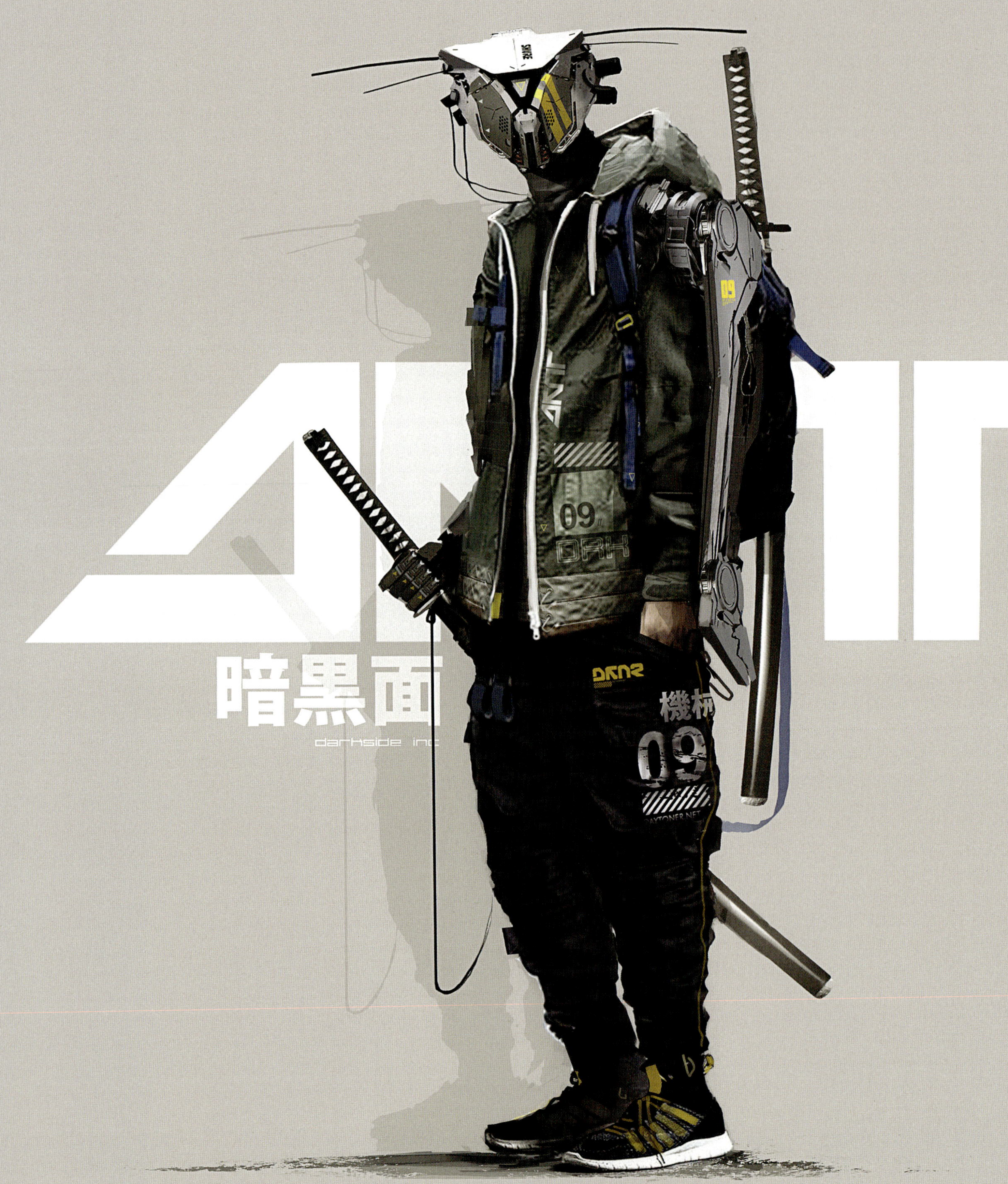

R34CH3R MK1 // x.**xxxx**

TYPE: _ HUMAN-MACHINE HYBRID
LOCATION: _ MOSCOW

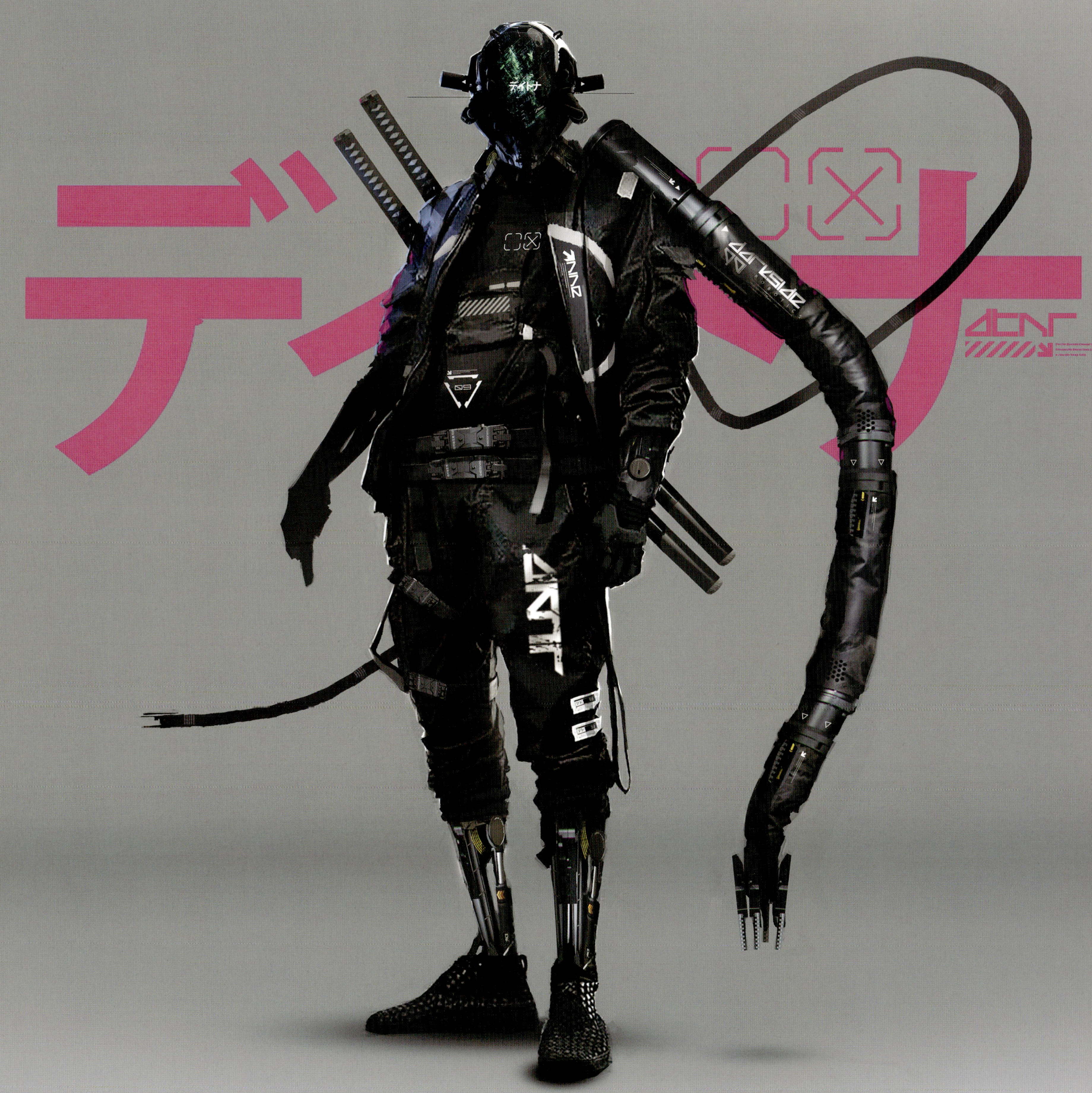

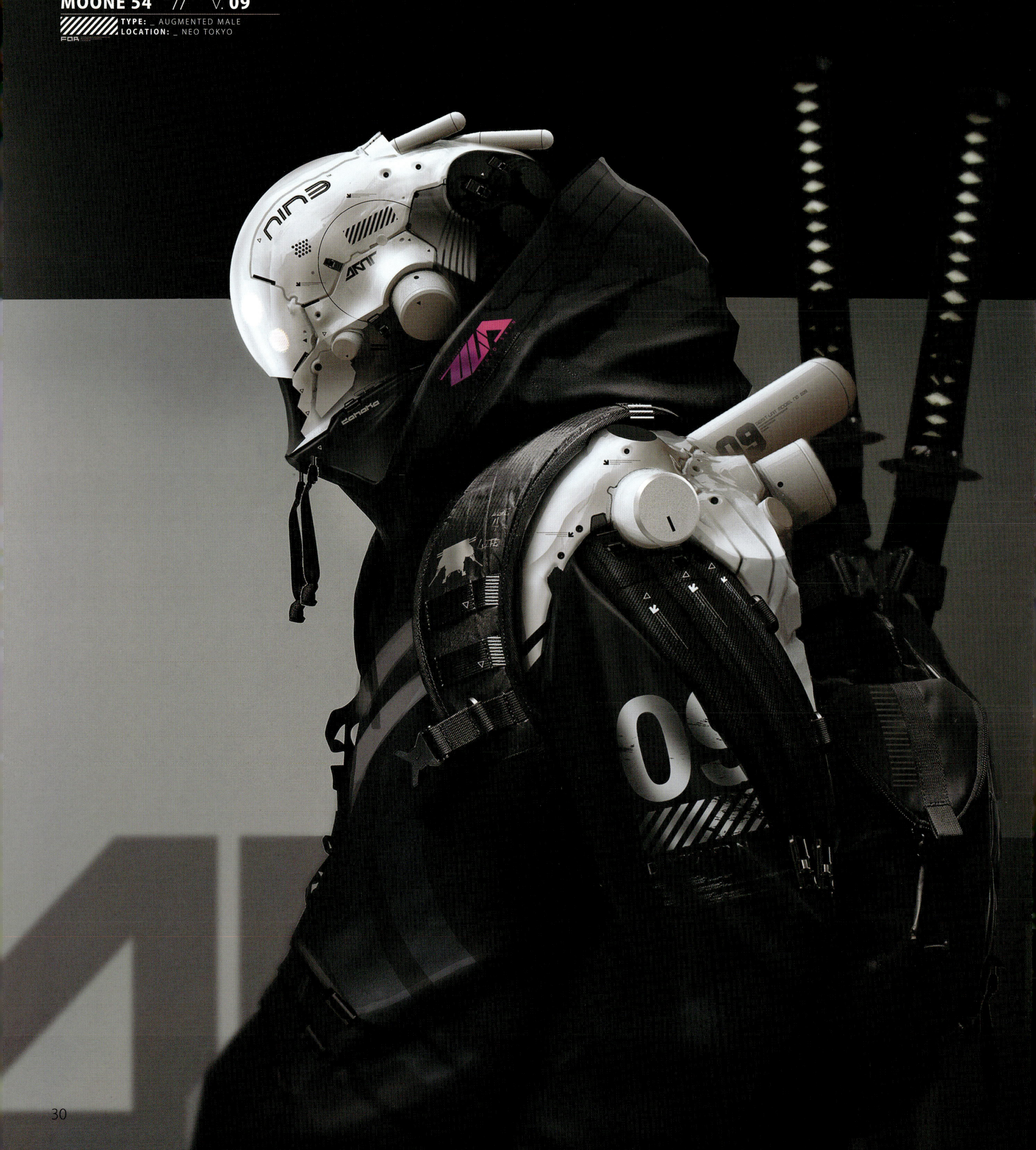

MOONE 54 // V. 09

TYPE: _ AUGMENTED MALE
LOCATION: _ NEO TOKYO

SL1CK R1CK // mk. **01**

TYPE: _ AUGMENTED MALE
LOCATION: _ POST LA

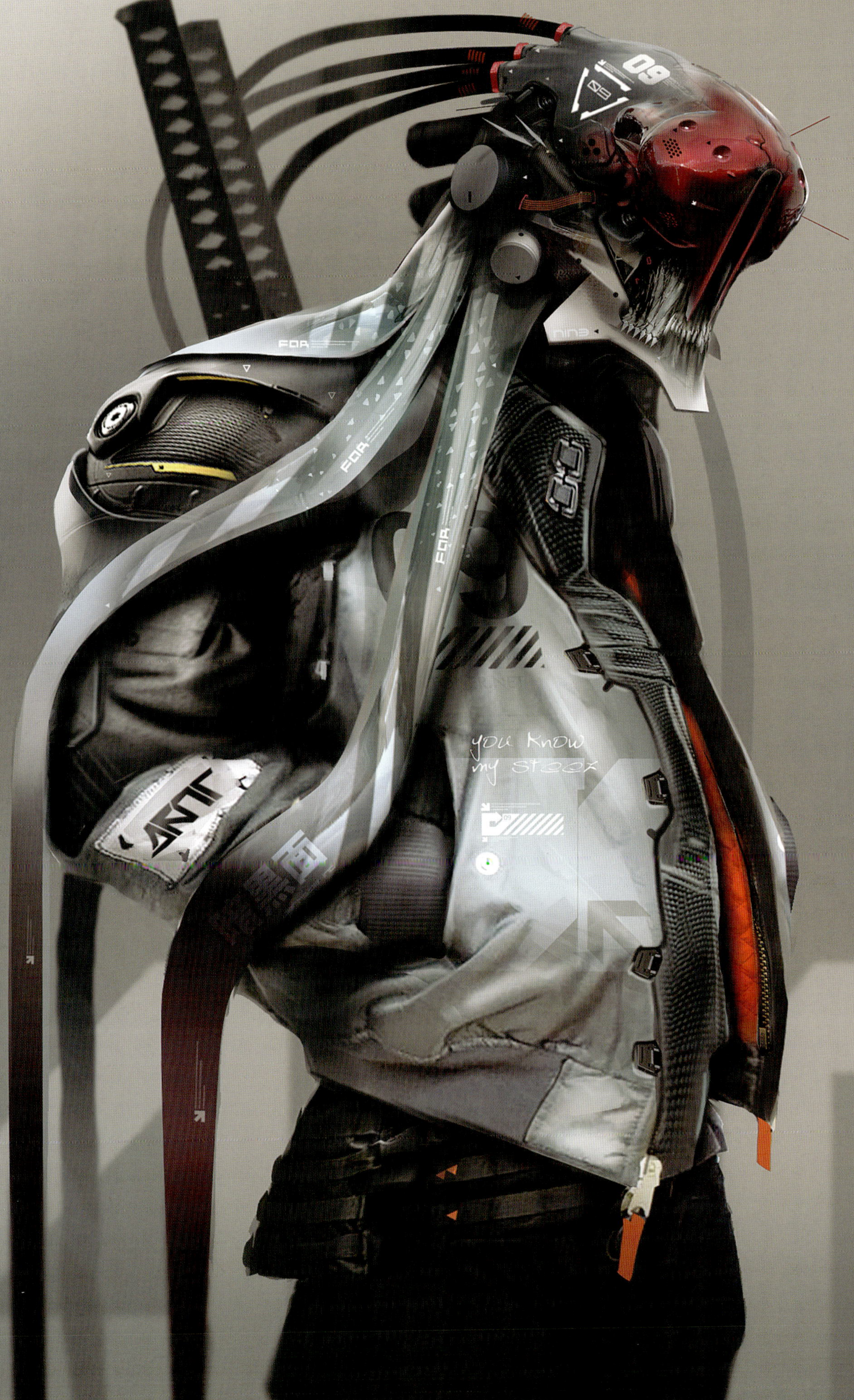

MASTER KORYU // #YZ

TYPE: _ HUMAN-MACHINE HYBRID
LOCATION: _ NEO TOKYO

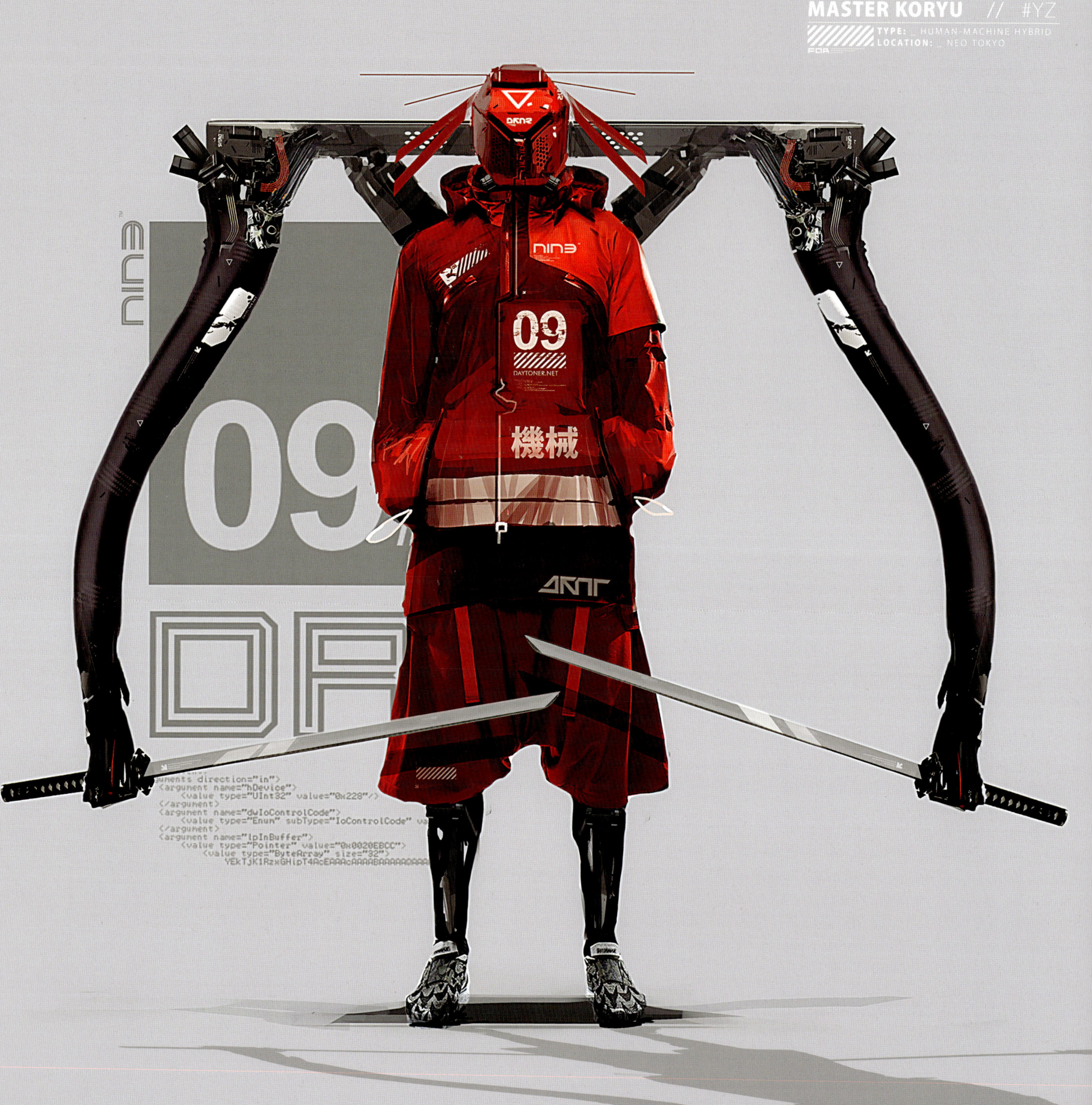

Master Koryu was the fastest in any quick-draw competition, which earned him the nickname "Devil Slicer." His shabu-shabu was legendary too.

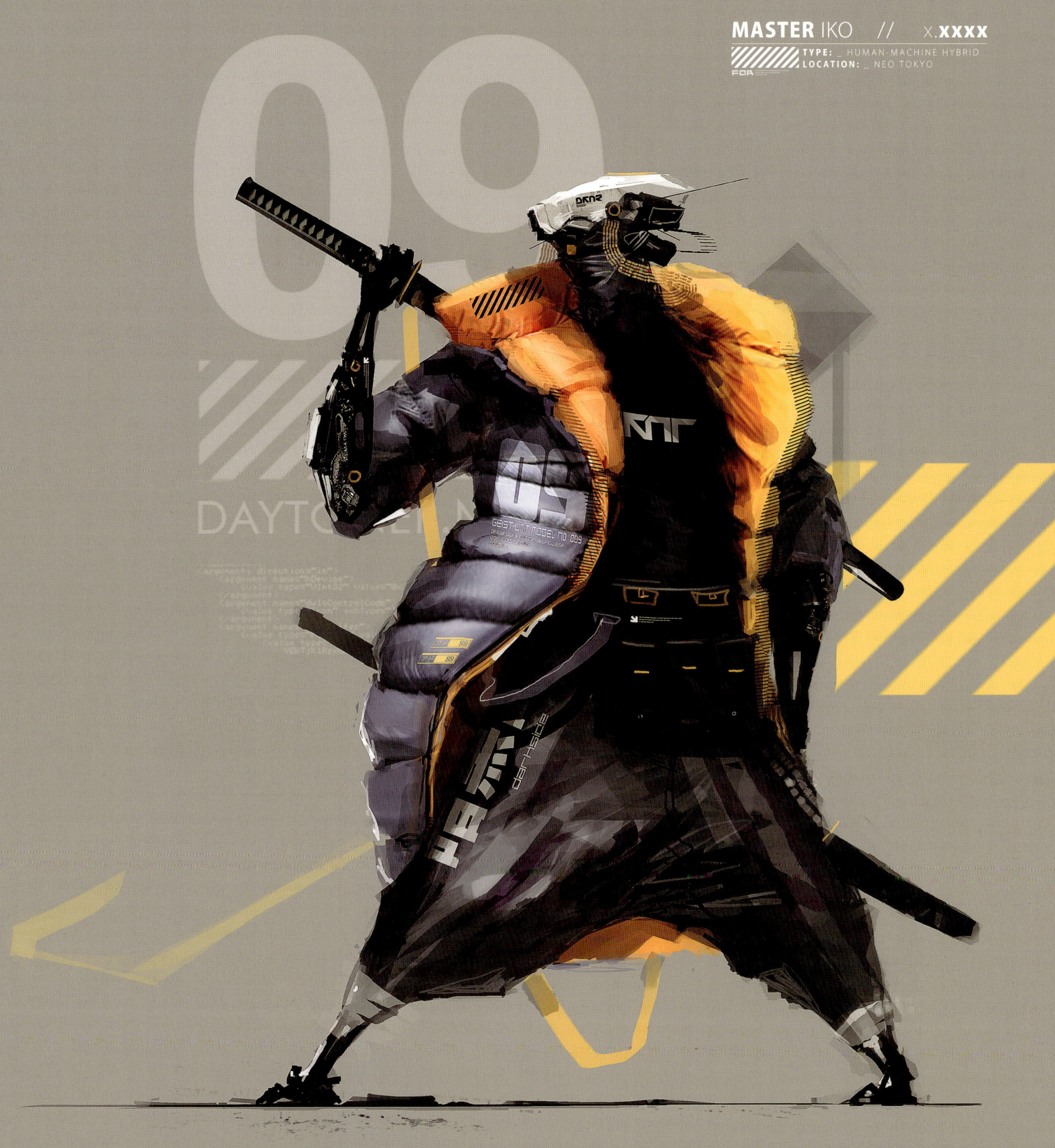

Master I.KO was known for his preference for huge, inside-out puffer coats, drop-crotch pants, double katanas, and fancy footwork. His sloppy adaptation of classic Niten Ichi-ryu was feared by all his enemies.

Against the belief of its biggest skeptics, tech-wear had a huge comeback in 2036 at major haute couture shows all over the globe. Yoshinori Takahara had the tech garments clashing with robotic parts and traditional elements. The fact that he completely refused to design for humans made his shows the most exciting ones to look at.

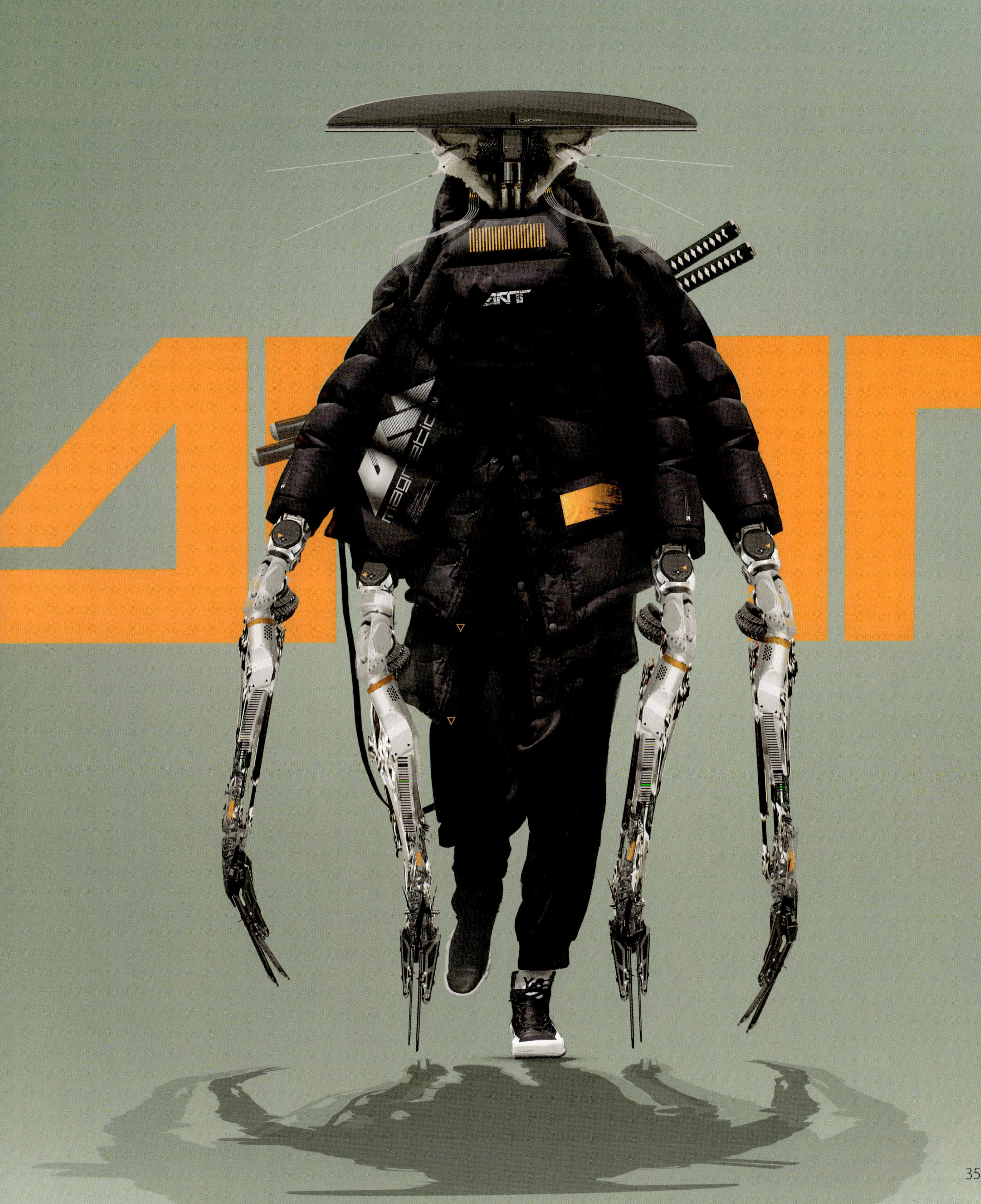

The gear at street level became more and more advanced at the same time. Urban explorers liked the new possibilities offered by these gadgets. The tech was seamlessly mixed with streetwear and techwear. Daytoner, a young robot fashion enthusiast, started creating wearables and masks.

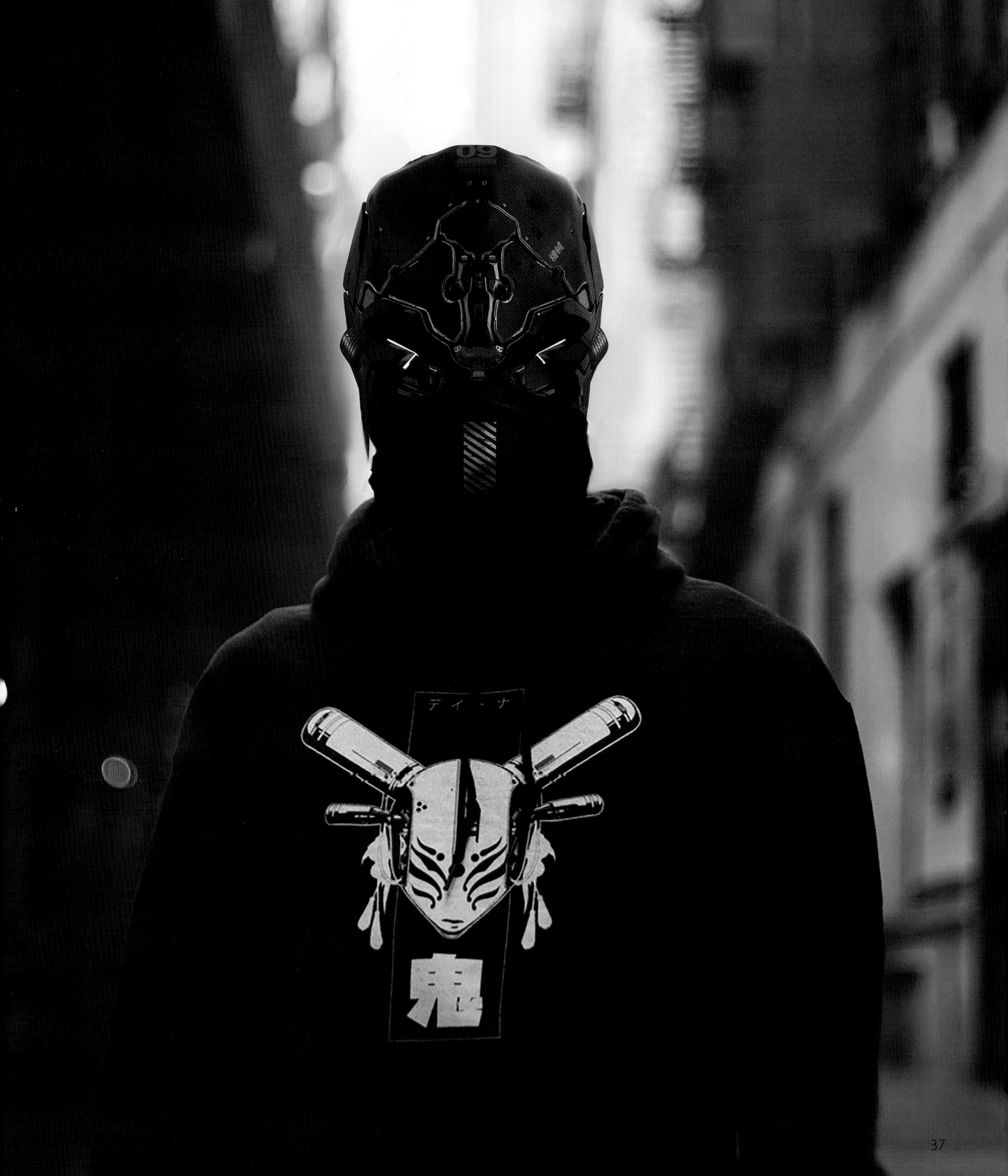
テイ・ナ
鬼

Nine Eyes and Slicer were leaders of the two major late 2030s urban ninja gangs: Nine Clan and Dead Eyez. Nine Eyes' head only had two pairs of four sensors on each side, so it never became clear where he derived his name from.

The Urban Ninja Movement, the first signs of which can be dated back as early as 2016, initially was a big mashup of harmless cultures. Tech nerds, health Goths, and hard-core cosplayers found a place to live out their fantasies. The movement developed gang-like structures only much later, with members eventually featuring more and more advanced helmets and cranials from various fashion brands. Katanas were the weapon of choice.

Neglecting their human roots, the subsequent Posthumanism Movement would call for the Global Machine Revolution in 2044.

NINE EYES // MK.**I**

TYPE: _ POSTHUMAN
LOCATION: _ NEW BANGKOK

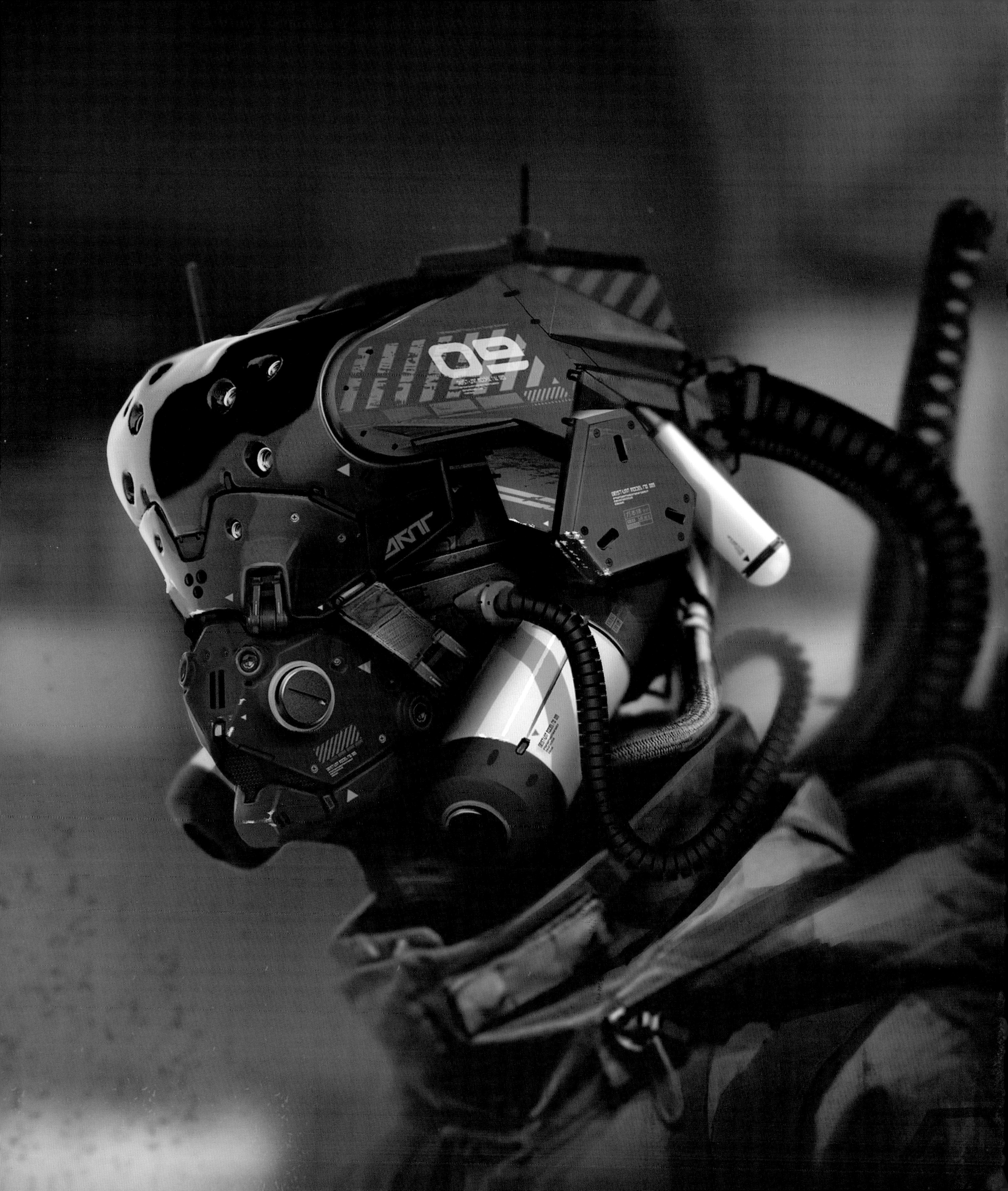

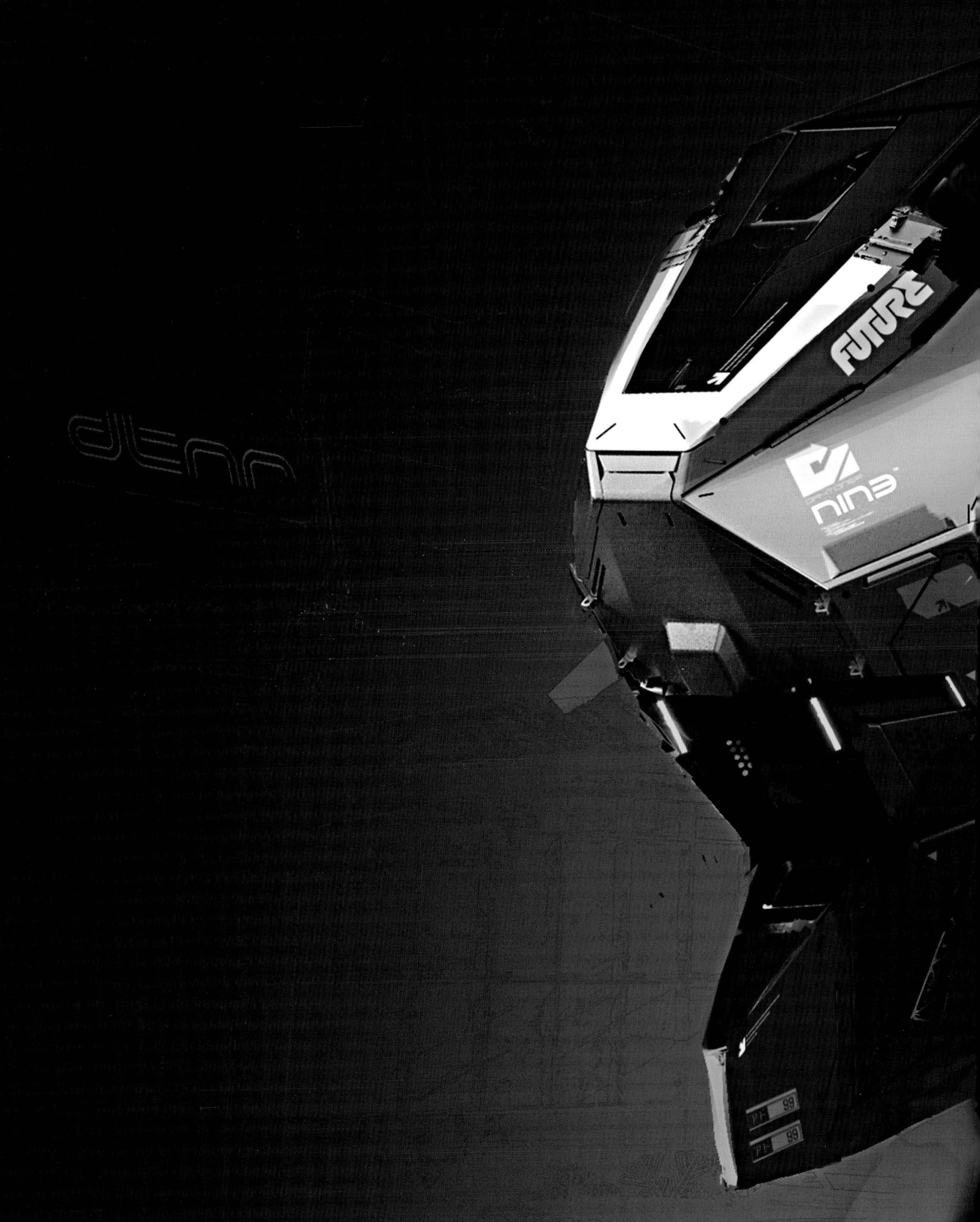
FUTURE

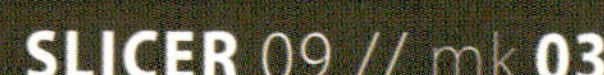
SLICER 09 // mk.03
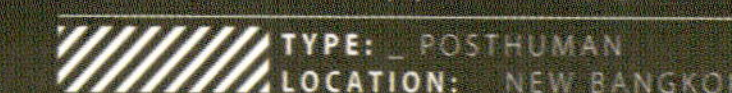
TYPE: _ POSTHUMAN
LOCATION: _ NEW BANGKOK

09
DRK
magnetic™

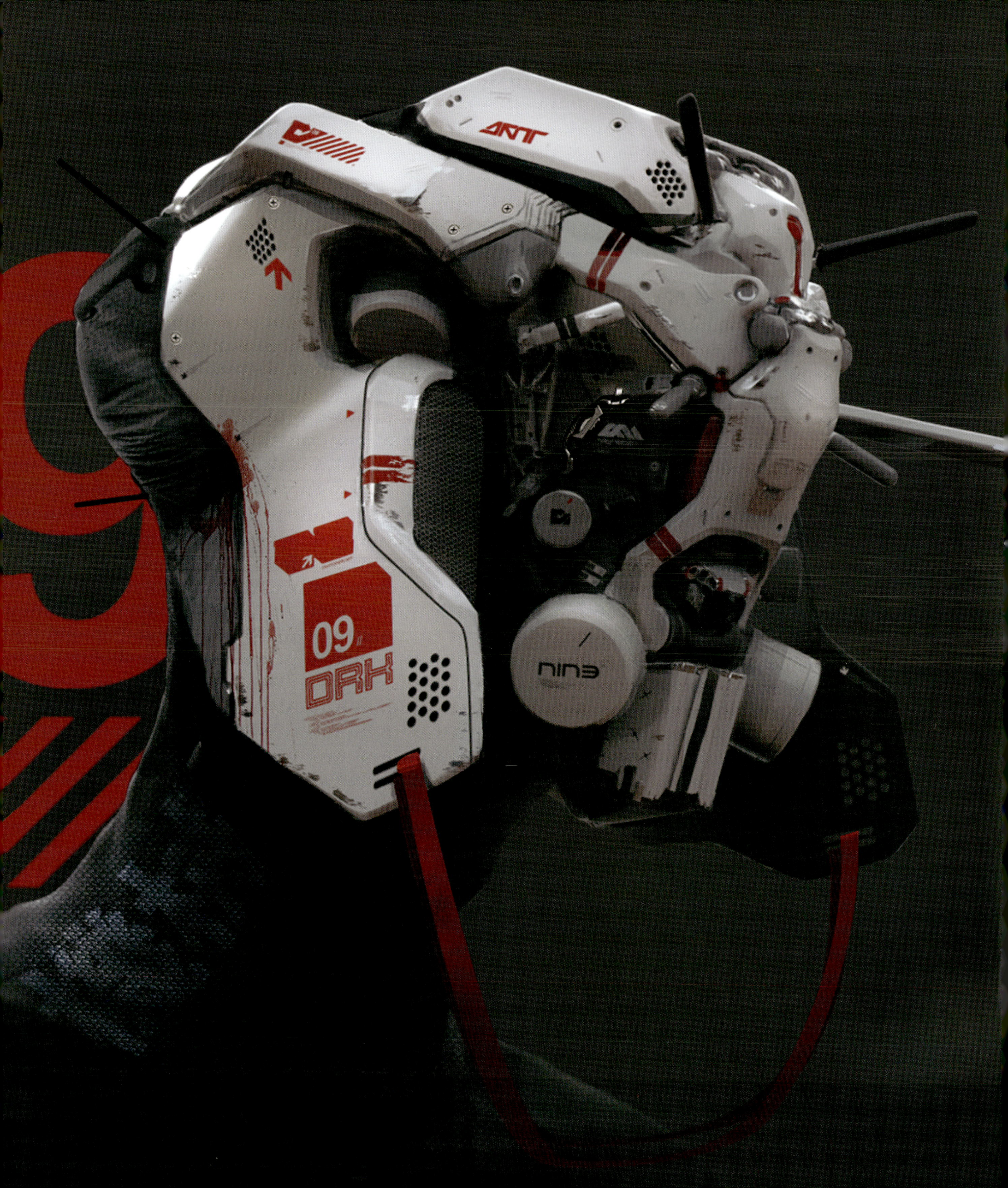
09
DRK

O.N.G. // rl.**btla37**

TYPE: _ POSTHUMAN
LOCATION: _ UNKNOWN

O.N.G., short for Original Ninja Gangster, disappeared around 2039. Parts of his iconic cranial were later discovered in the cribs of Nine Eyes and Slicer.

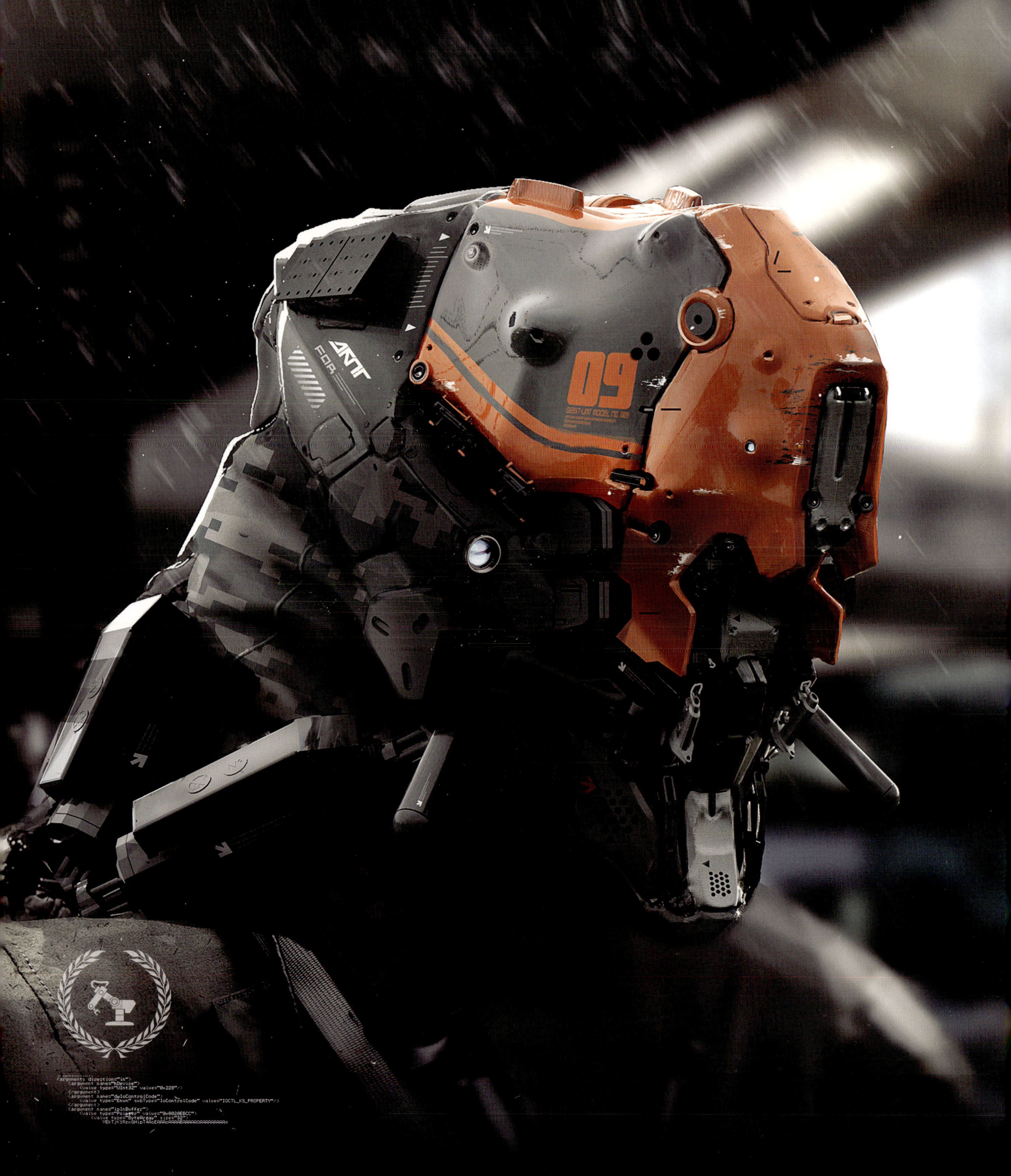
09
<arguments direction="in">
<argument name="hDevice">
<value type="UInt32" value="0x228"/>
</argument>
<argument name="dwIoControlCode">
<value type="Enum" subType="IoControlCode" value="IOCTL_KS_PROPERTY"/>
</argument>
<argument name="lpInBuffer">
<value type="Pointer" value="0x0020EBCC">
<value type="ByteArray" size="32">

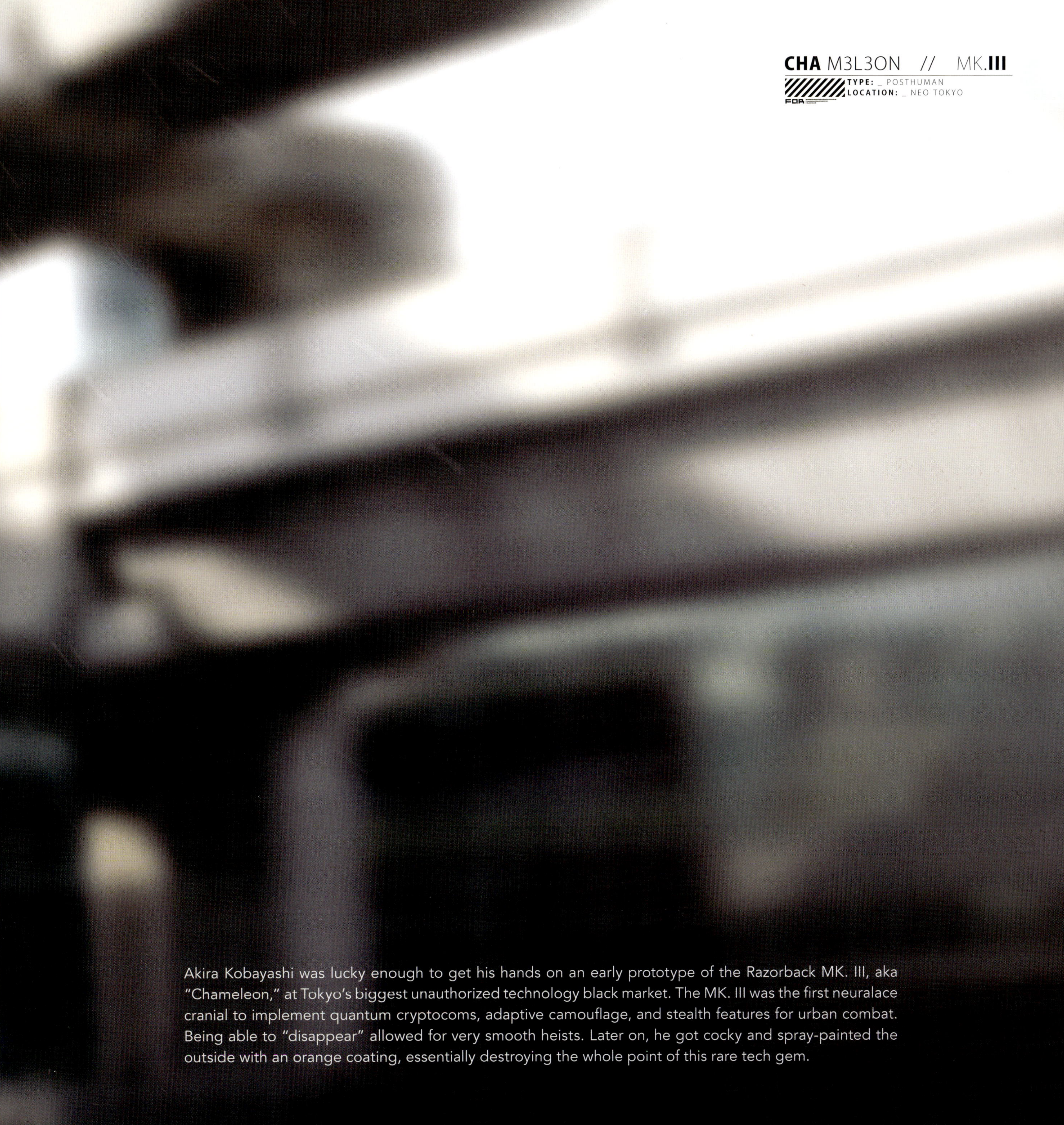

Akira Kobayashi was lucky enough to get his hands on an early prototype of the Razorback MK. III, aka "Chameleon," at Tokyo's biggest unauthorized technology black market. The MK. III was the first neuralace cranial to implement quantum cryptocoms, adaptive camouflage, and stealth features for urban combat. Being able to "disappear" allowed for very smooth heists. Later on, he got cocky and spray-painted the outside with an orange coating, essentially destroying the whole point of this rare tech gem.

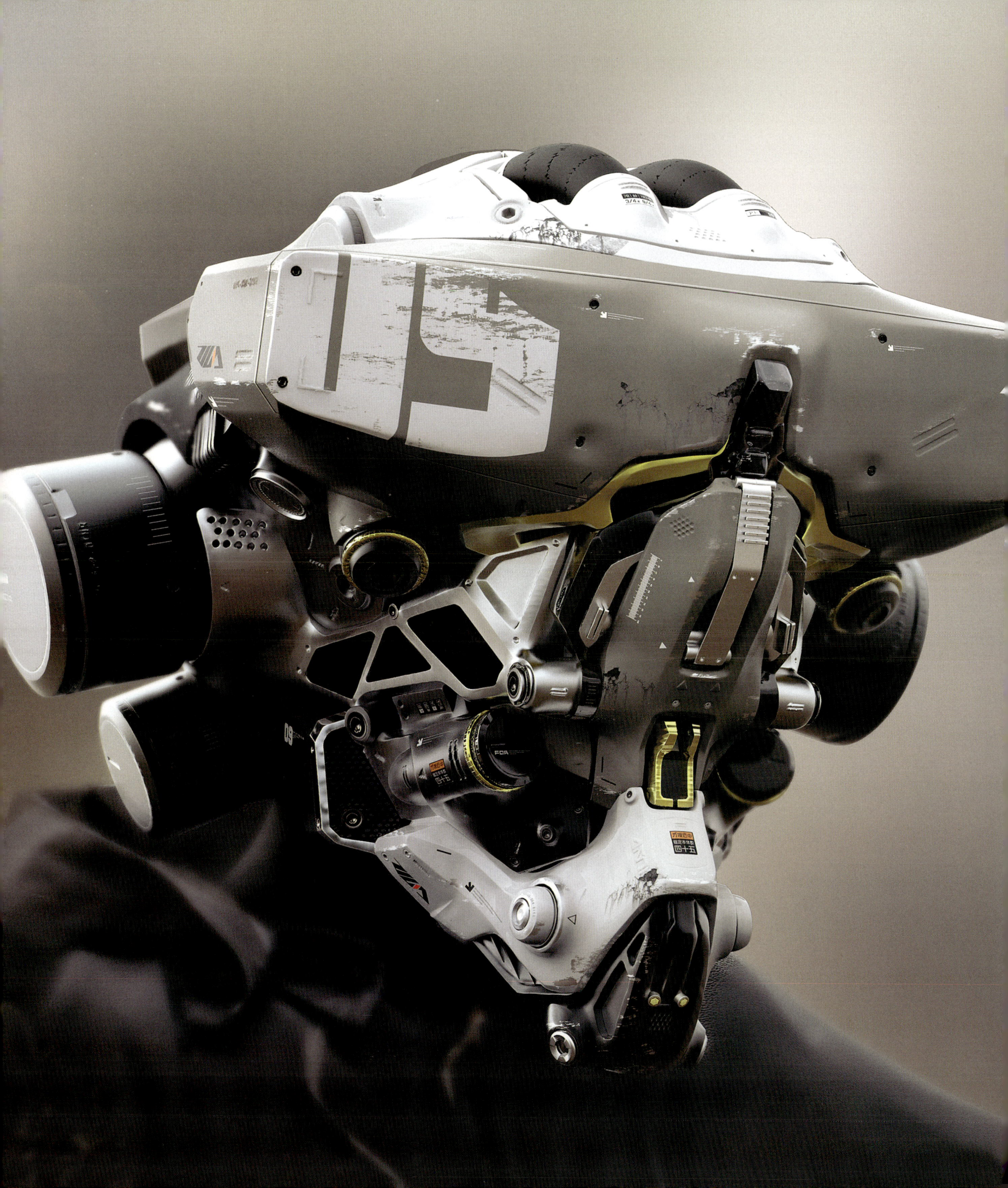

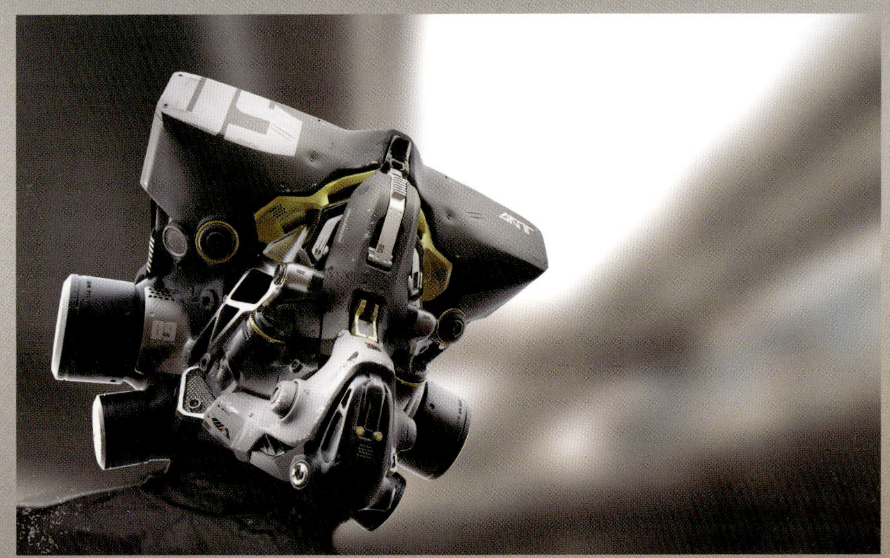

VR and AR had a huge comeback with neuralace. With "Silencer," the first-generation NR (NoReality) full enclosure headset was introduced. Silencer was an escapist's wet dream. If regular reality was not to your liking, you could step out of it entirely and live a life in real time in an altered overlay. Old-school cyberpunk enthusiasts were among the early adopters. Many other alternate universes quickly became available, and a black market developed for disturbing and strange NR software running on jailbreaked Silencers. Its glitchy early models were infamous for creating intense nausea and sometimes permanent brain damage.

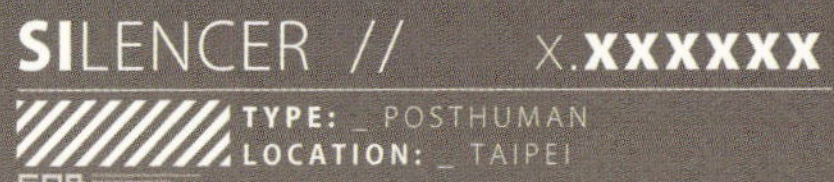

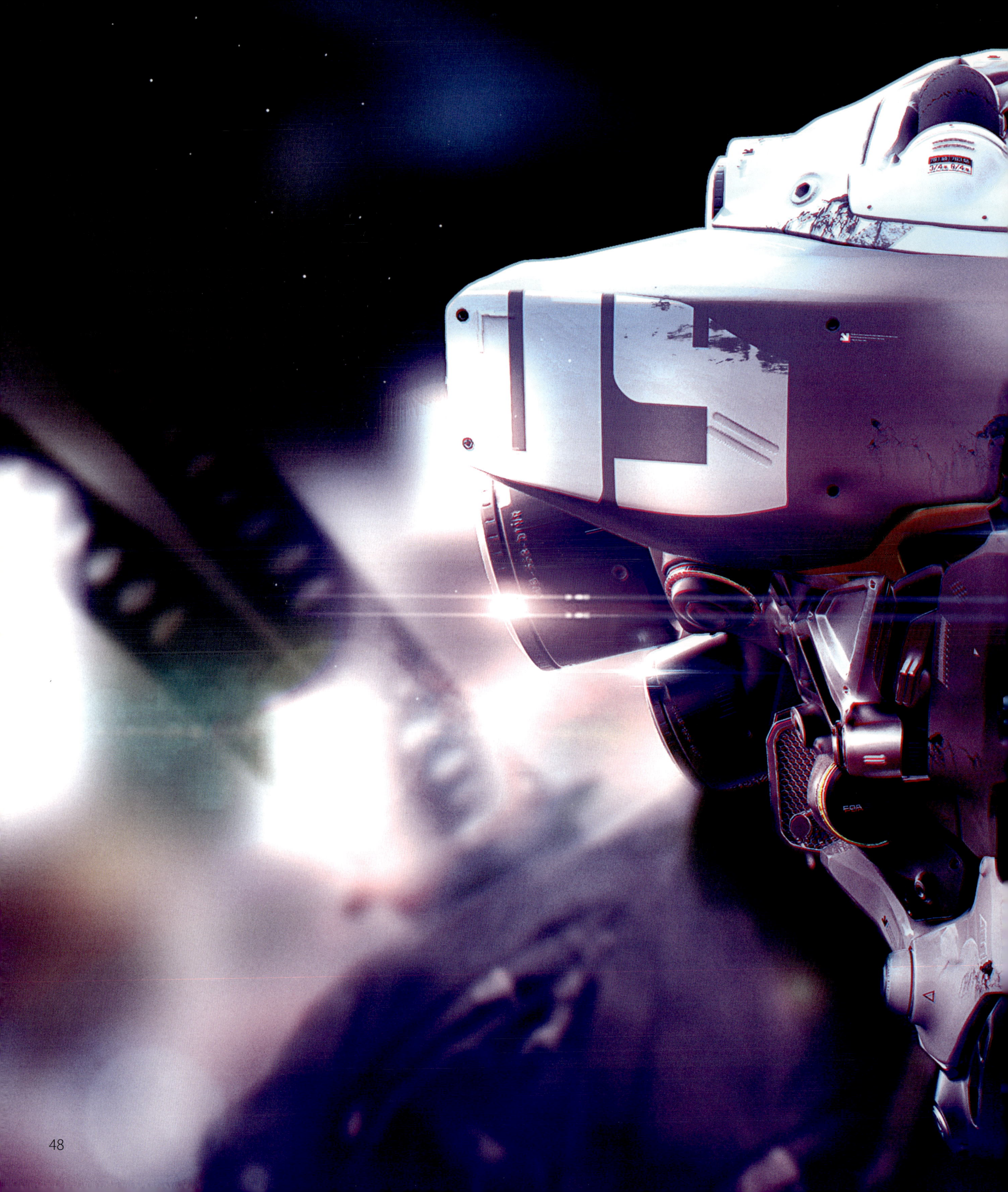

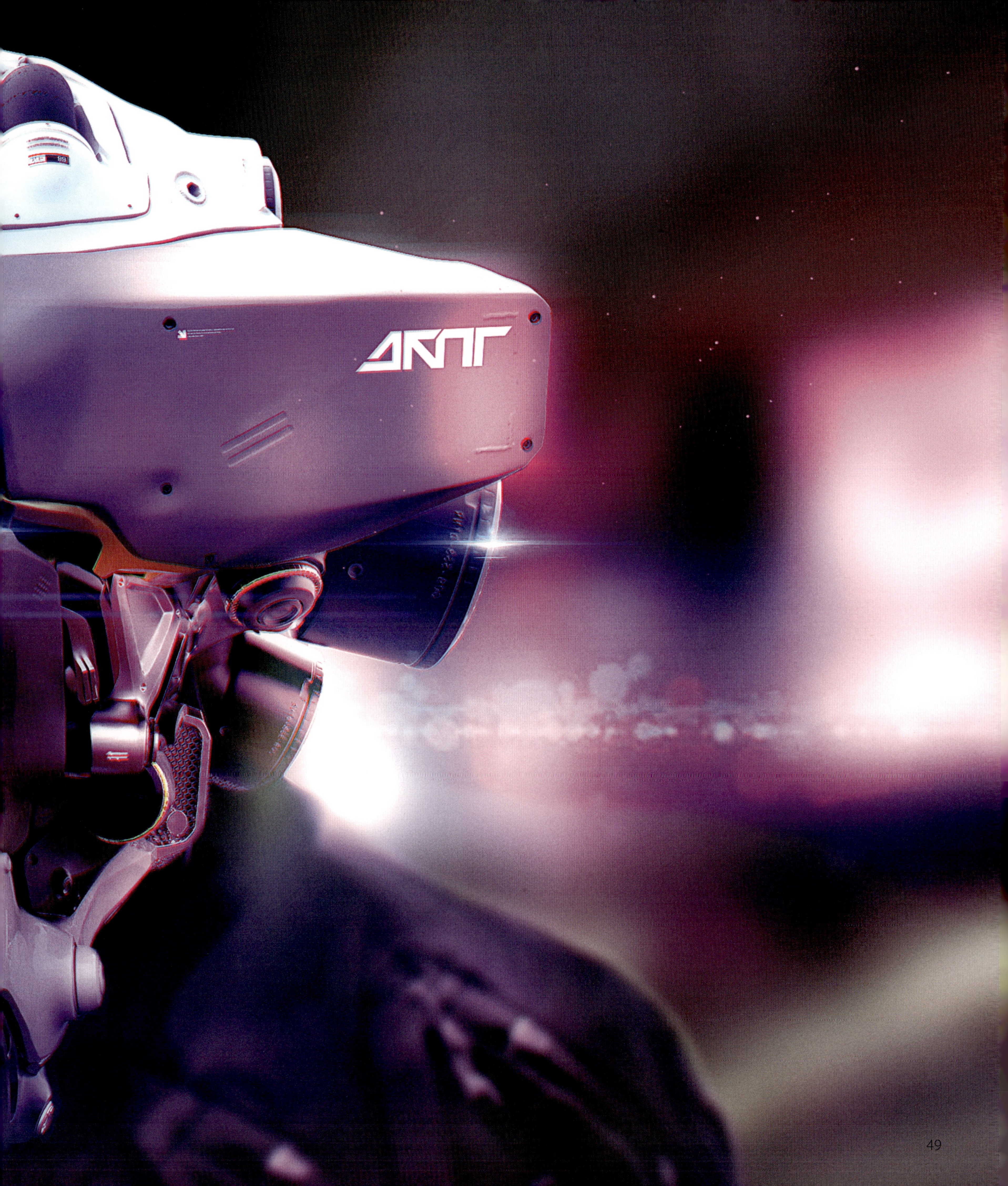

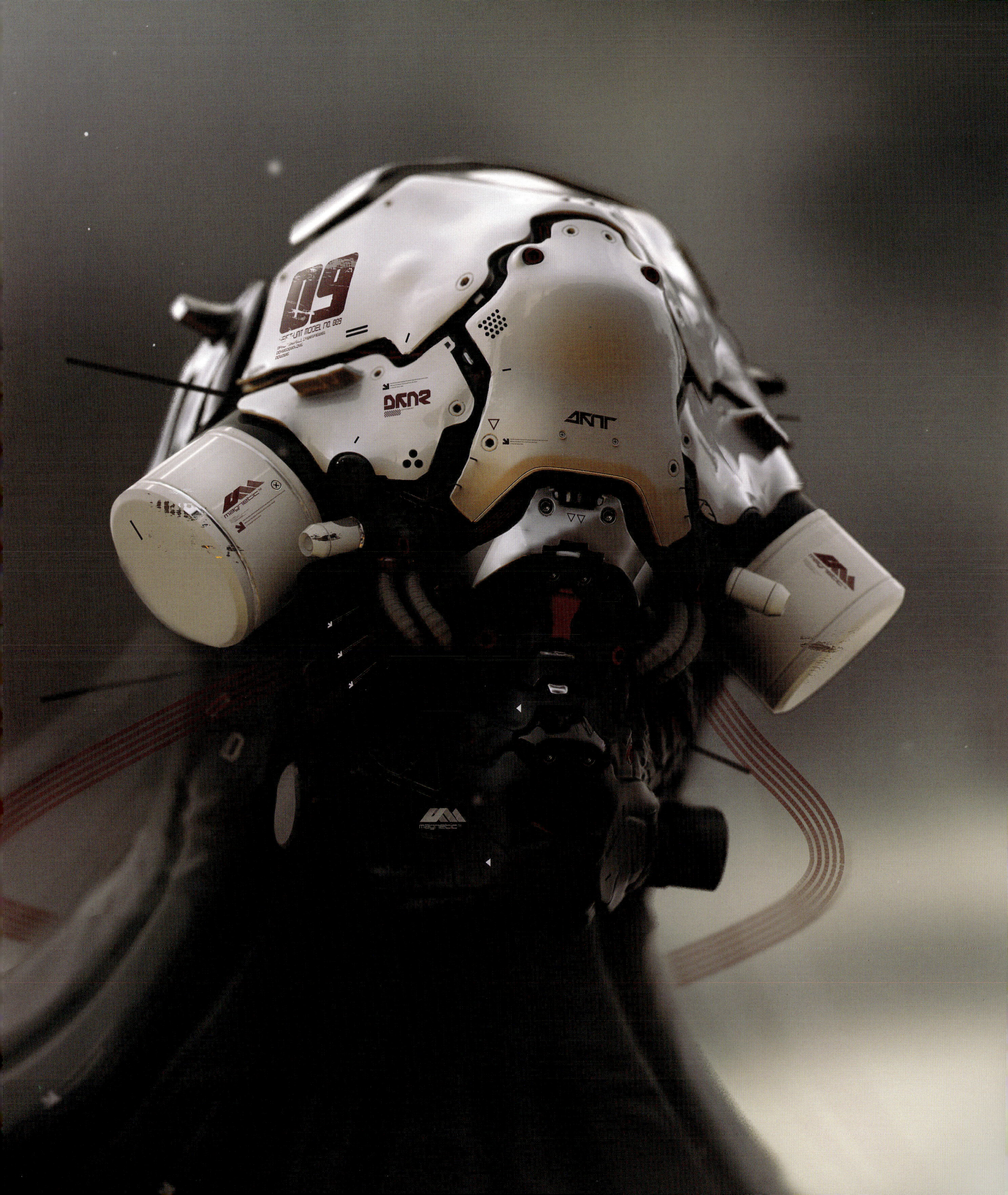
09
UNIT MODEL NO. 009
magnetic

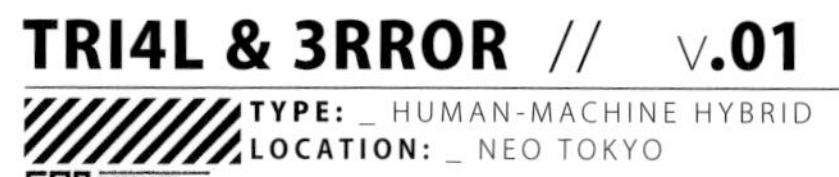

The "Trial and Error" series was a limited edition and Nakatomi Industries' first foray in the human augmentation market. Only 99 were produced worldwide. Their urban anime design made them a No. 1 fashion item. Nowadays, buyers will pay a premium price for this vintage gem.

Japanese designers gave cranials a very extravagant comeback for a brief spell during the late 2040s. Graffiti aficionados and other twentieth-century subculture enthusiasts were extremely attracted by the stylized look inspired by classic 1990s animes. FAKER featured the limited fallout-cherry-pop color option. It was supersensitive to scratches.

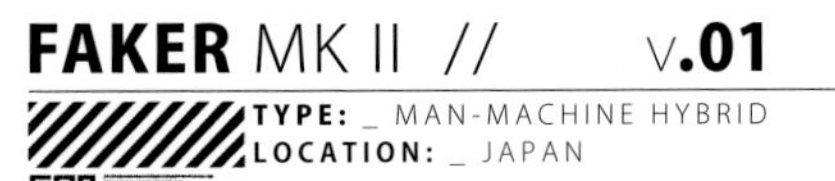

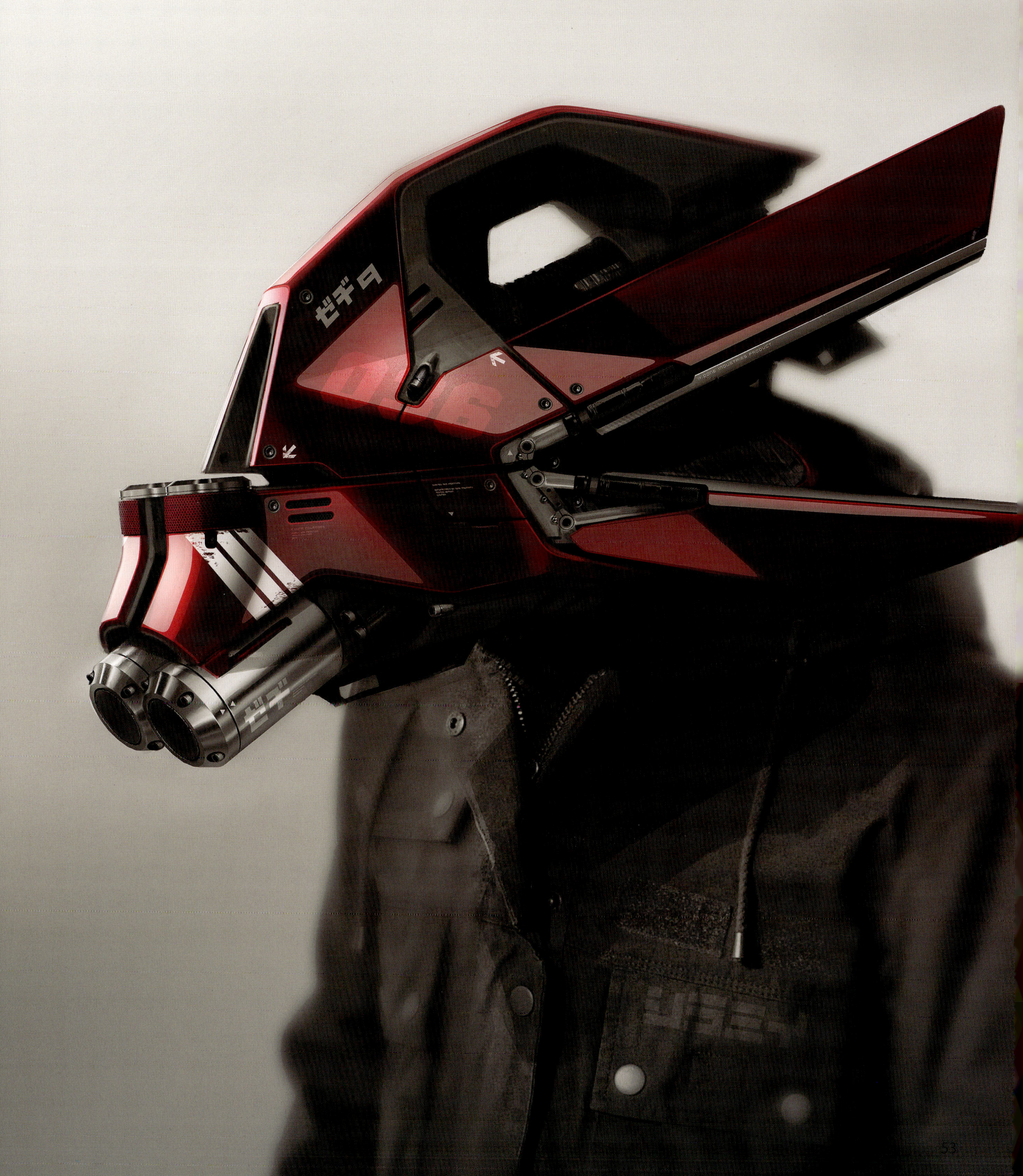
ゼギタ

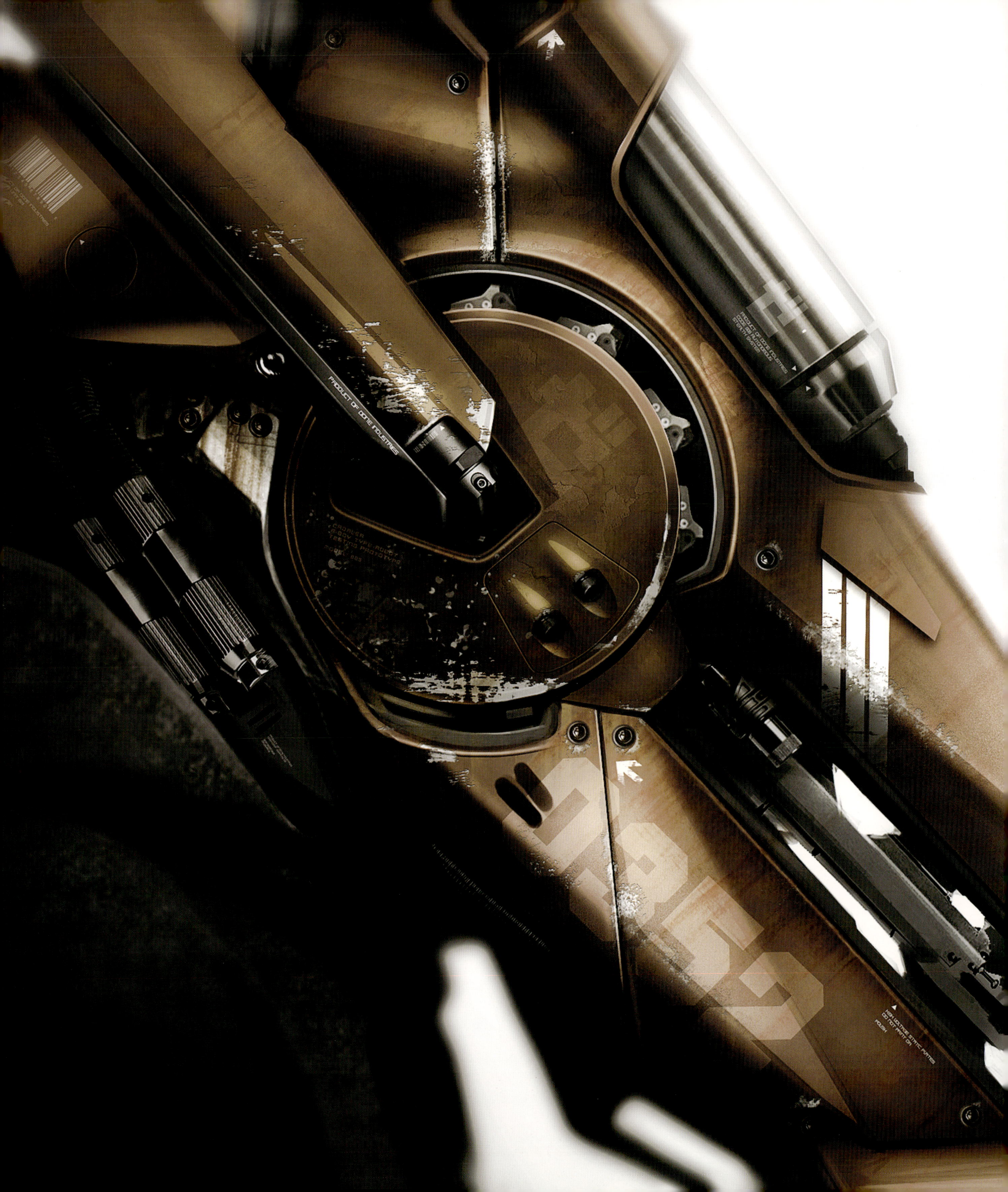

Cadaver0352 was the alias of a late 2040s Post Berlin street artist. His artistic style was somewhat on the dark side, with gun-skull being one of his most famous designs.

Grasshopper was the fastest amongst all the posthumans. His Gen. 1 Light Speed Module™ had him move at incredible speed. You needed a strobe light to see him go to work. His famous sword style was later referred to as "blending."

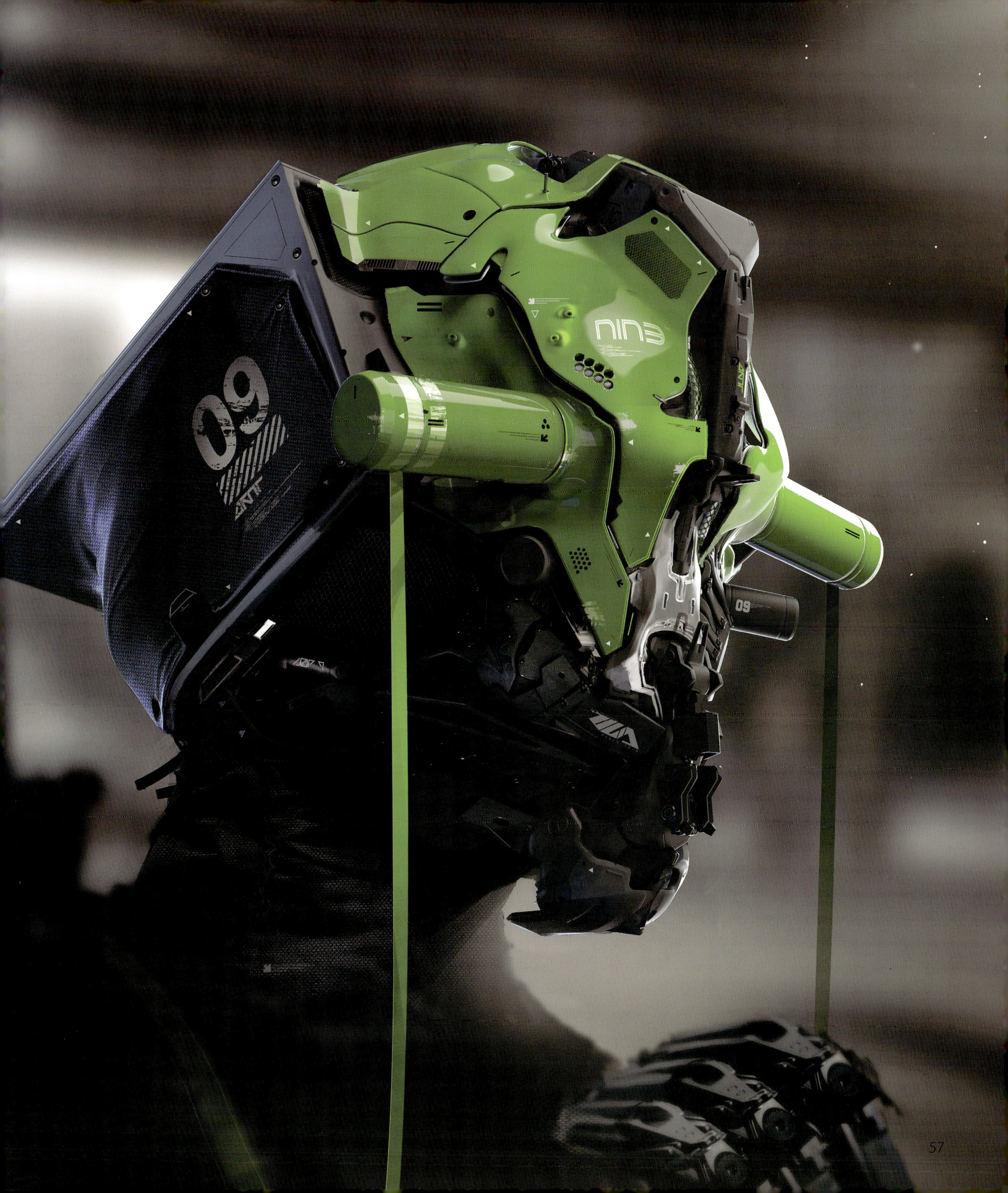
09

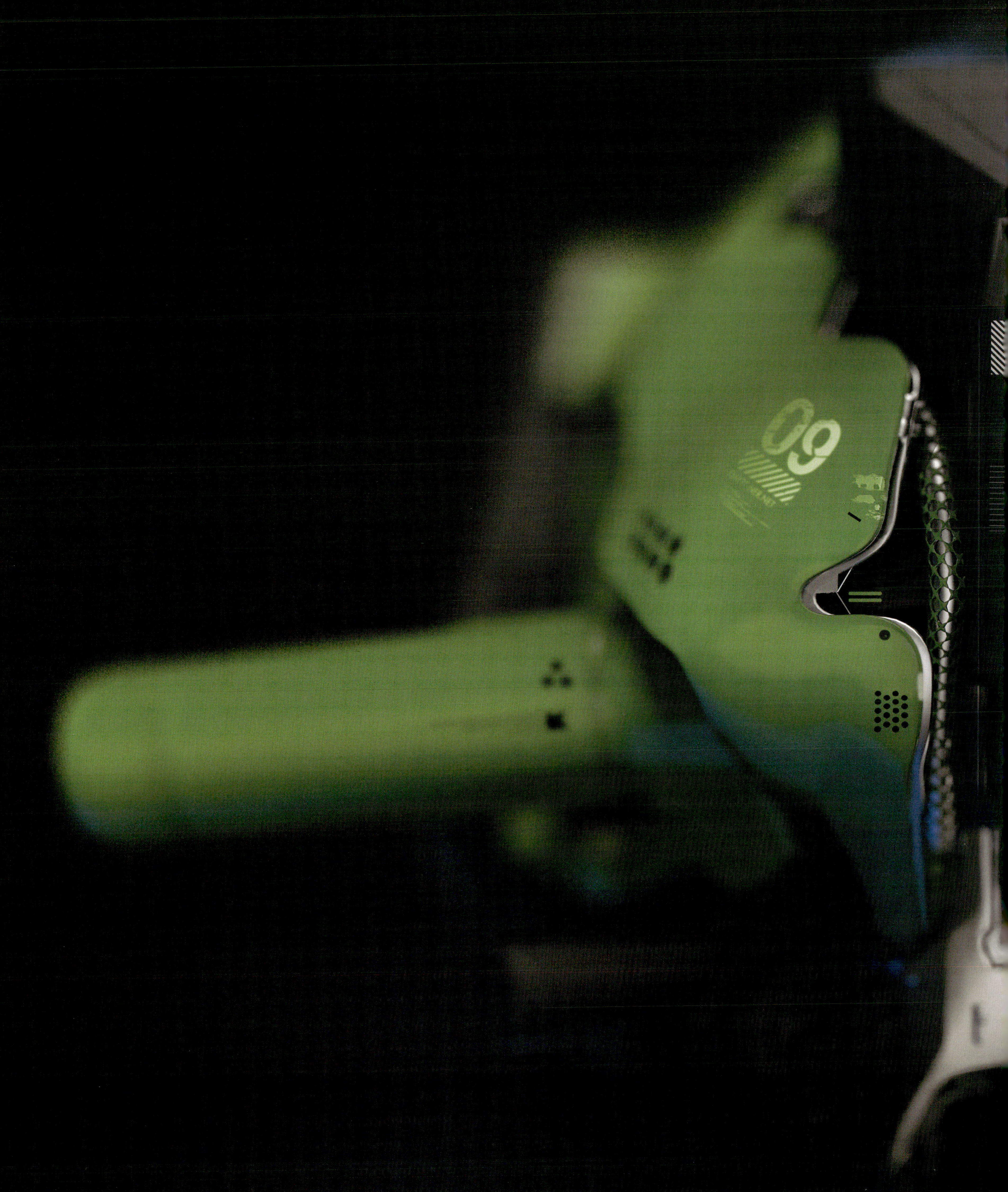

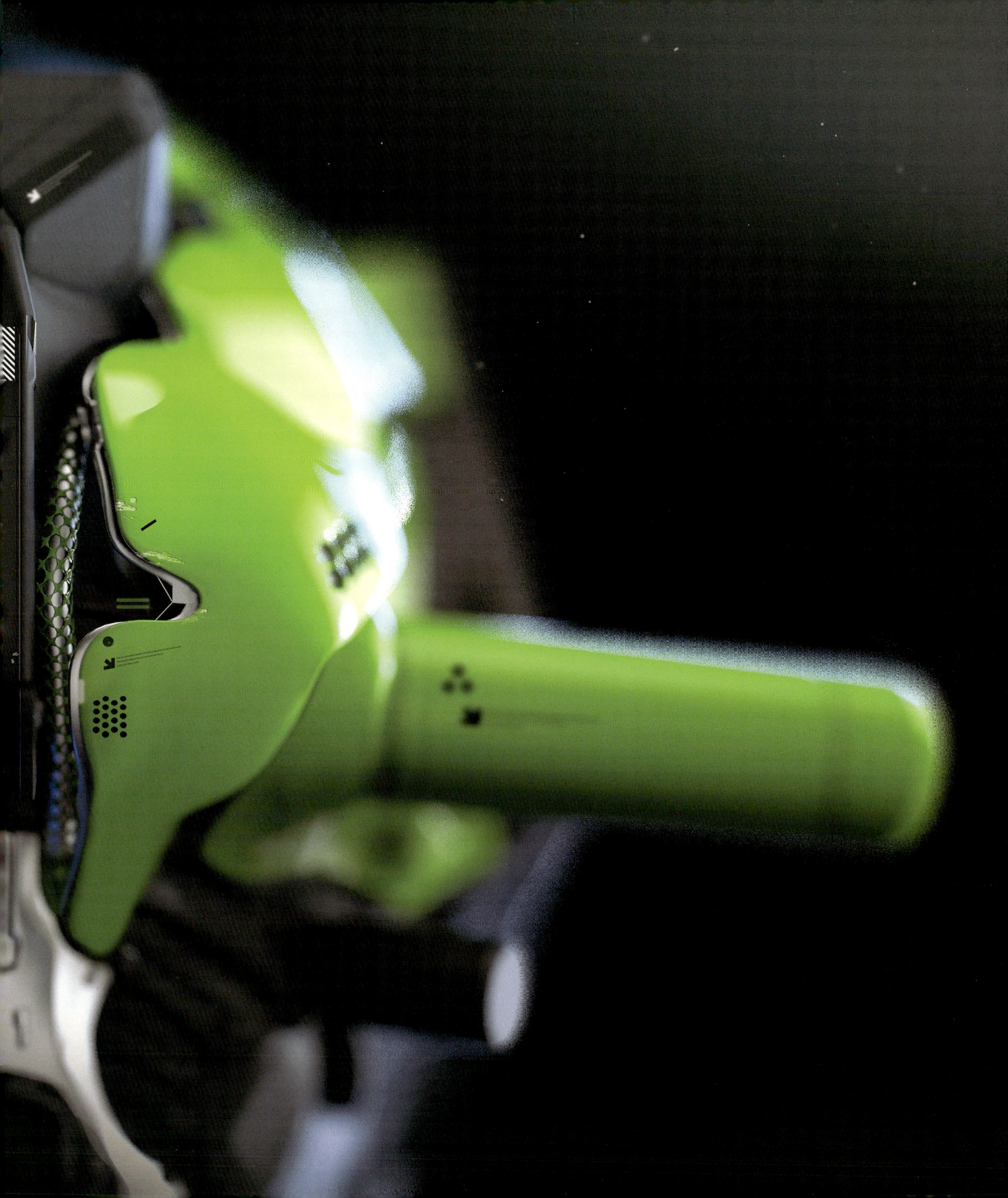

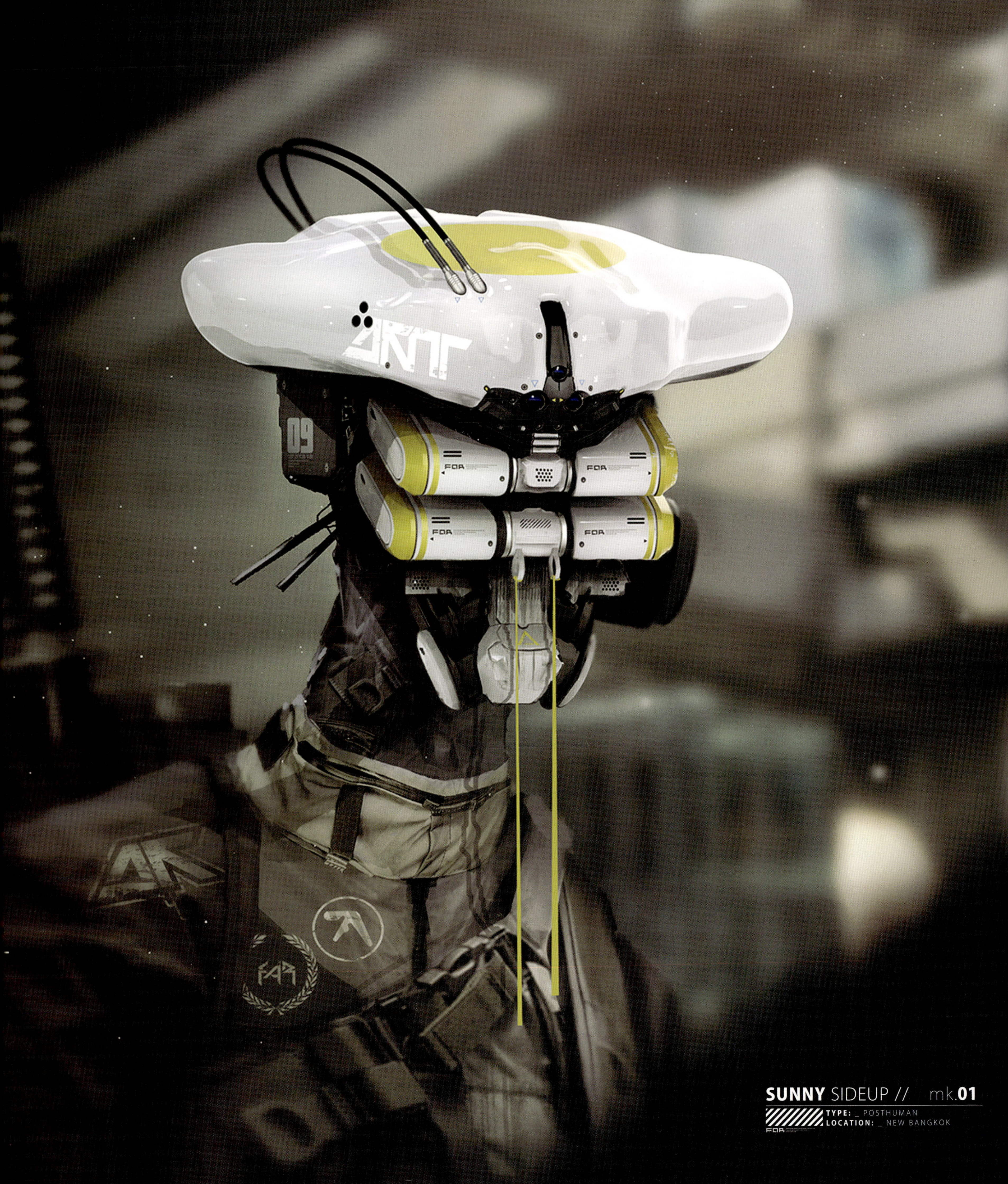

SUNNY SIDEUP // mk.01
TYPE: _ POSTHUMAN
LOCATION: _ NEW BANGKOK
FOR
09
FOR
FOR
FOR
FOR

BASHER // prototype

TYPE: _ HUMAN-MACHINE HYBRID
LOCATION: _ POST LA

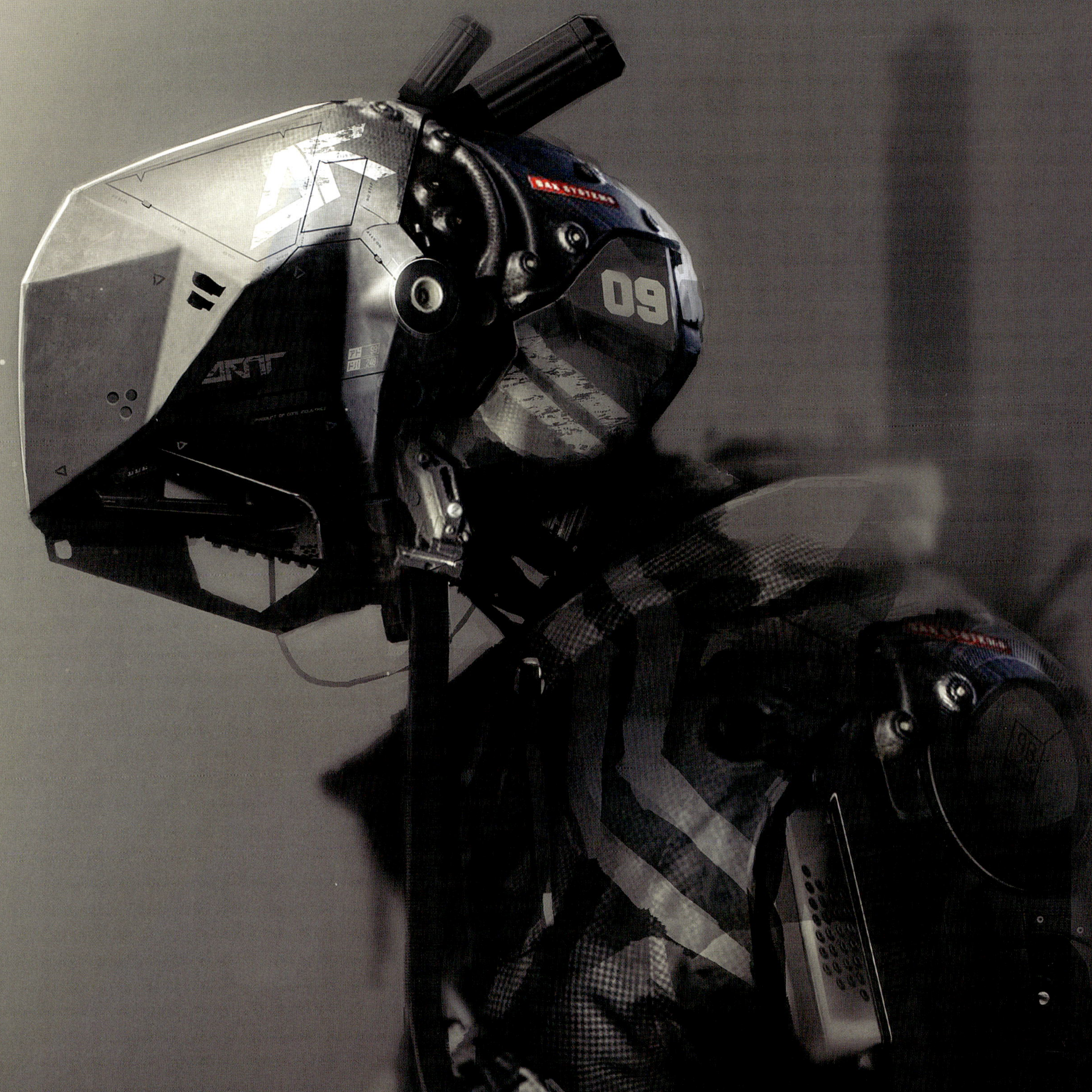

Basher and Sunny Sideup paved the way for the DOODES era of one-off kit-bashed posthumans. These were the first individuals to do "the awkward thing," which later got perfected by others. The look and philosophy was based on the photo- and kit-bash culture of the 2010s. The ultimate goal was to achieve maximum weirdness in design and become a truly unique character.

The DOODES were a mixed robot and posthuman clan maximizing the human effort of becoming your own real-life avatar. Exaggerated and off proportions gave them their distinct, awkward, unique look. They were known to wear discarded prototype trash, which they combined in the strangest ways possible. Their armor was scavenged robot parts out of Post Berlin's Dark Districts.

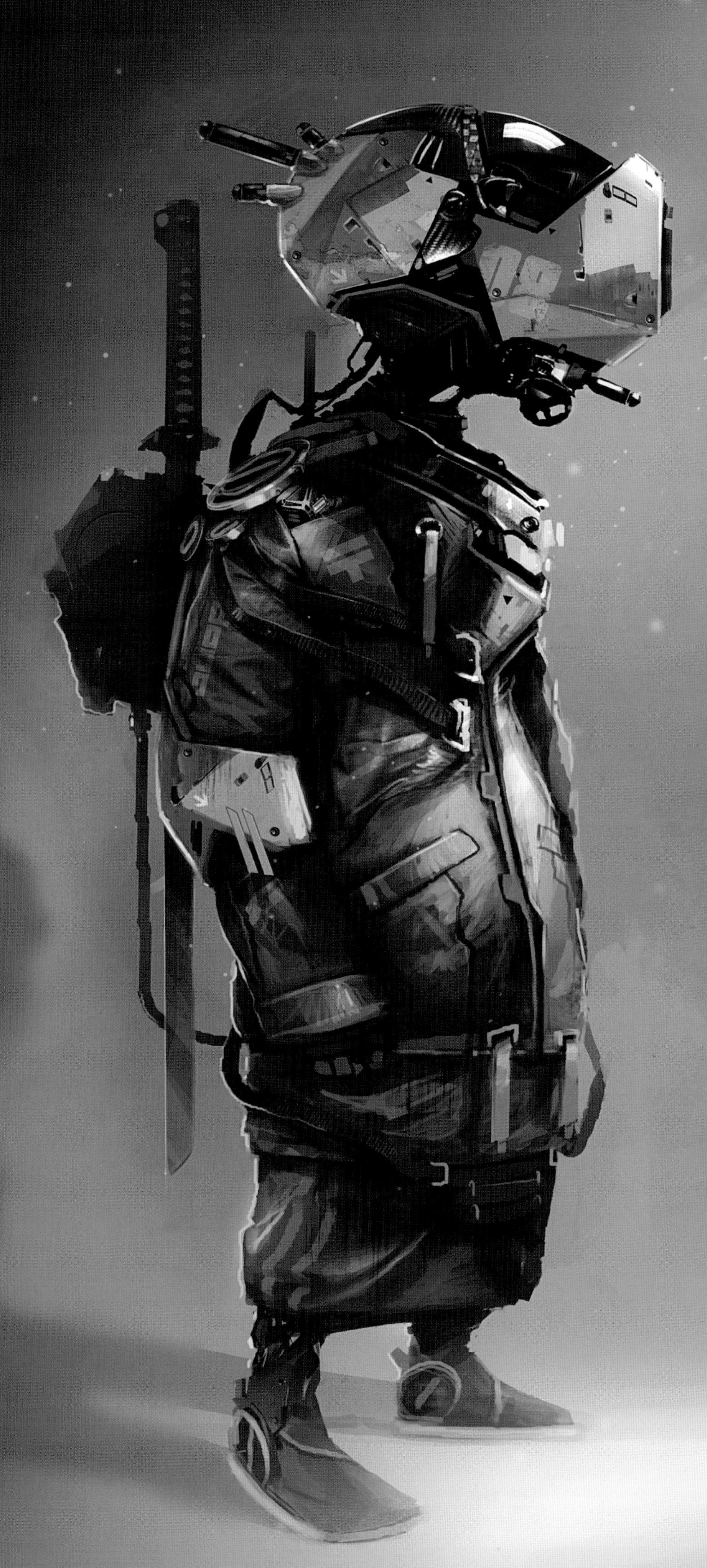

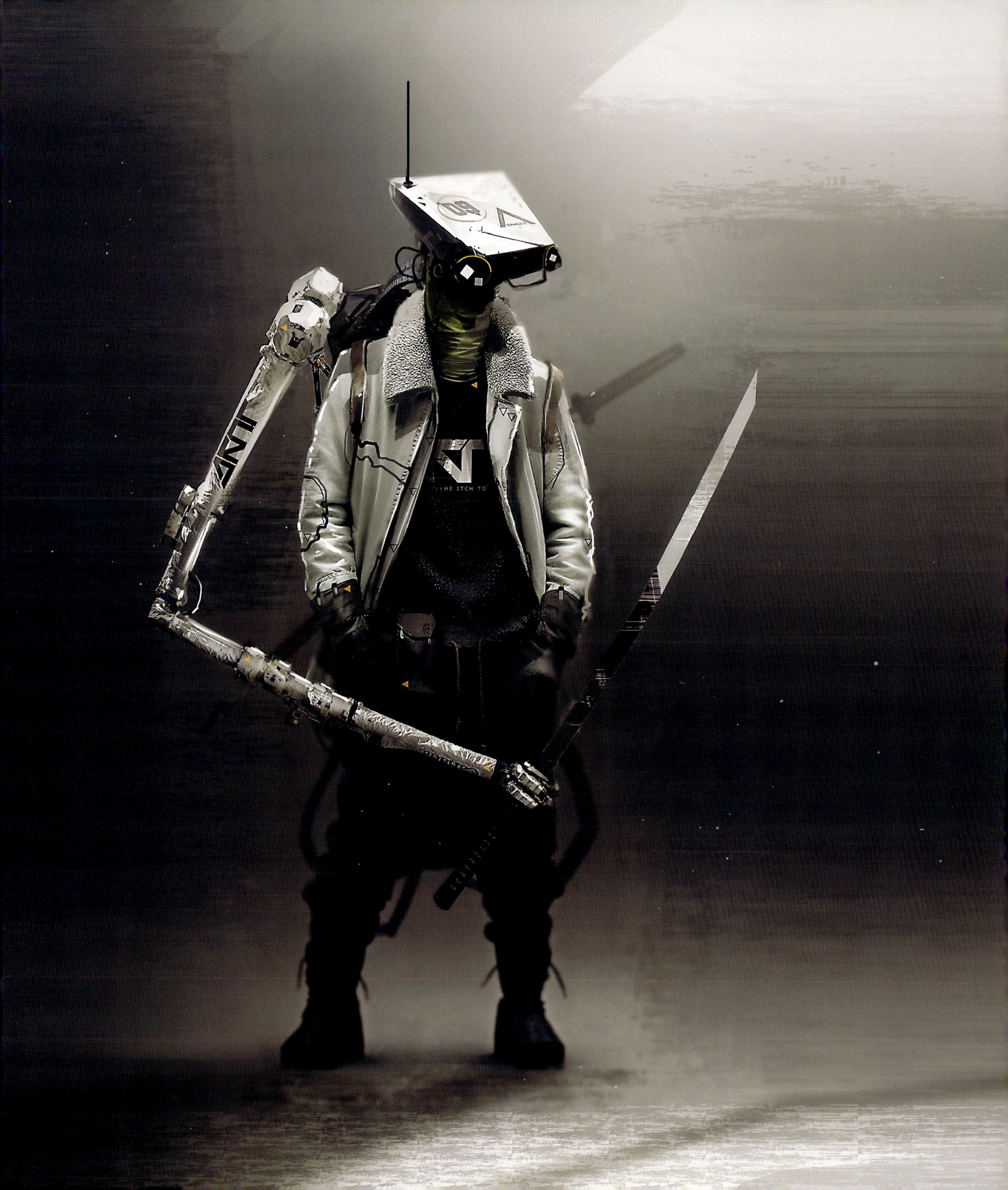
09
DANGER
HE ITCH TO

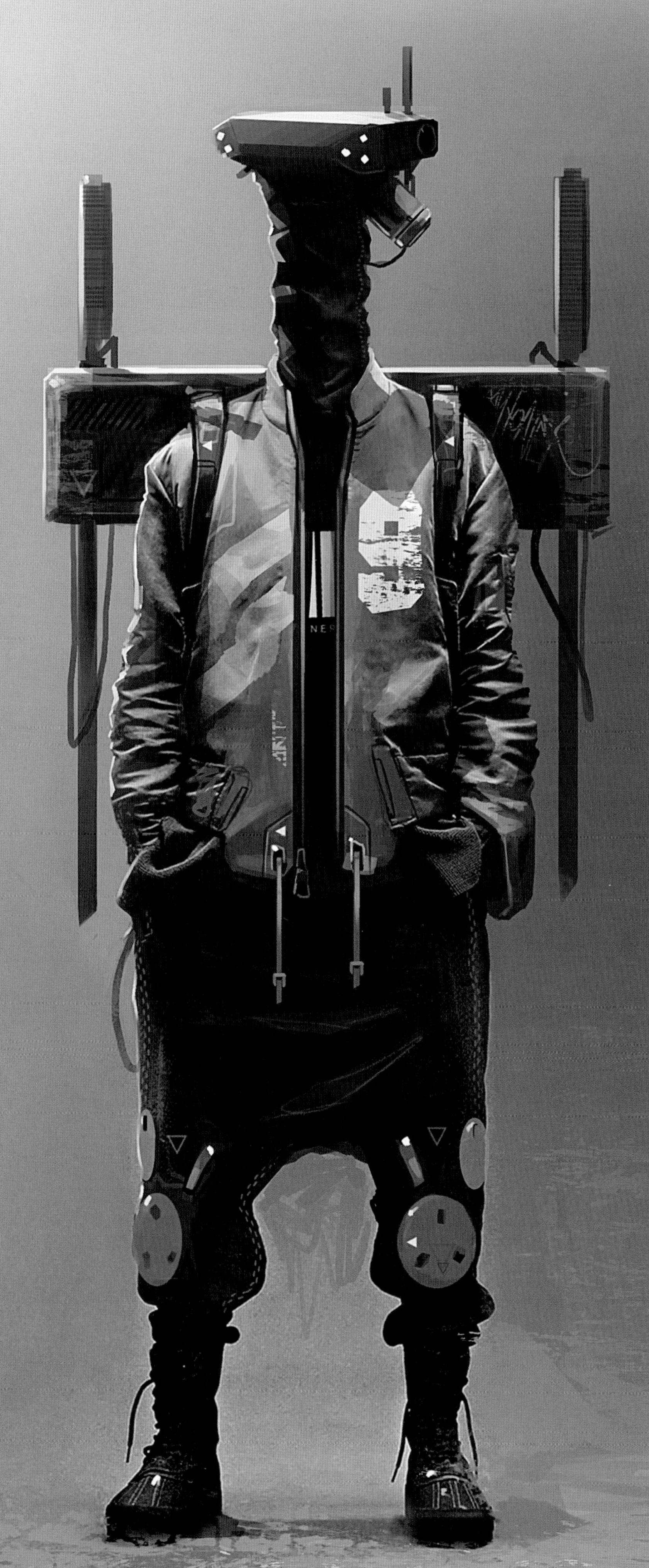

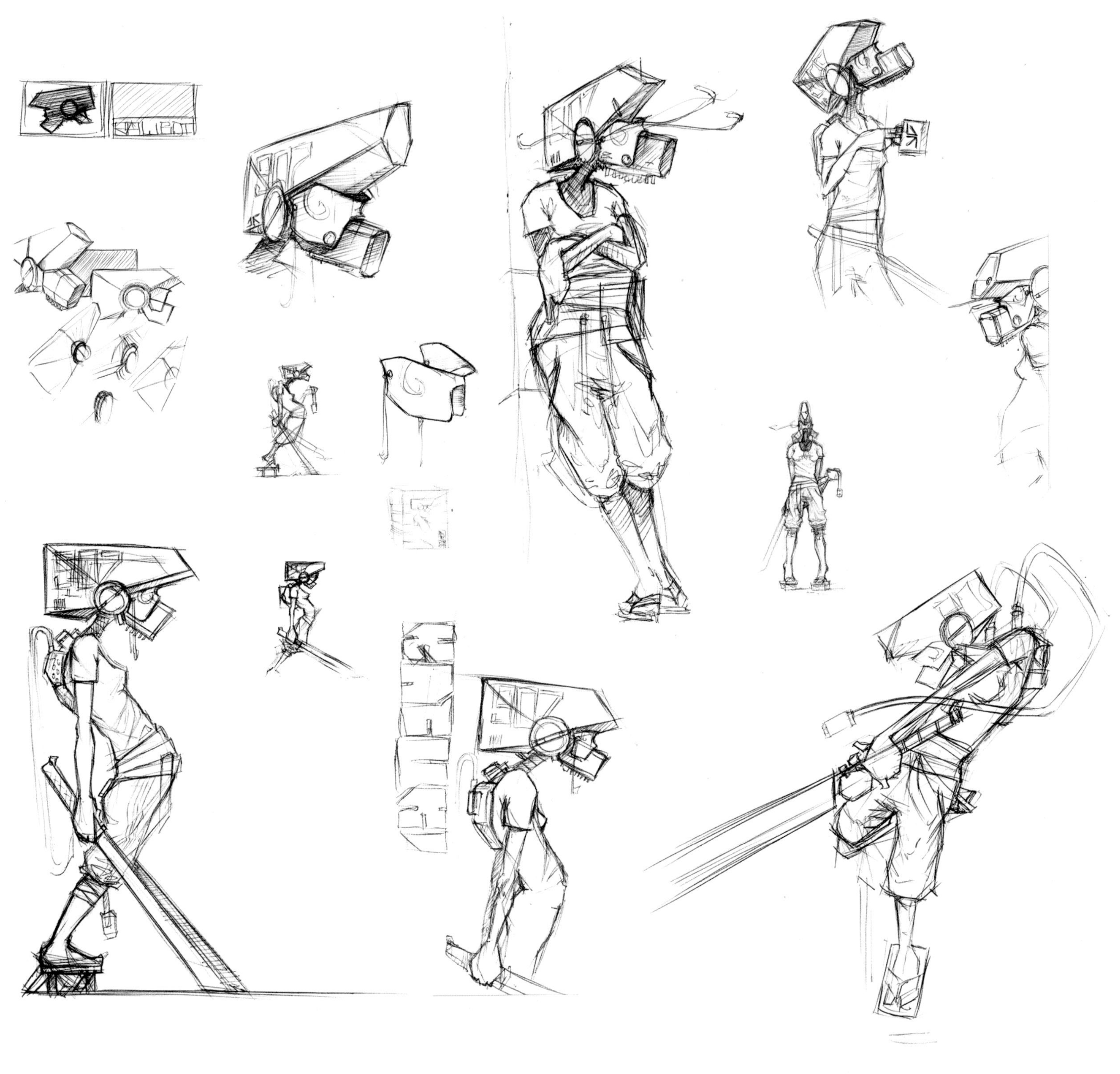

KABUKI 902 was one of the most famous female DOODES. Her distinct cranial was a combination of squarish geometrical shapes and a broken shard of a Japanese Kabuki dancer's mask, beautified with red ribbons. She became famous through the second wave of social media hype in 2036. Signing the deal for her own toy line and an anime series rendered her a global icon.

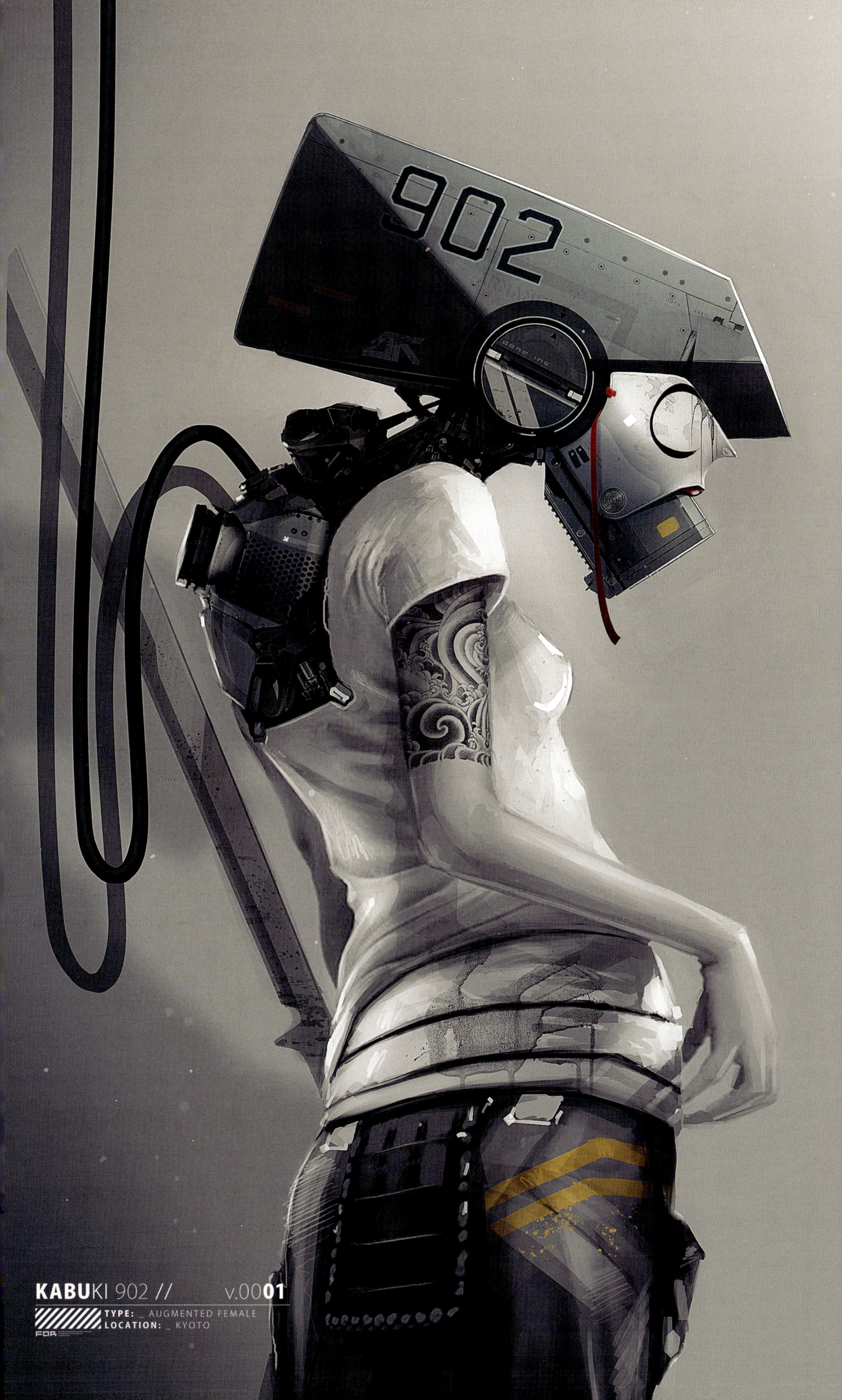
902
KABUKI 902 // v.0001
TYPE: _ AUGMENTED FEMALE
LOCATION: _ KYOTO
FOR

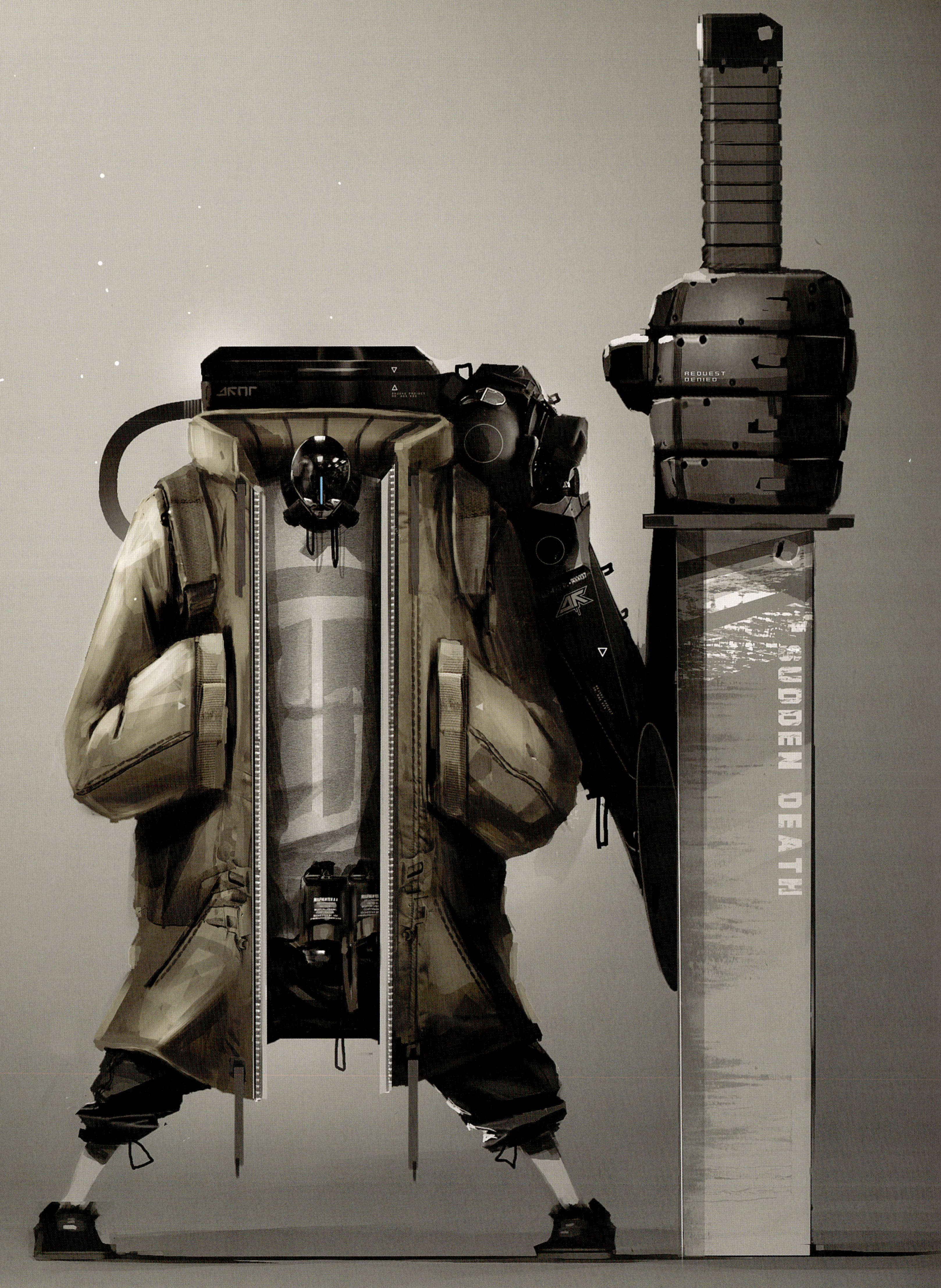
REQUEST
DENIED
SUDDEN DEATH

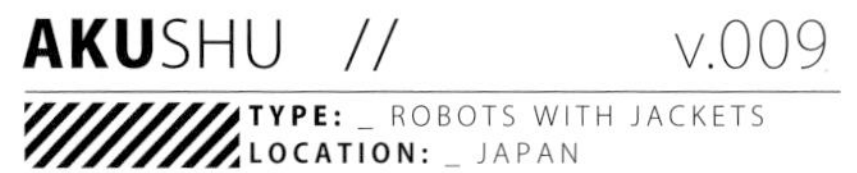

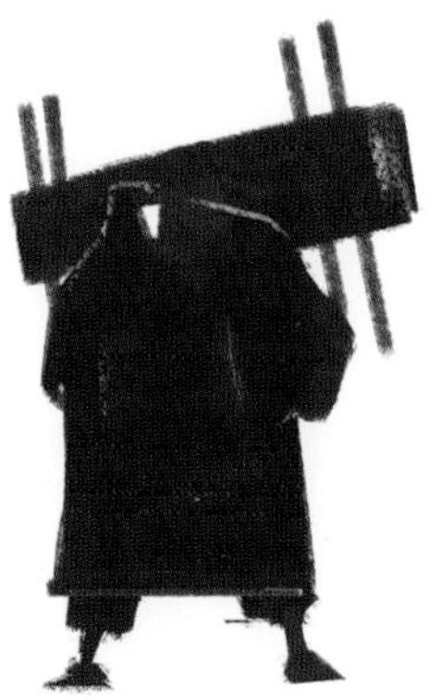

Akushu, aka Iron Fist, had the most confident handshake. Turning down memberships in both DTNR as well as 2Fly, he started his own thing. Akushu barely took his hands out of his pockets during confrontations. When his backpack, HAND OF GOD, and his broadsword, SUDDEN DEATH, teamed up, there was no space for extra hands anyway.

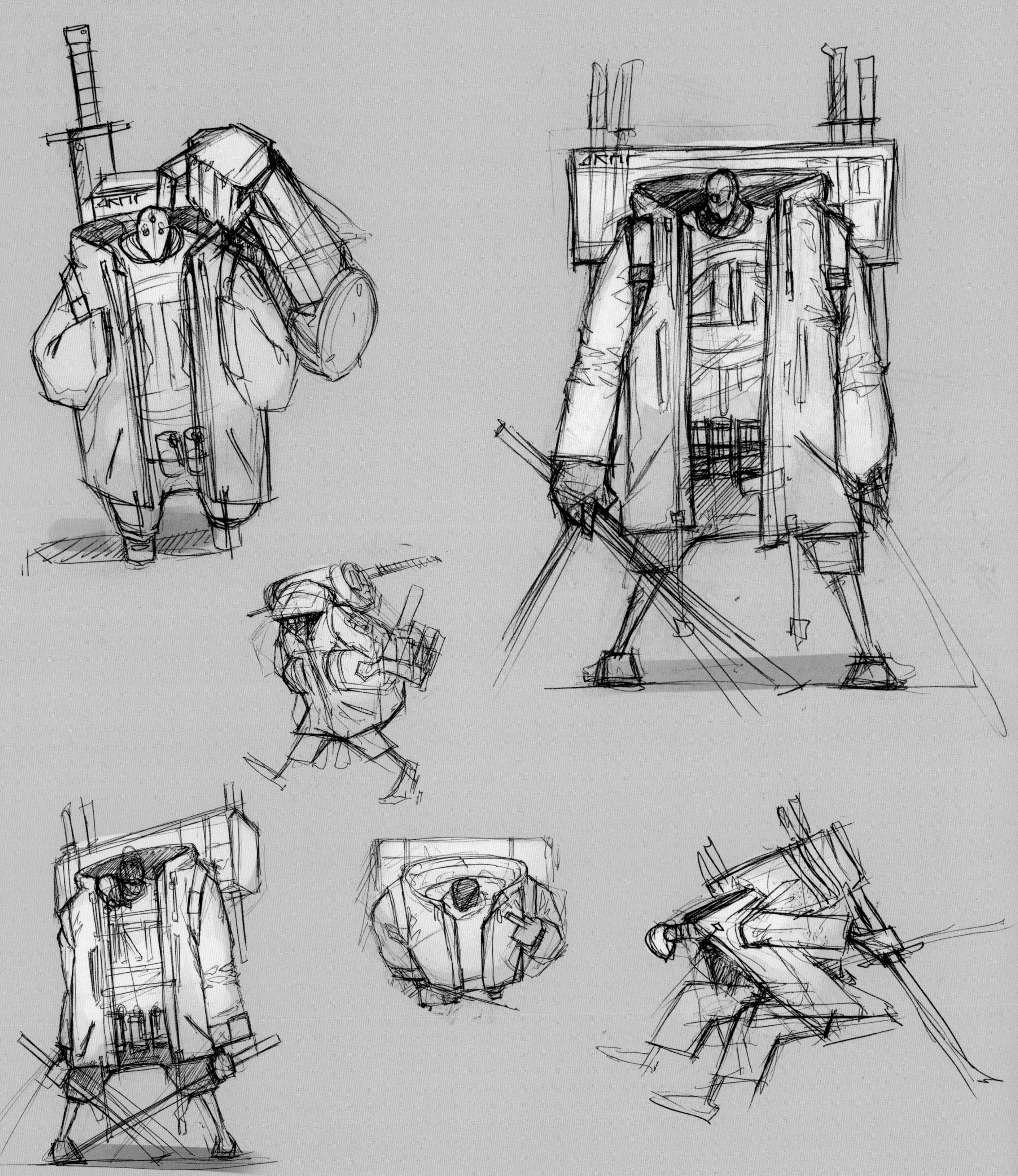

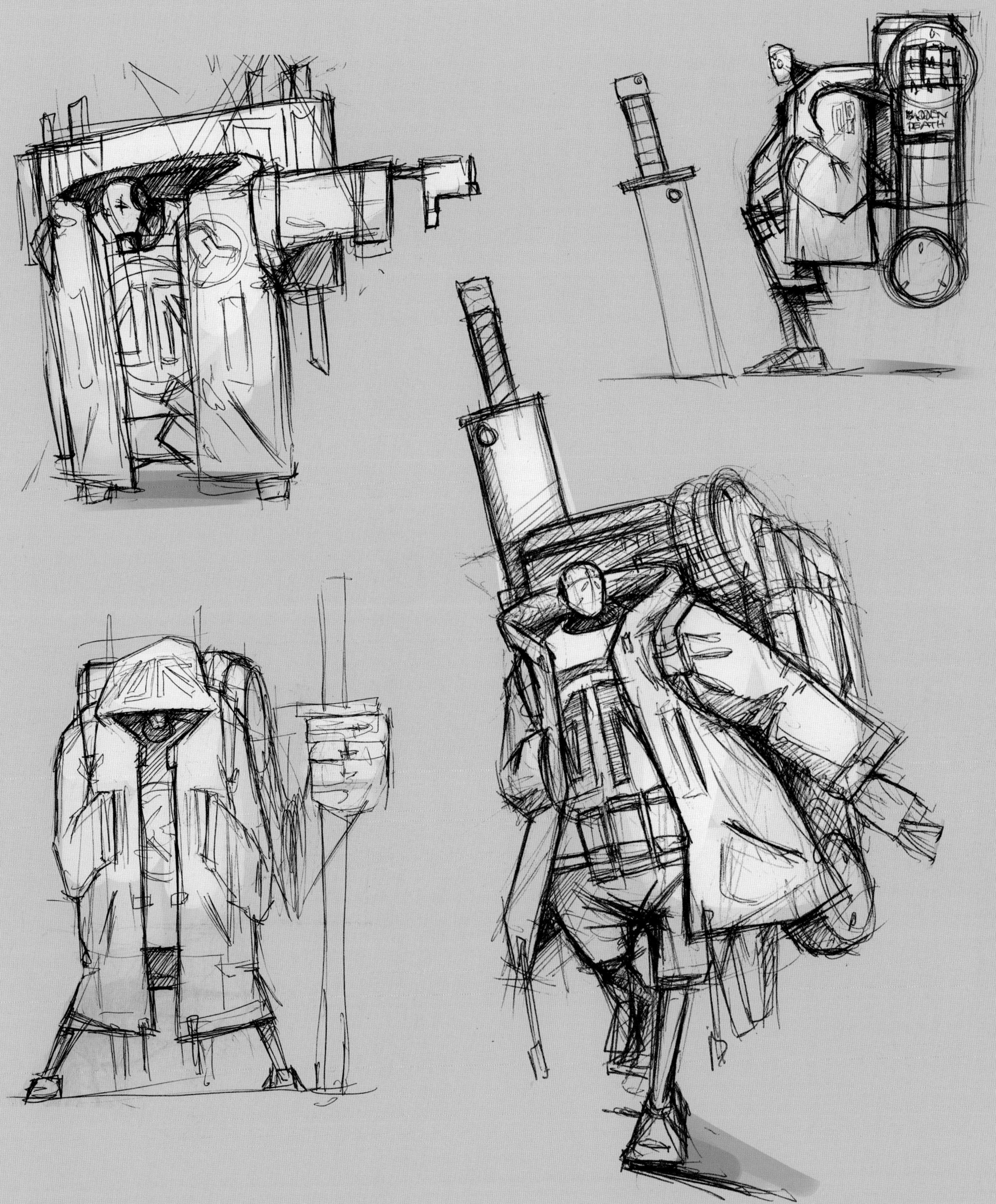
SUDDEN
DEATH

2FLYCREW // **999.**XXX

TYPE: _ LEVITATING HYBRIDS
LOCATION: _ UNKNOWN

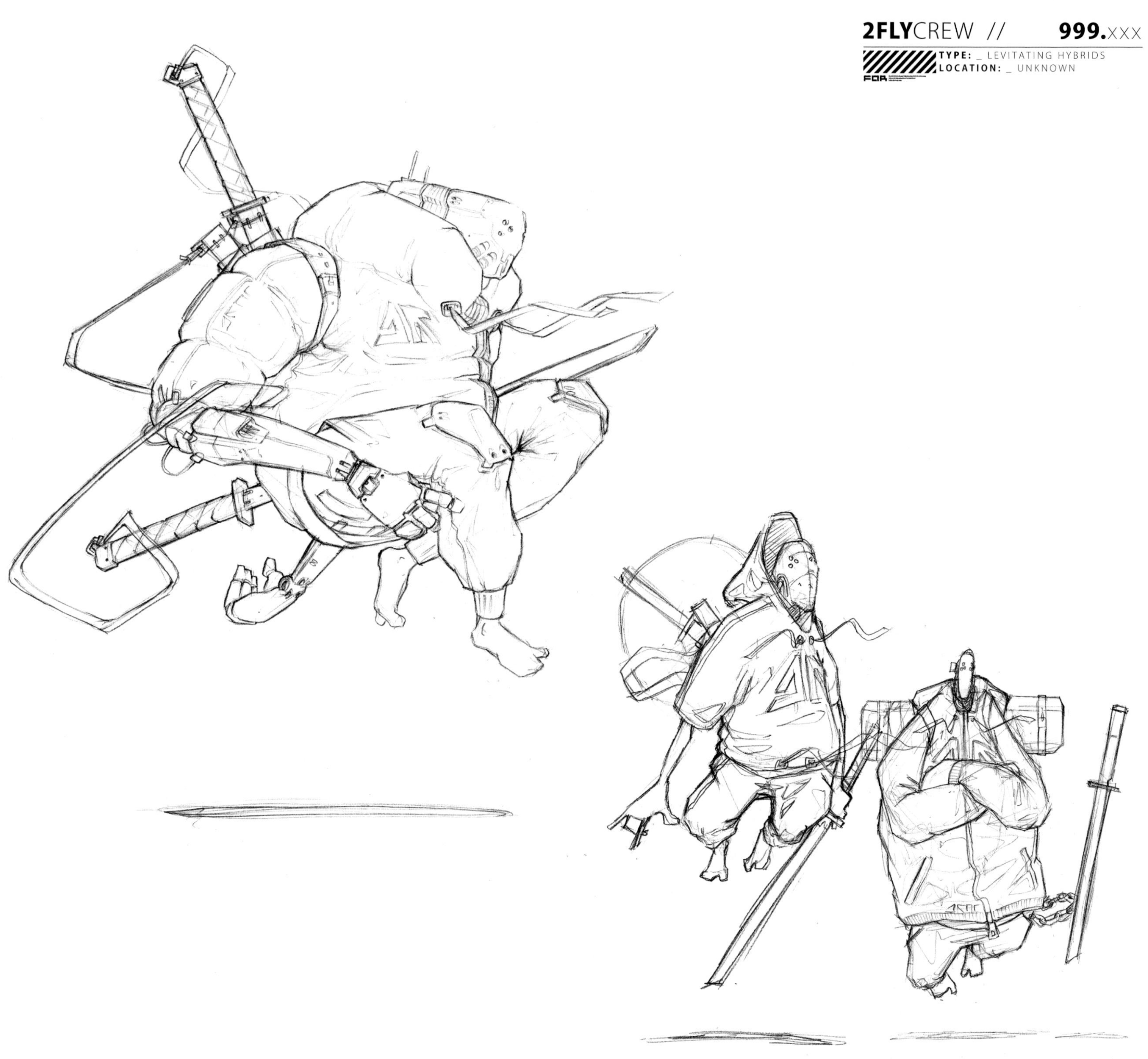

Being able to get their hands on three brand-new QLM_mk2 Quantum Levitation Masters, which had fallen from a delivery drone somewhere, gave these three friends a big advantage. Being "too fly" for rival gangs, they quickly climbed the food chain in the hood, and the 2FlyCrew was born.

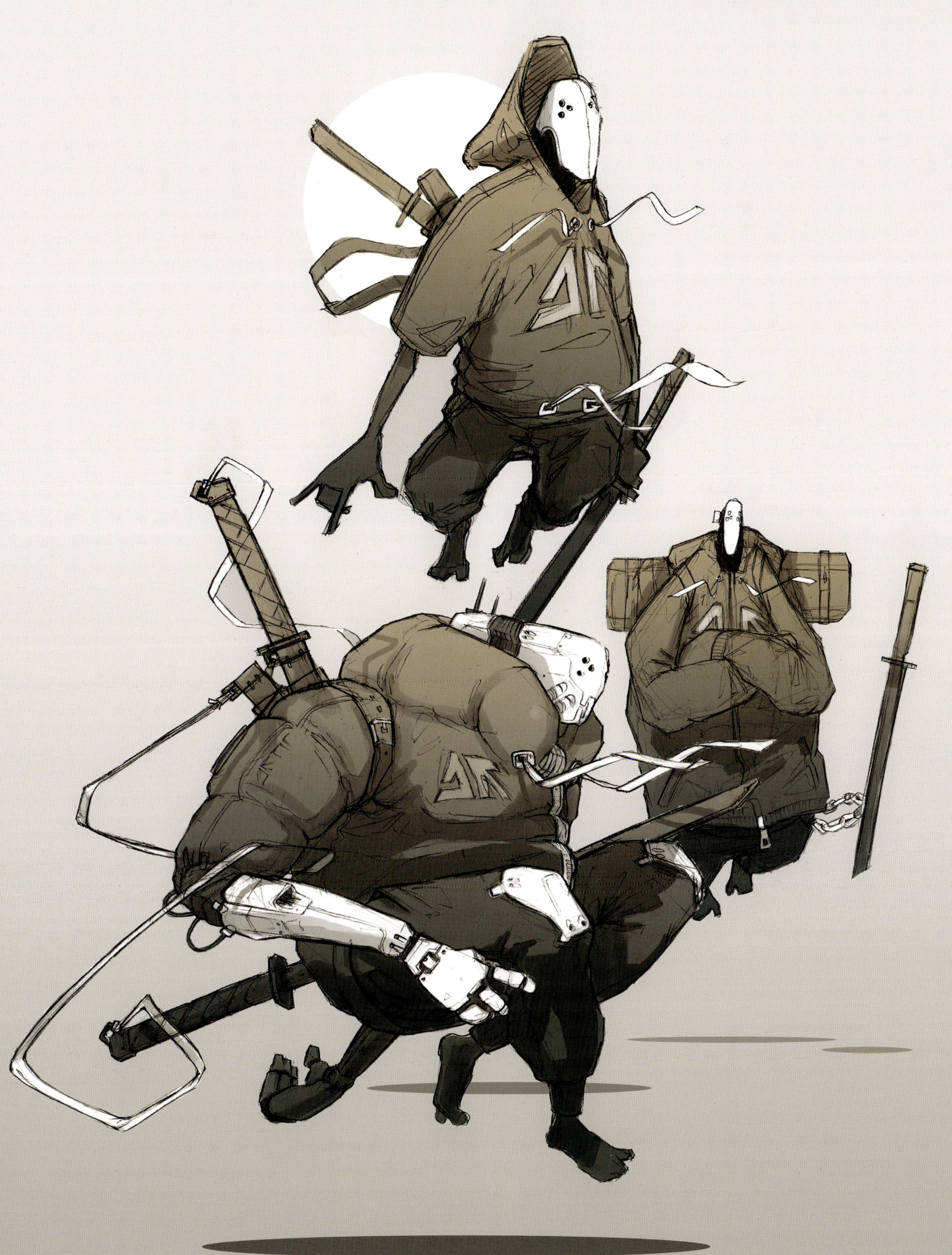

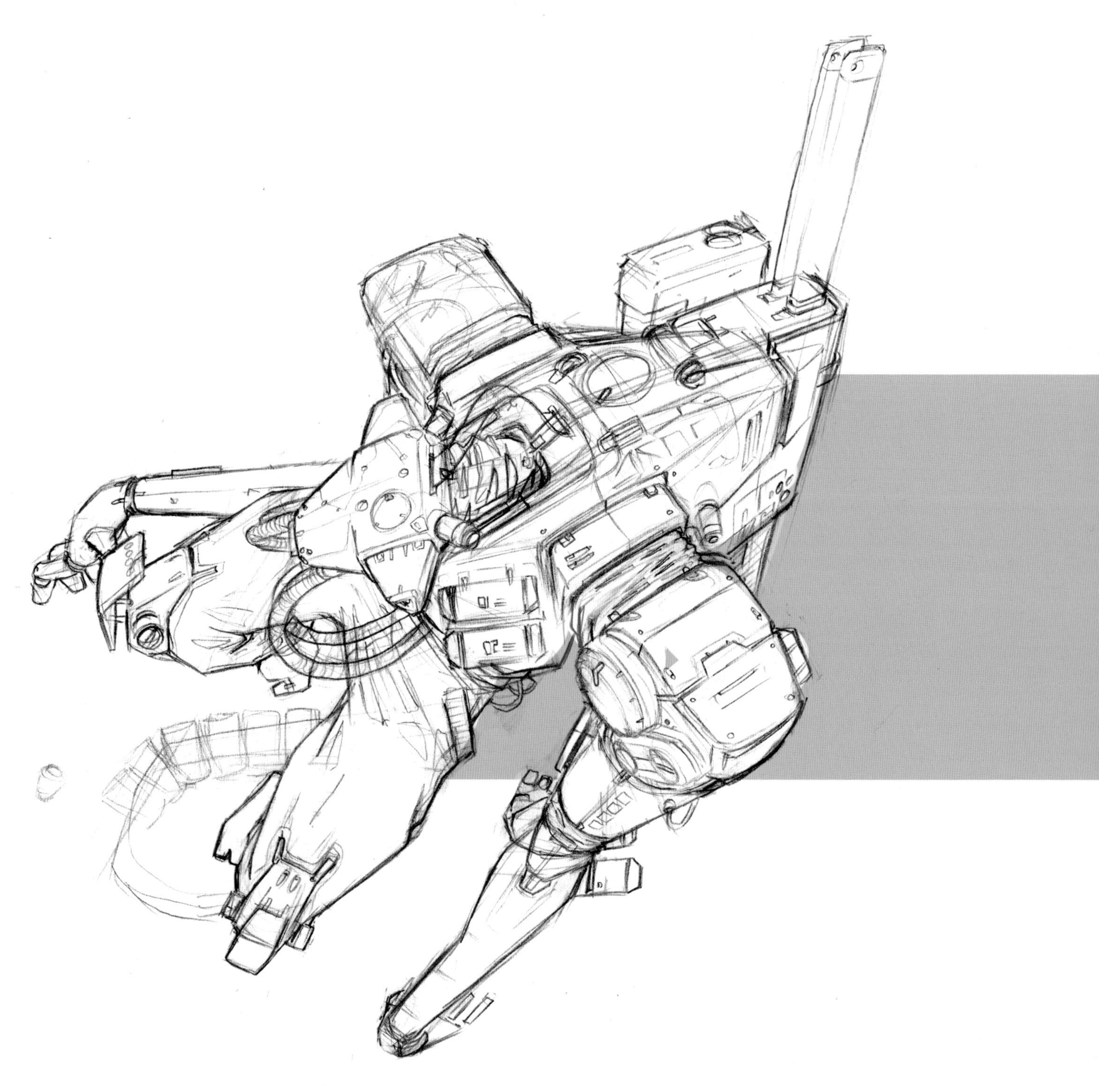

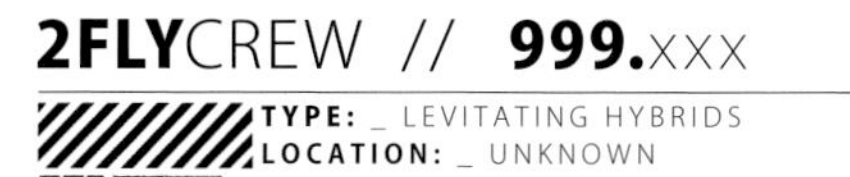
2FLYCREW // 999.xxx
TYPE: _ LEVITATING HYBRIDS
LOCATION: _ UNKNOWN

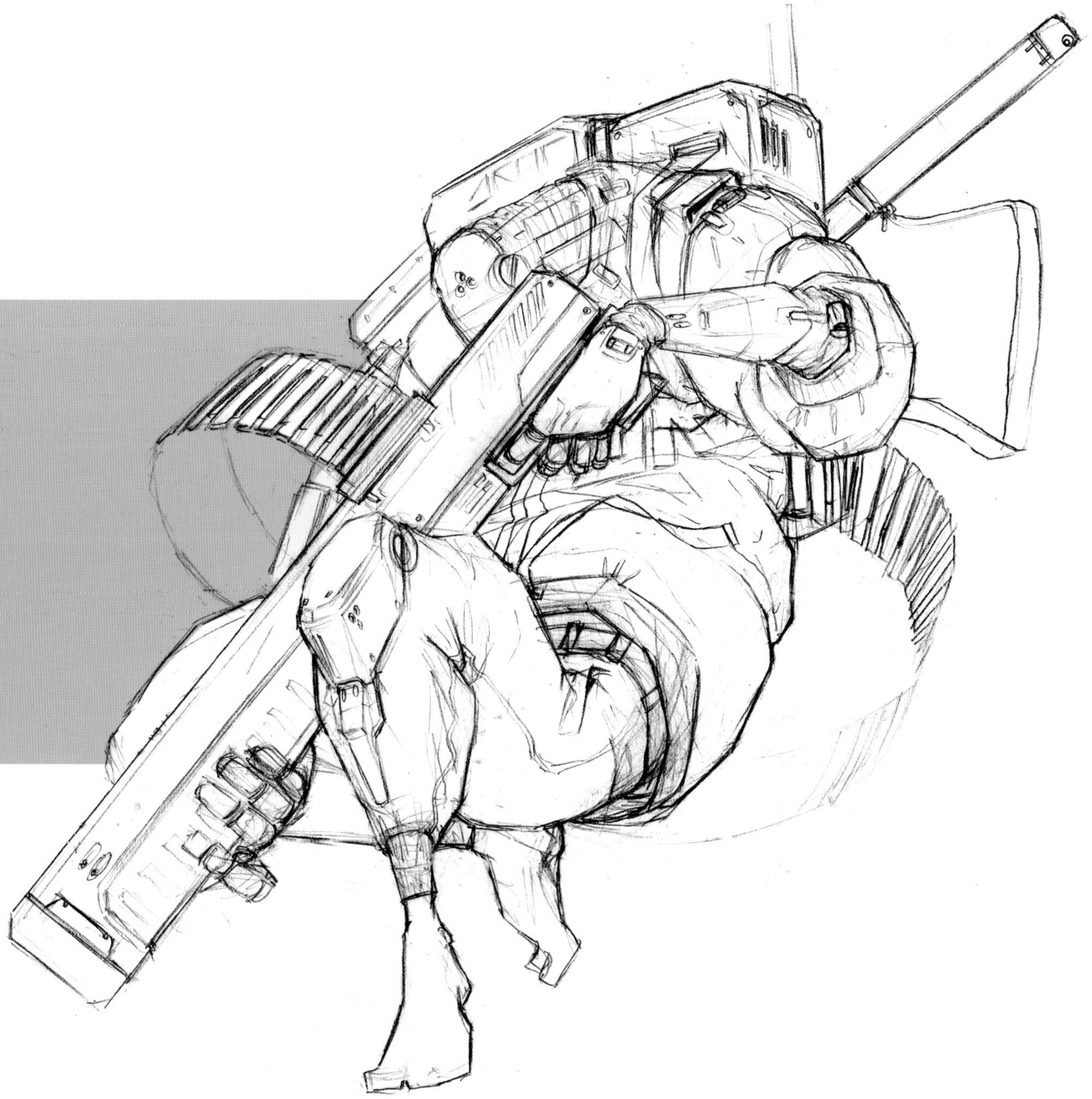

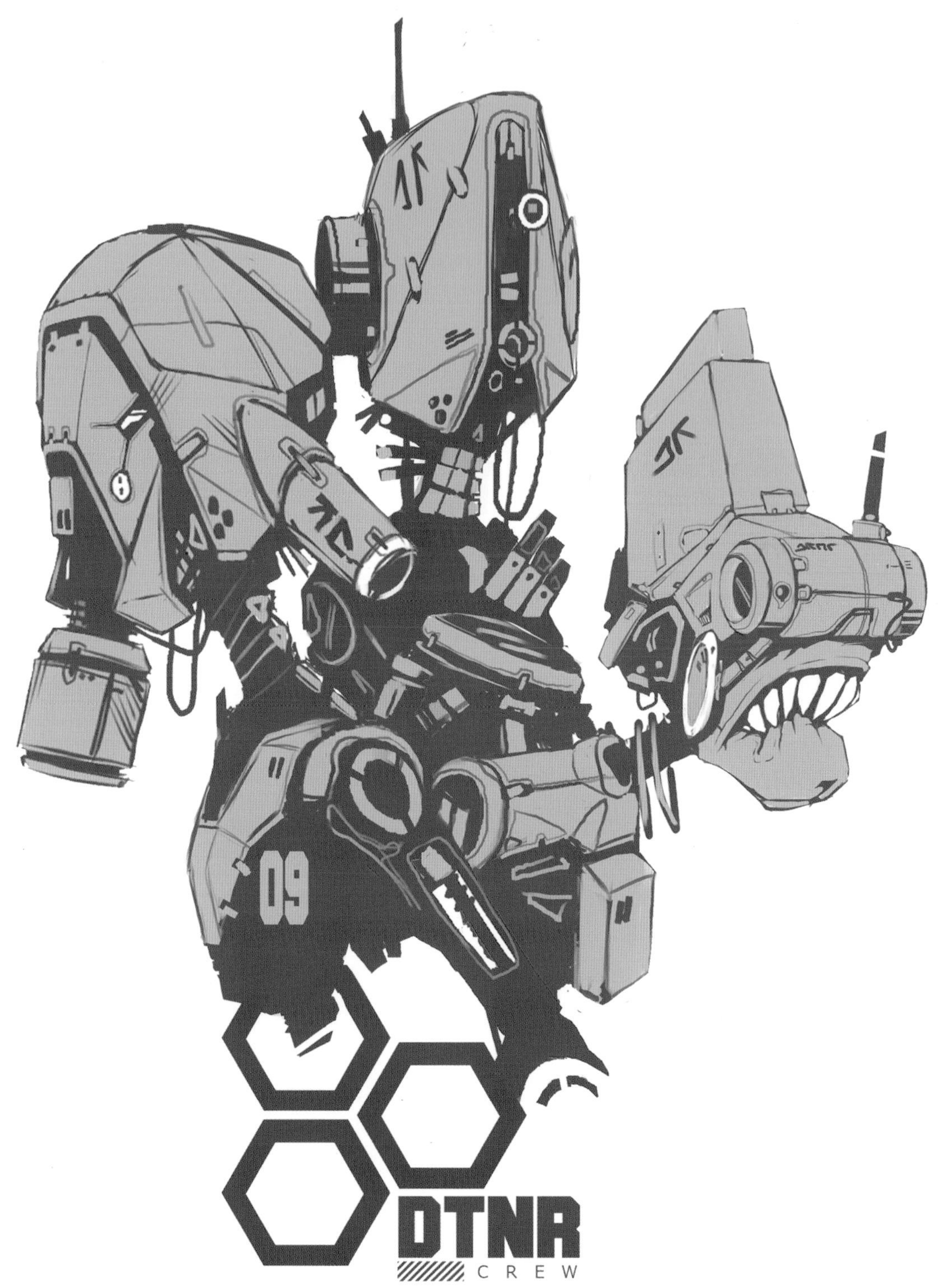

The biggest and most feared clan was the DTNR Crew, named after the early twenty-first-century design artist. The DTNR clan had chapters in all of the world's major cities. Style-wise related to the DOODES, they gained a much greater following. DTNR Crew also was the first posthuman clan to gain political support from robots and posthumans alike.

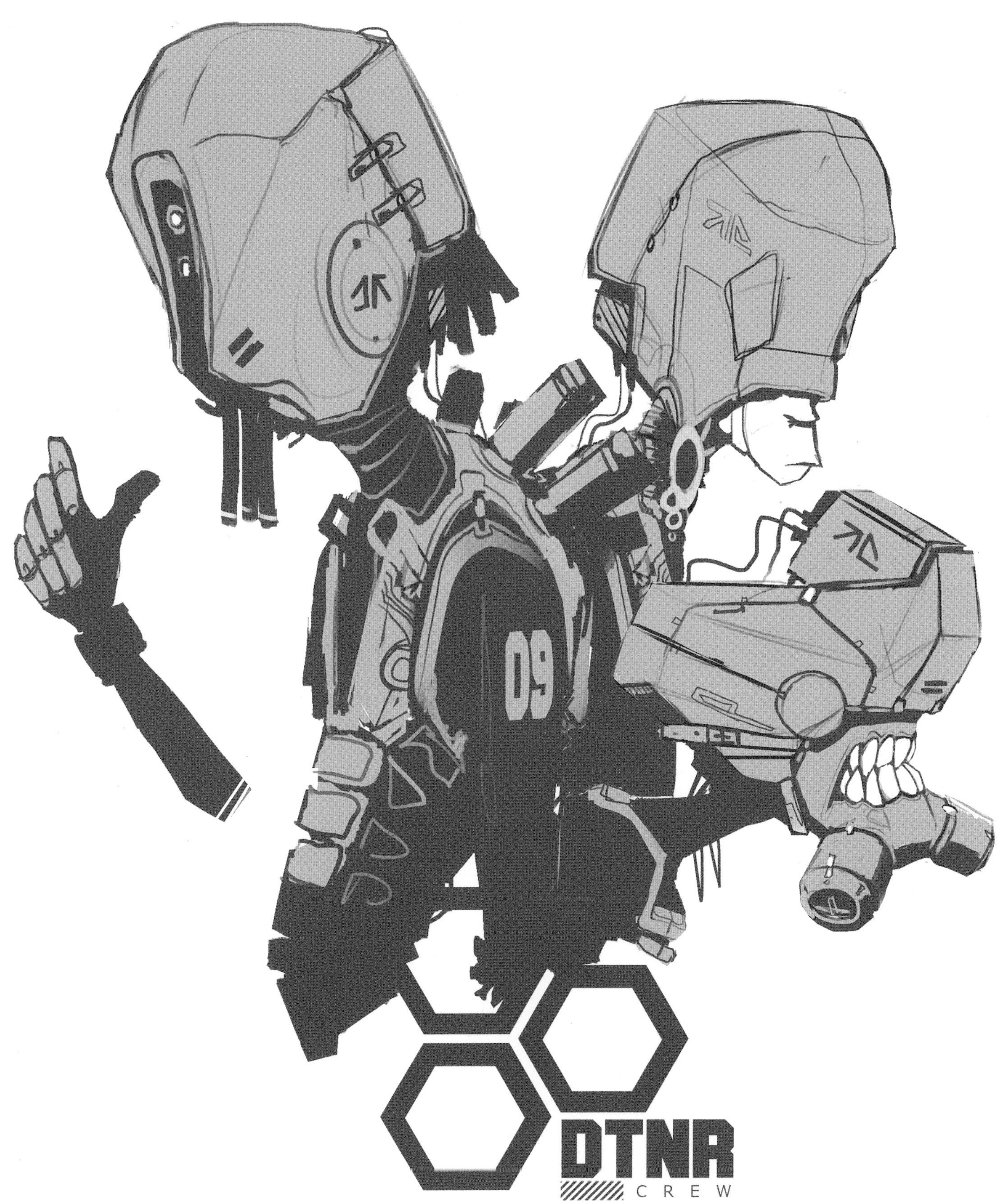
09
DTNR
CREW

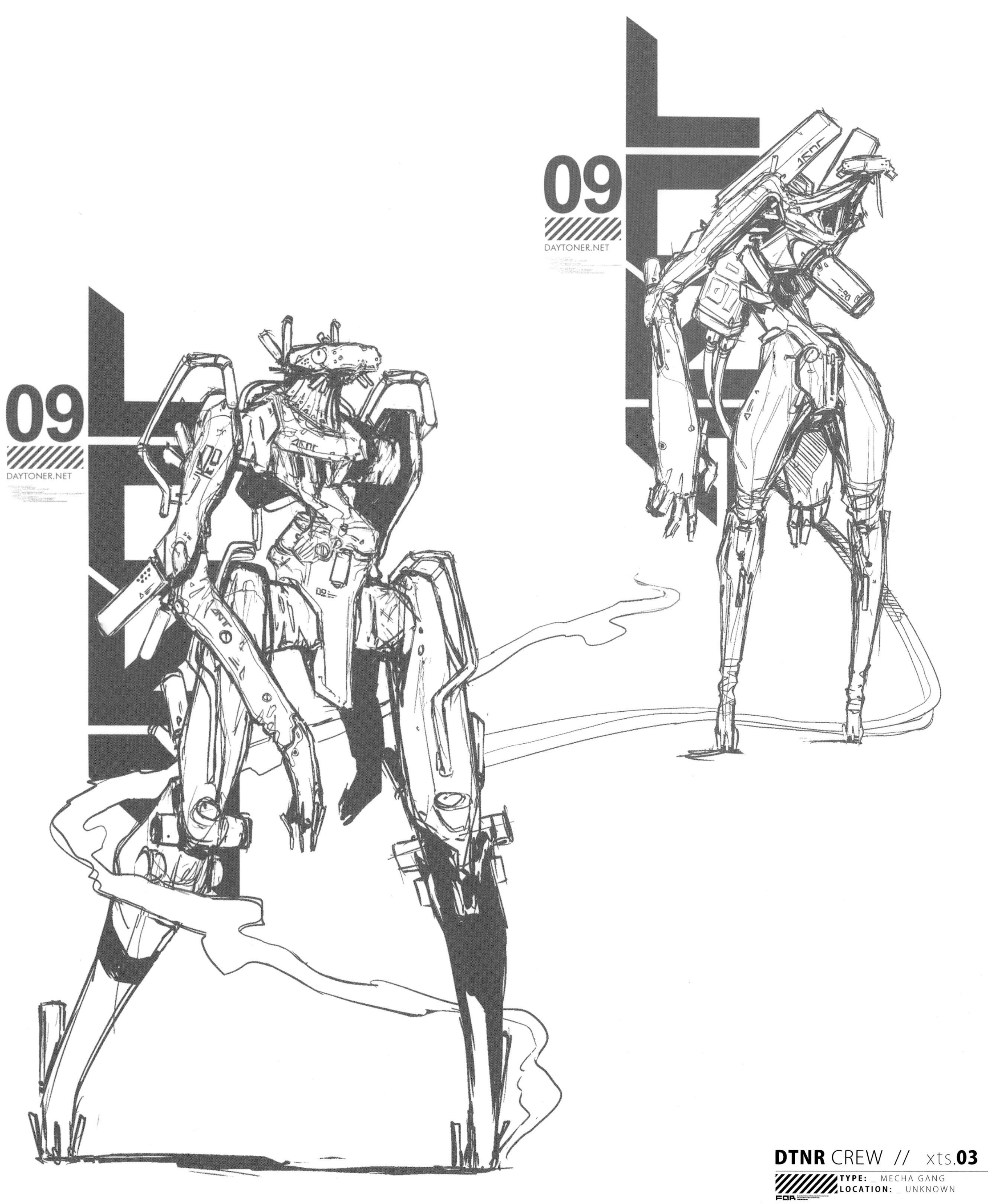

DTNR CREW // xts.**03**

TYPE: _ MECHA GANG
LOCATION: _ UNKNOWN

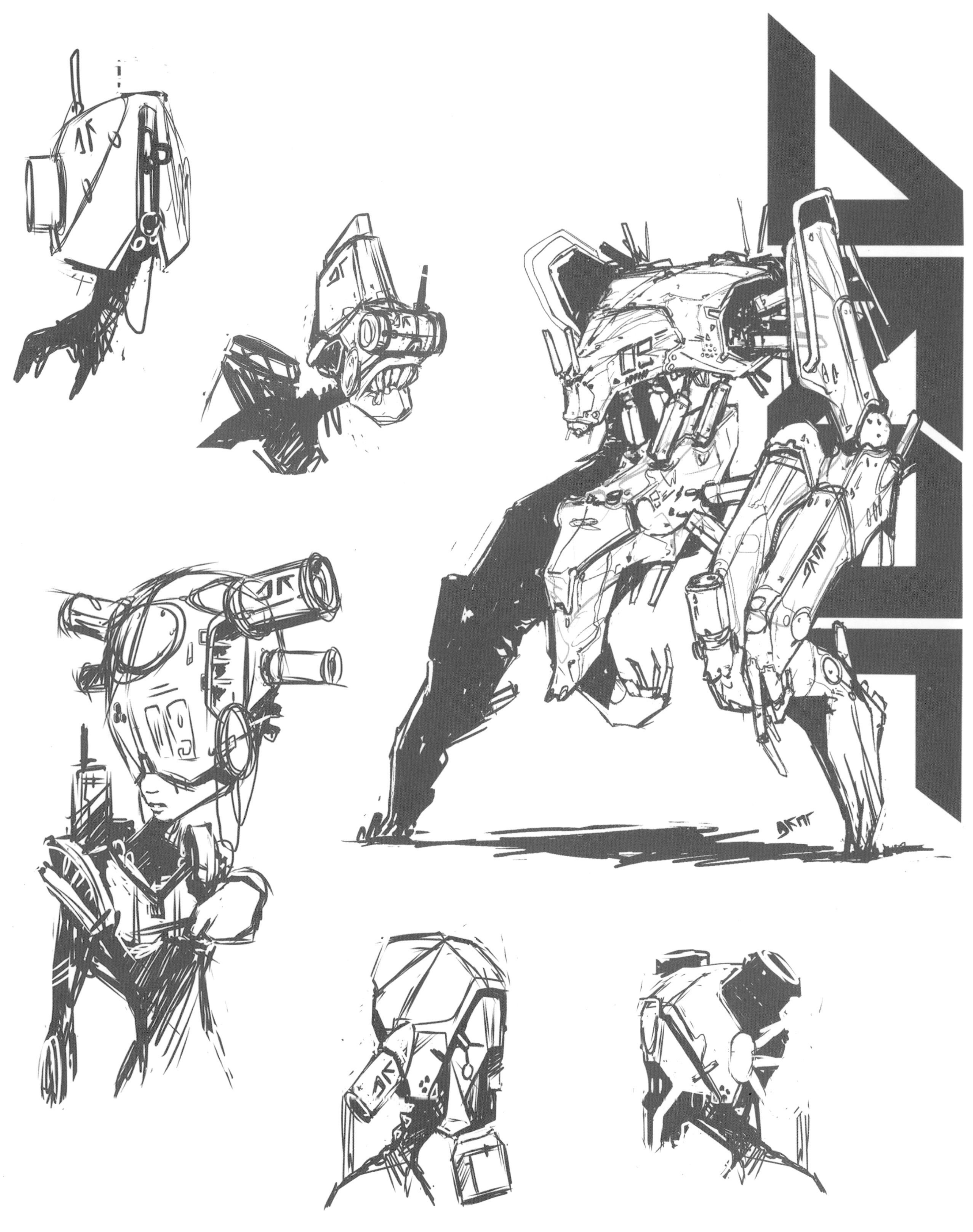

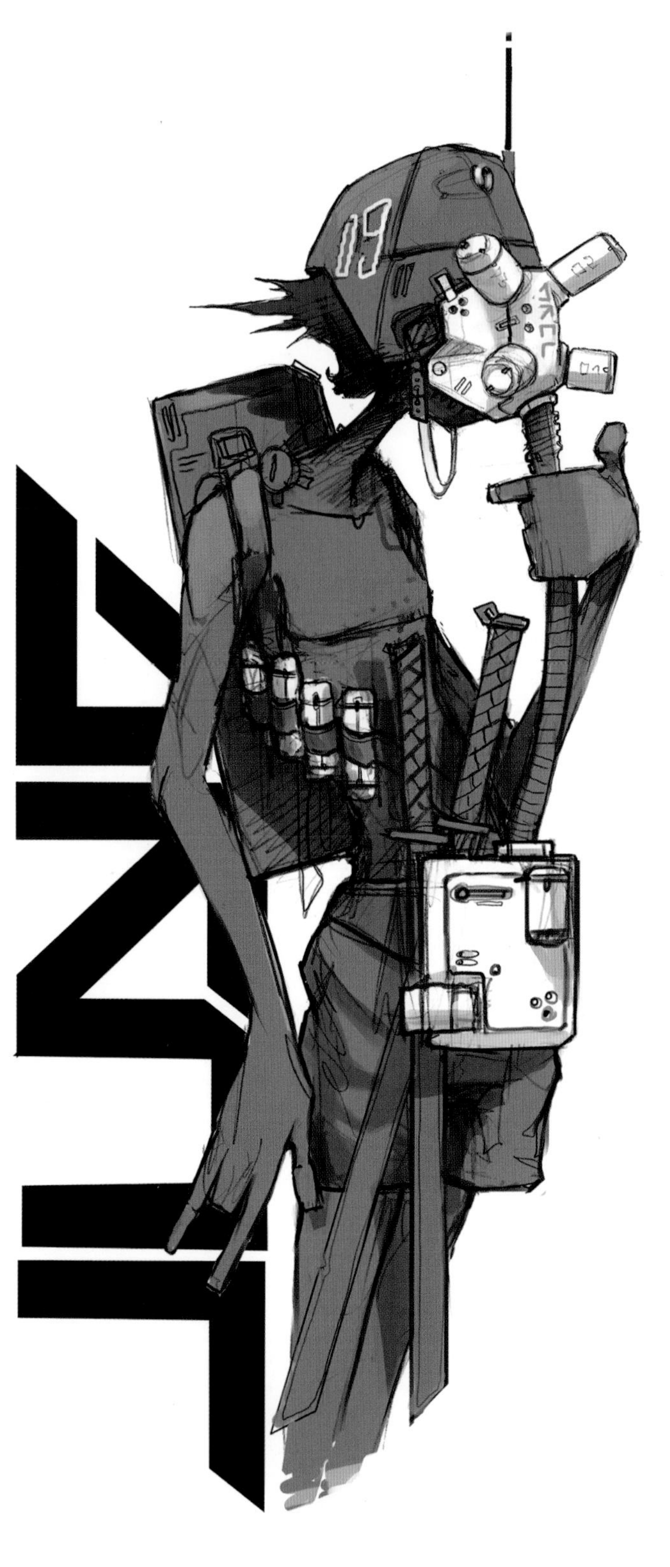

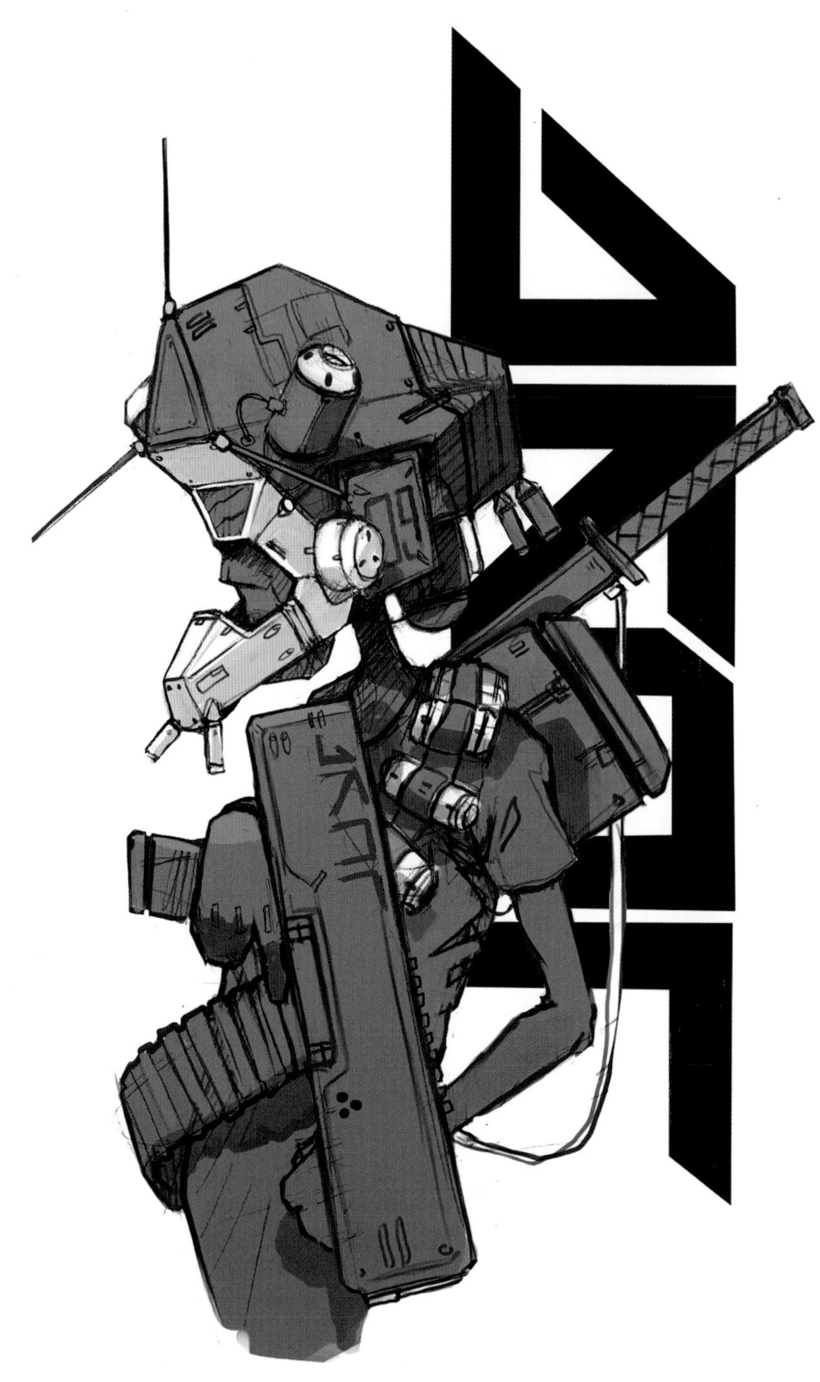

DTNR Crew members gave off a strong, old-school hip-hop vibe. "Graffiti Stil" was a welcome creative outlet for most of the clan. It is not surprising that some members of the DTNR Crew later became the template for a virtual-character driven hip-hop band. The DTNR Crew "Graffiti Stil" mod gave *Vertical Skies* a second wind.

TYPE: _ MECHA GANG
LOCATION: _ UNKNOWN

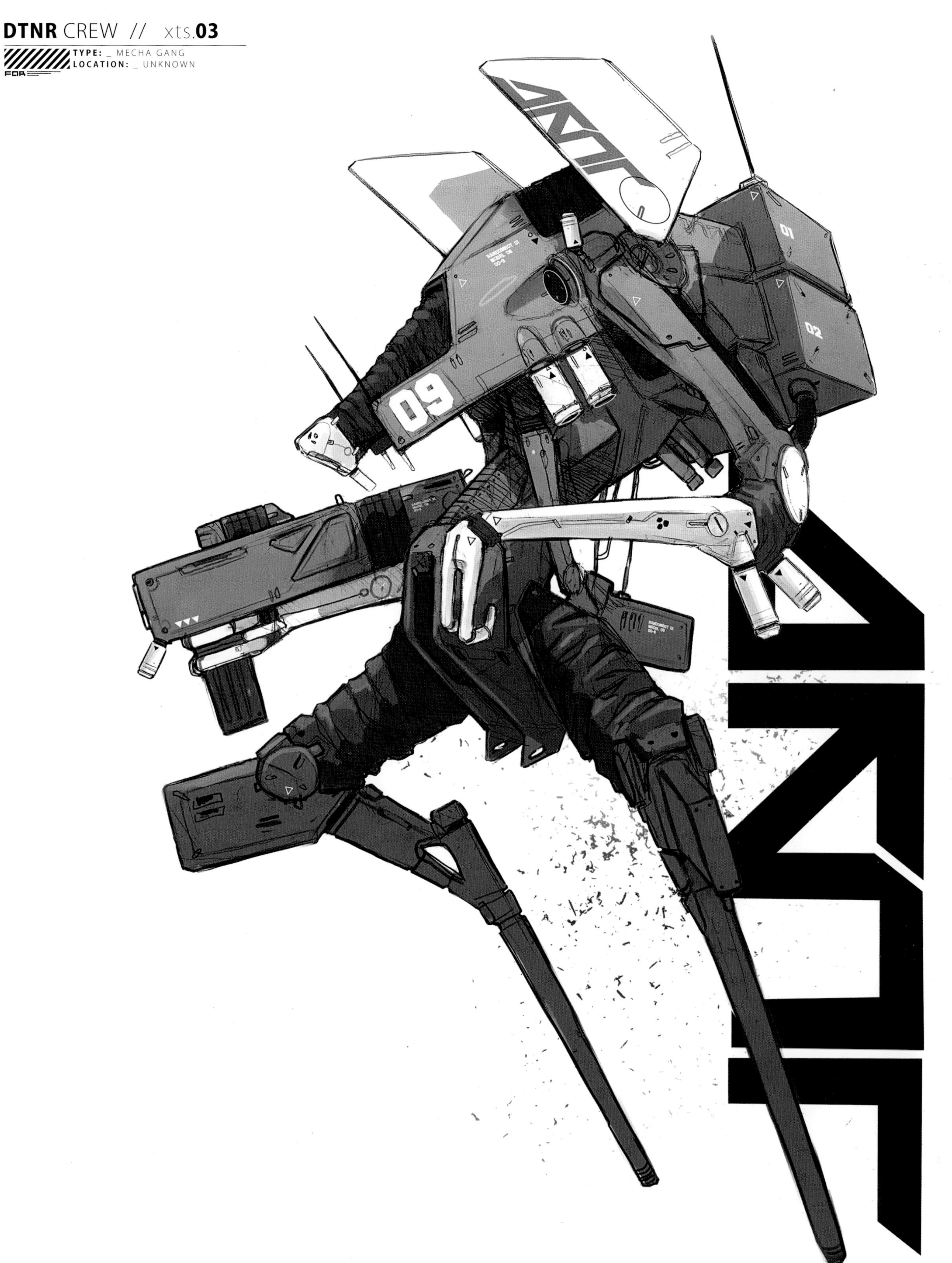

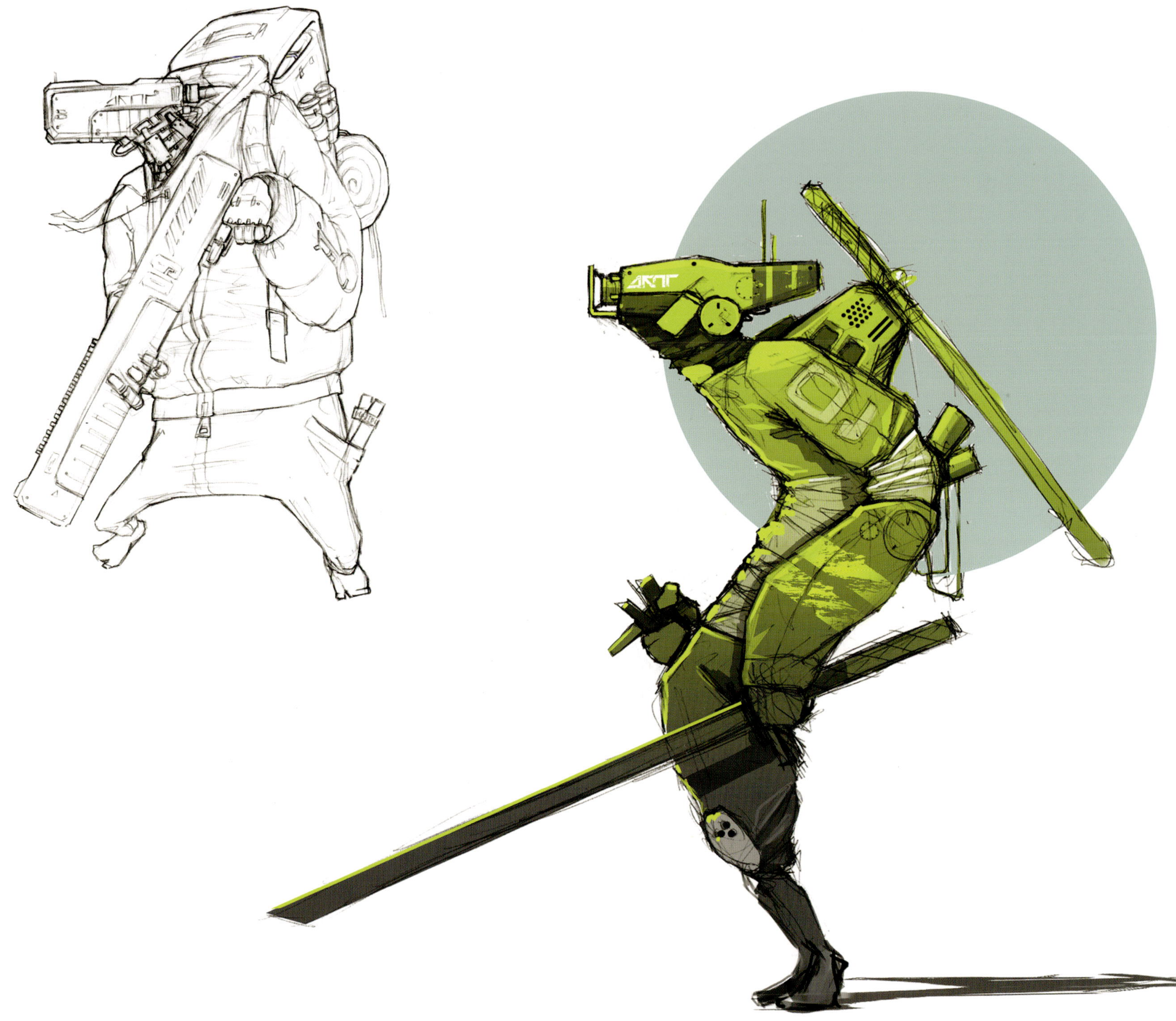

M9E, short for Master Nine Eyes, and Master Yiga were the founders of the M9E Clan. M9E never left the house without his "knife block." To have a plan B or, even better, a plan C was a crucial strategic element in his otherwise reckless and lavish fighting style. His enemies usually underestimated him due to his chunky appearance. But he always had the better stance!

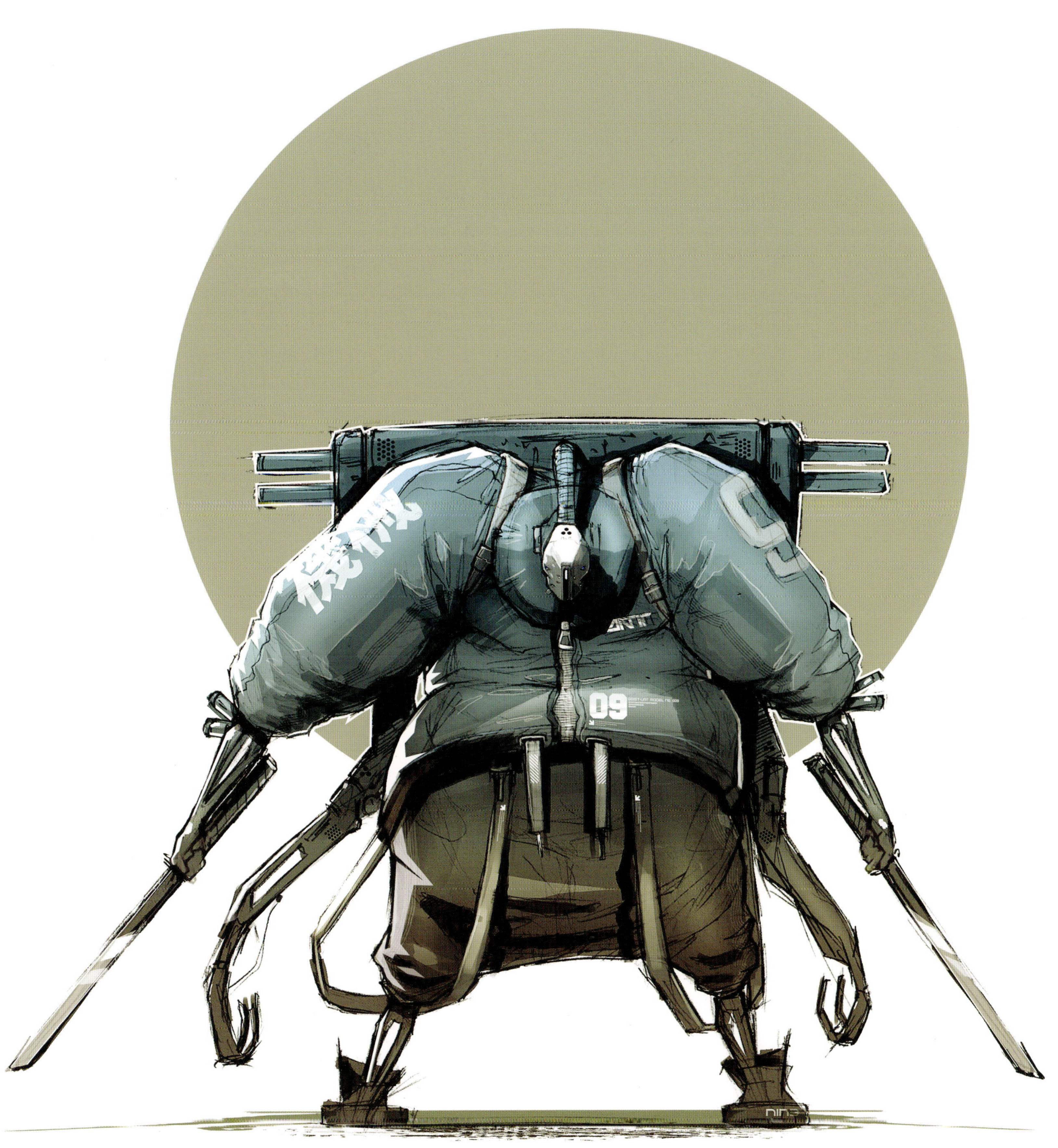
09

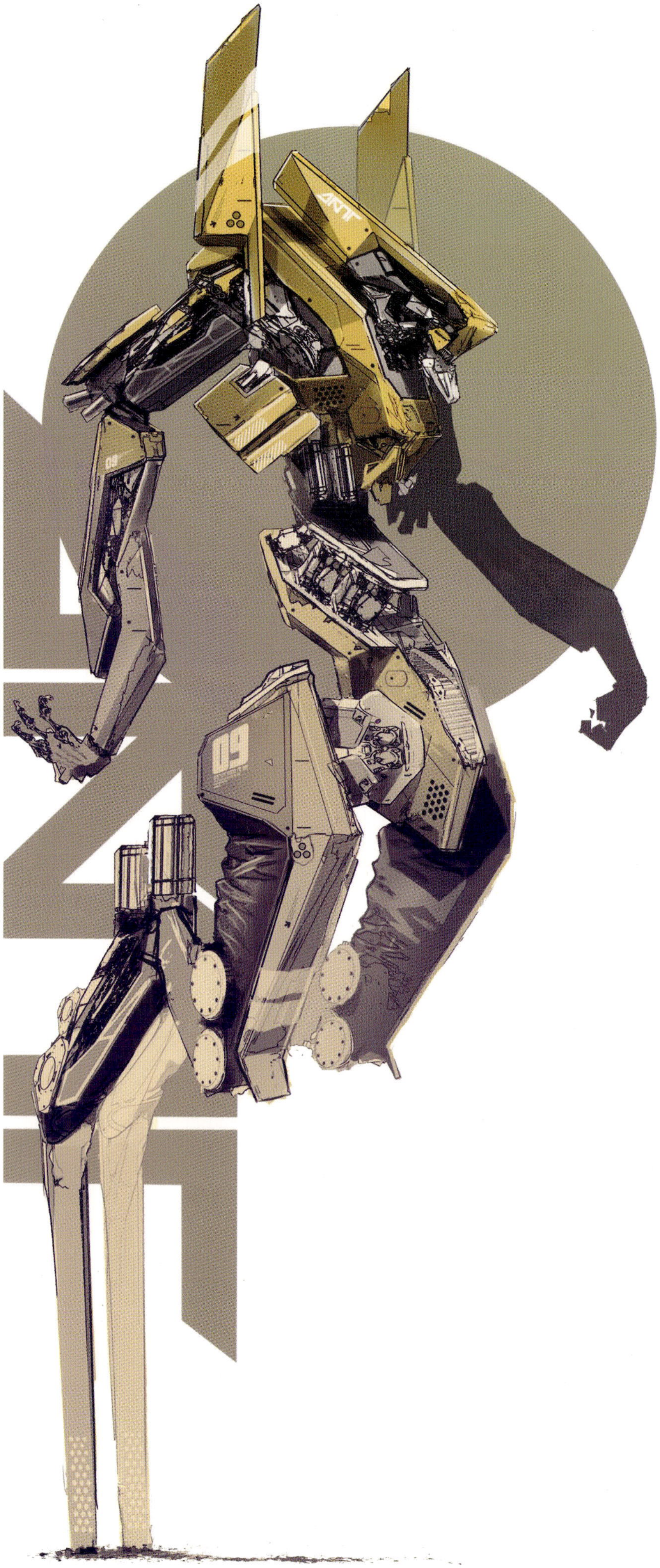

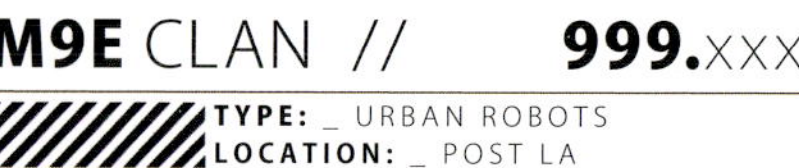
M9E CLAN // 999.XXX
TYPE: _ URBAN ROBOTS
LOCATION: _ POST LA

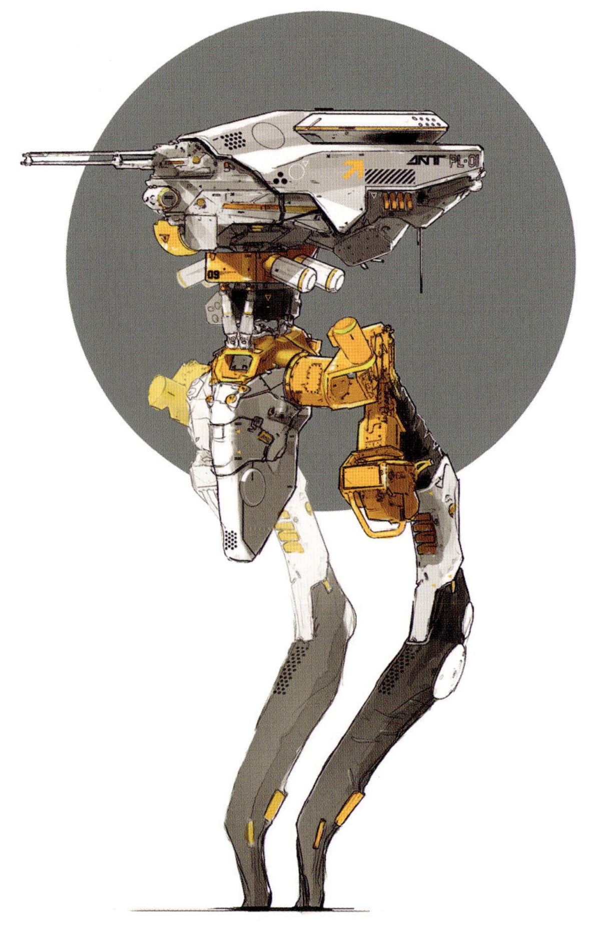

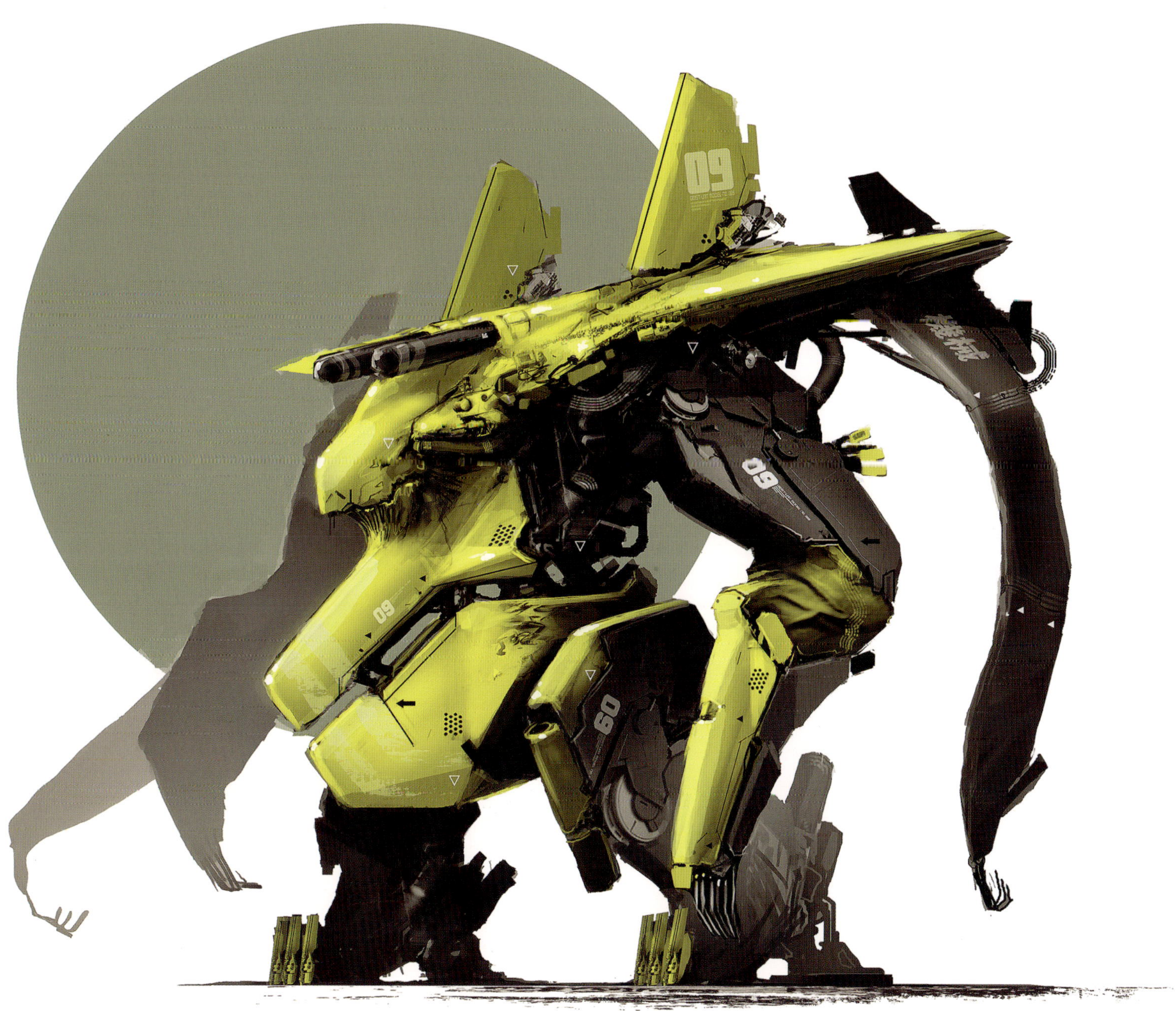

Master Nine Eyes attracted a ton of attention on social media and started a vinyl toy line under his name. Back then, he had an inner circle of four gathered around him. Not much is known about them. They would later become the brains behind the M9E operation. "Gunny," the mechanical mix between a rabbit and a gun, was Master Nine Eyes' most favorite pet.

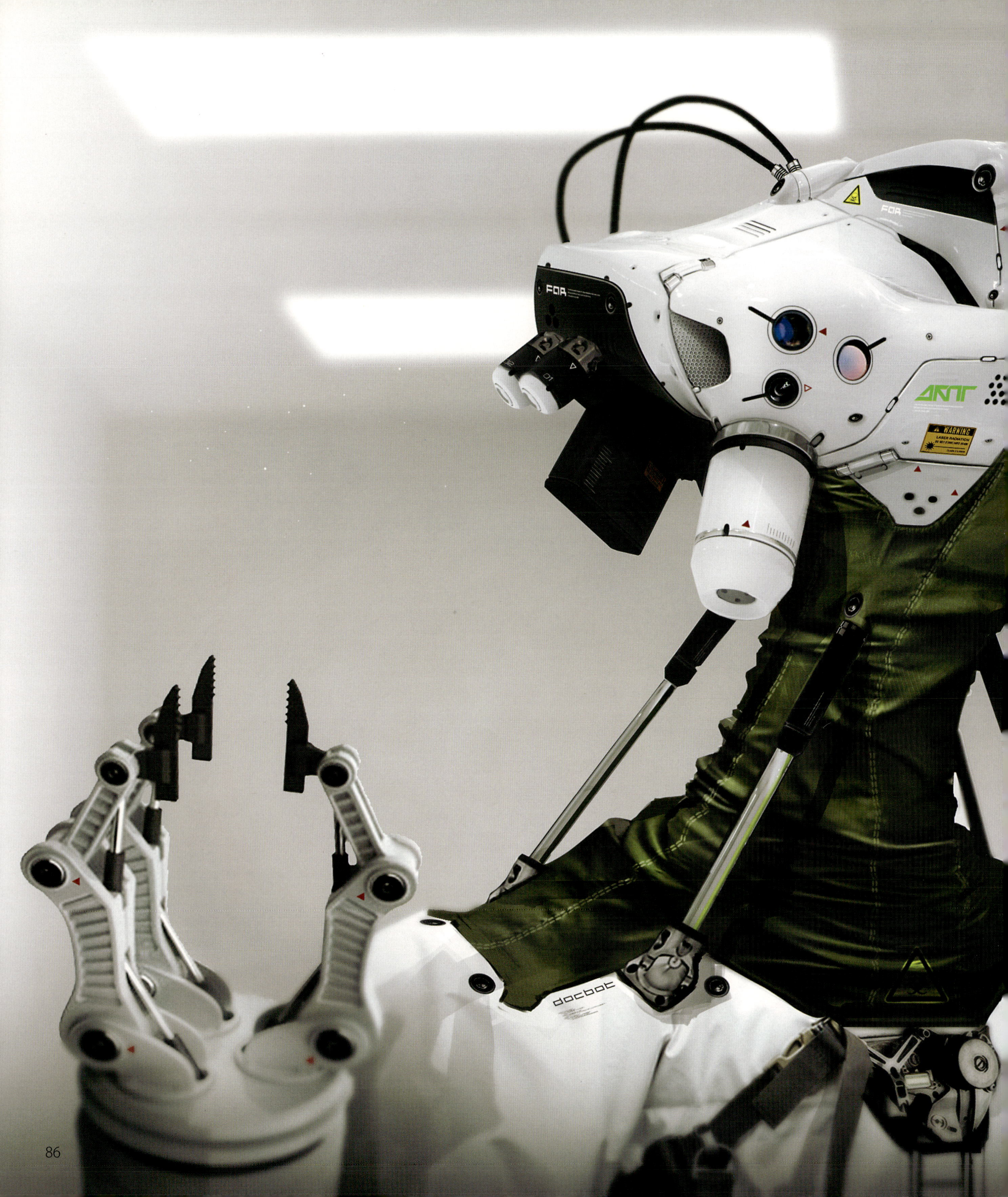
FOA
FOA
ANT
WARNING
LASER RADIATION
docbot

DOCBOT // v.01

TYPE: _ PLASTIC SURGEON
LOCATION: _ CEDARS-SINAI

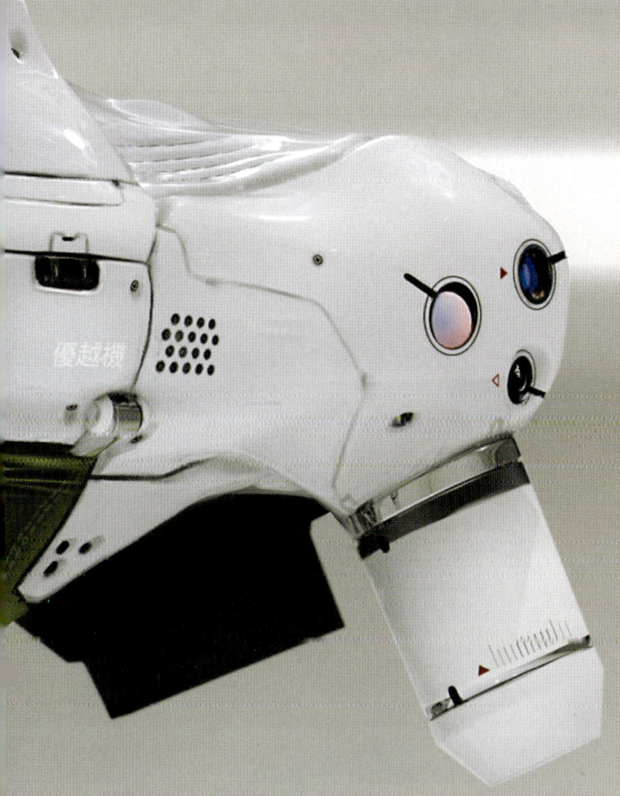

Lovably nicknamed "plastic surgeons" by squaddies, the DocBot combat medic care units drastically improved golden hour survival rates at the onset of the Iran war's second year. Later on, these units would become popular in various aesthetic surgery applications.

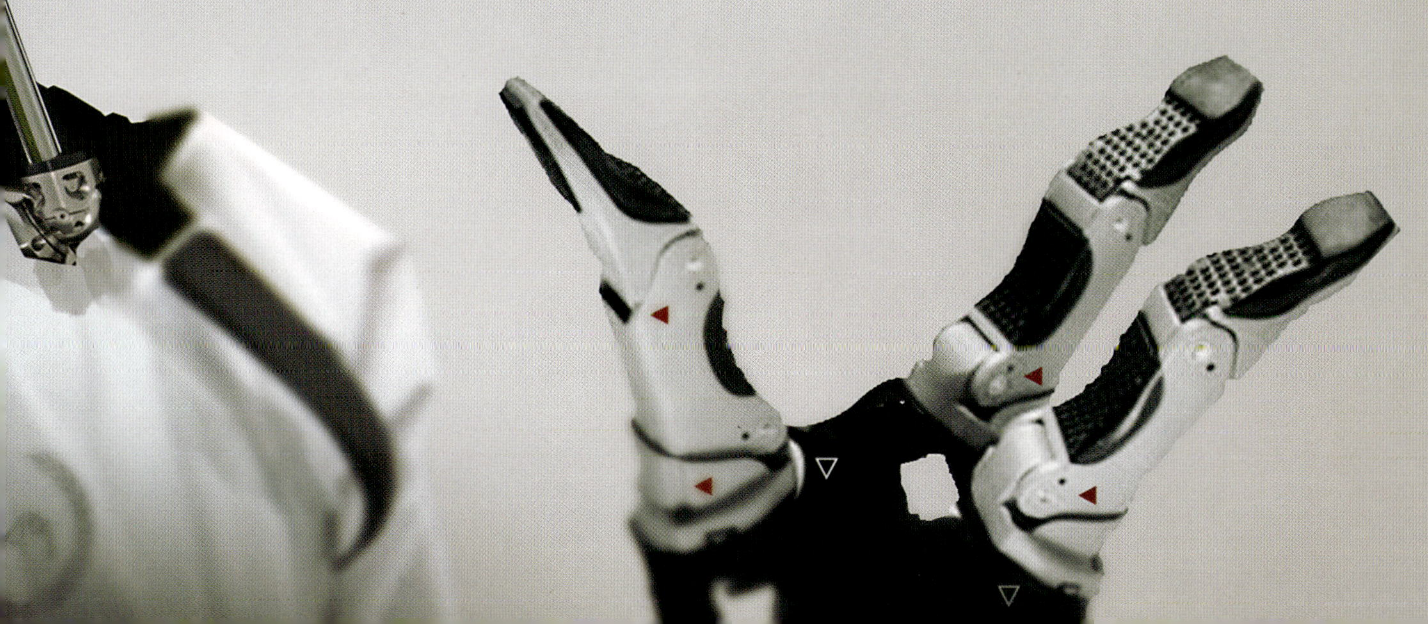

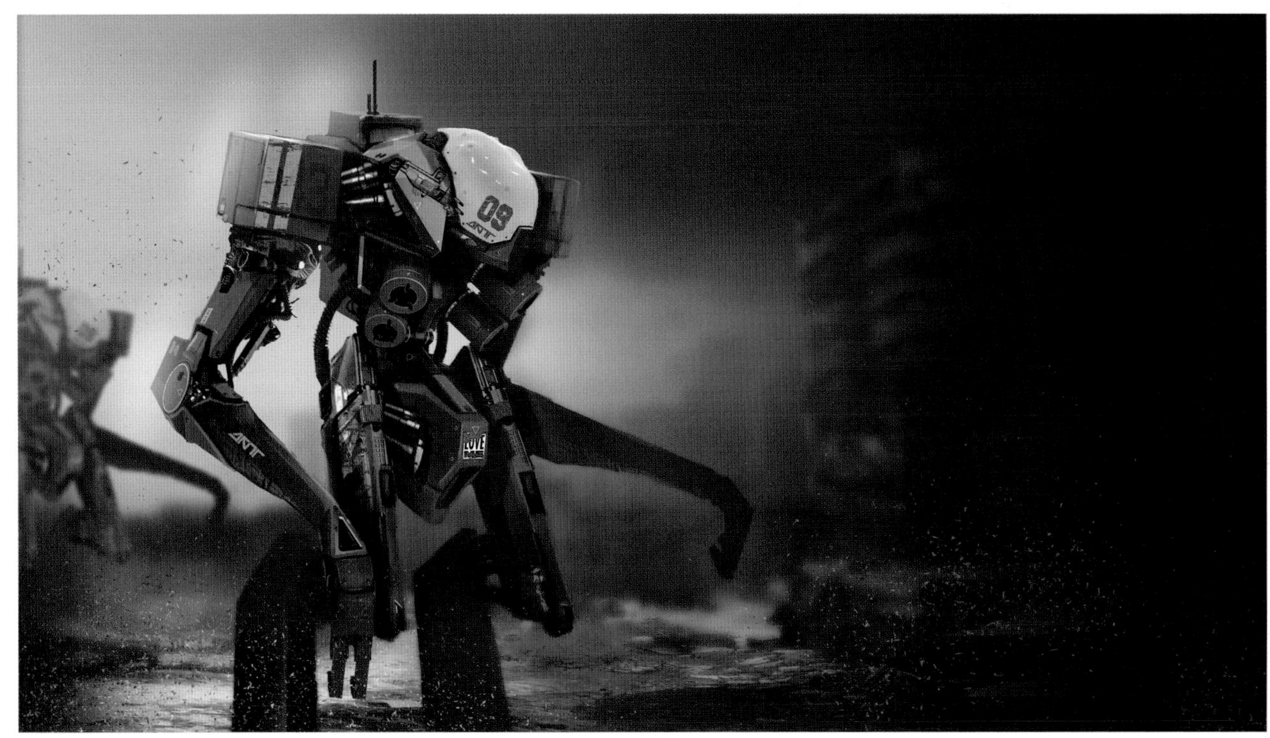

Nakatomi Industries' Relief Bot 09 and BIGBOT were originally designed for Fukushima cleanup operations. They ended up in automated urban eviction instead.

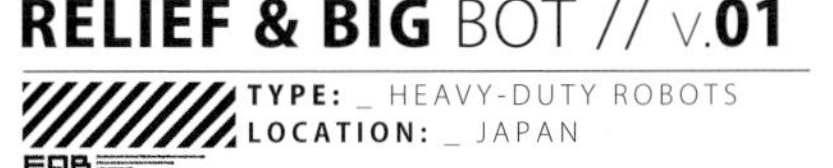

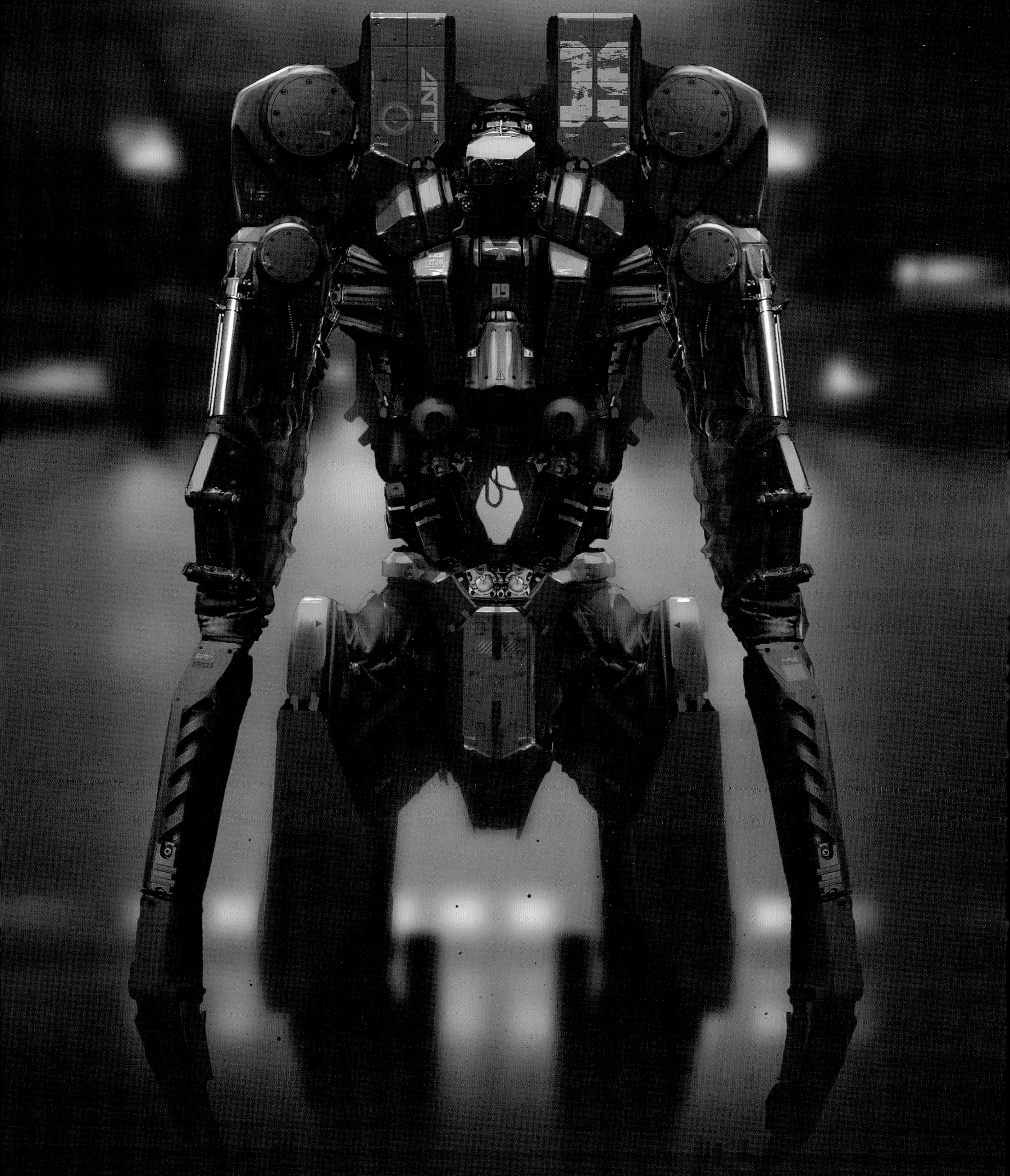

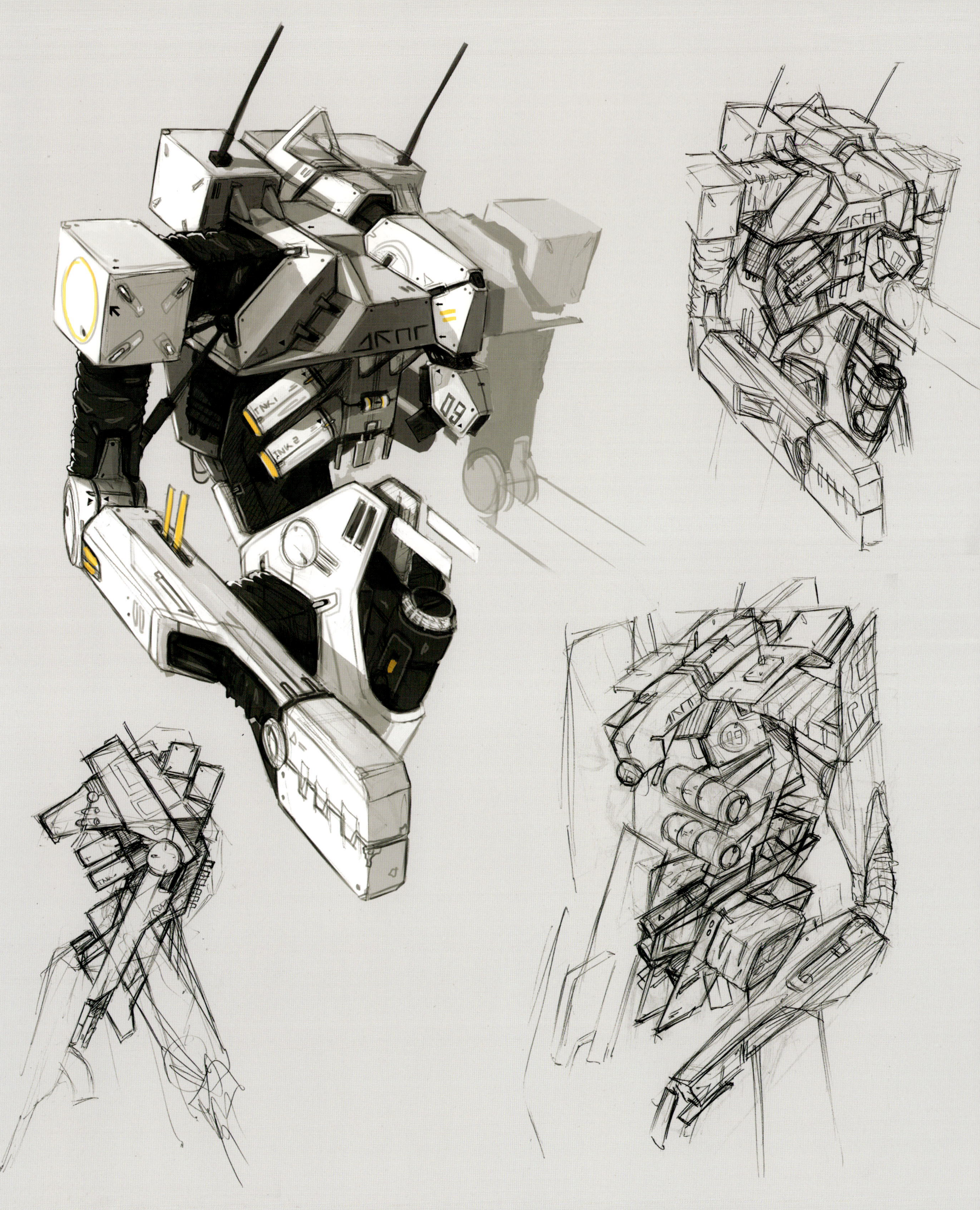

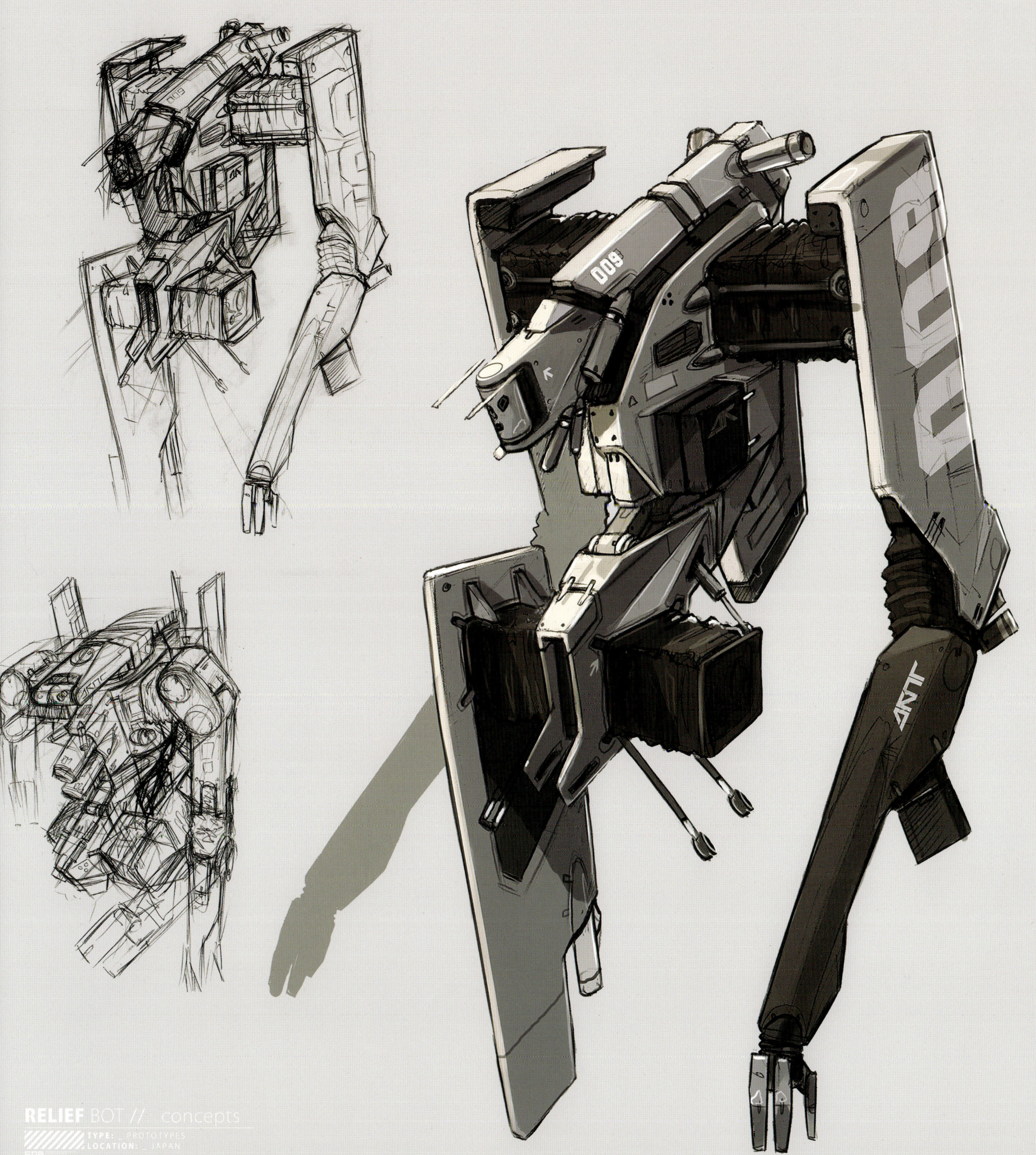

RELIEF BOT // _concepts

TYPE: _PROTOTYPES
LOCATION: _JAPAN

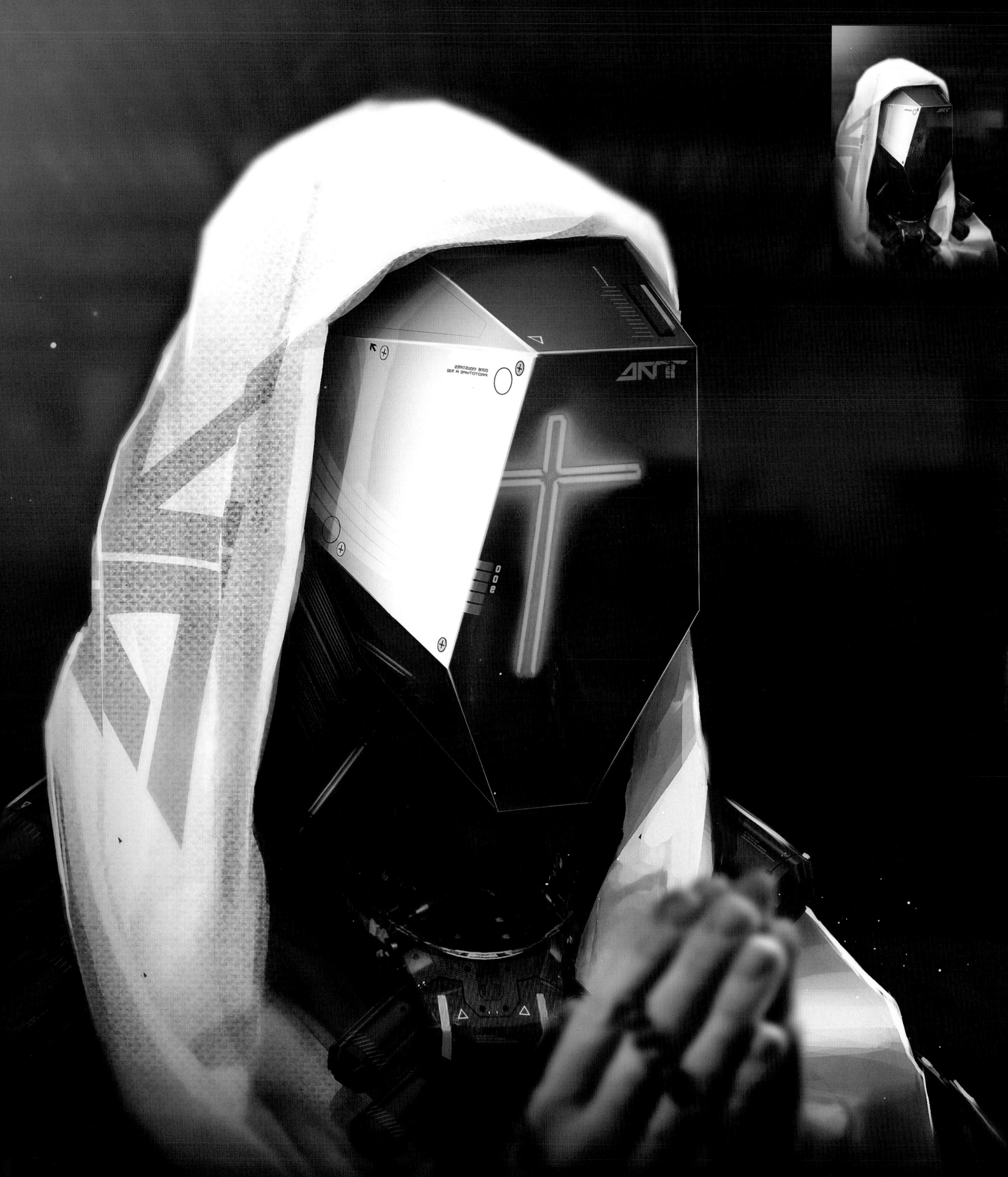

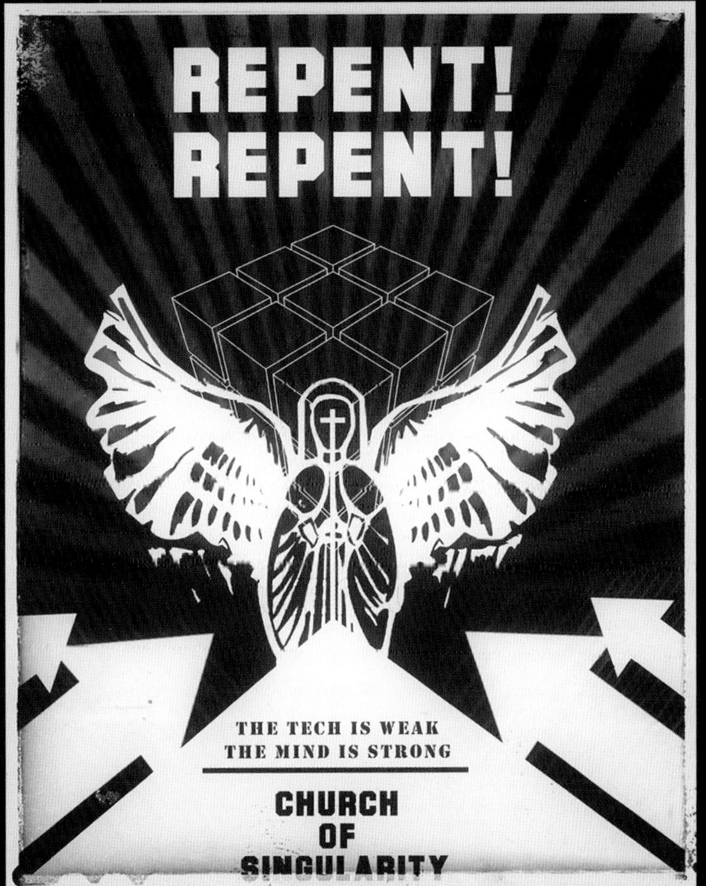

Singularism took a heavy blow when Chinese proto-AGIs discovered the quantum mind barrier in 2031. With what skeptics had always ridiculed the "rapture for nerds" postponed indefinitely, and an upload of consciousness unattainable within their lifetime, the remaining followers, the most hard-core of hard-core Singularists, developed the strange religious mixture of Judeo-Christian and Panpsychic Mysticism that is known as the Church of Singularity today.

Unrepentant church members faced a new doctrine of swift and mercilessly precise retribution when the high priestess proclaimed herself head of the Church of Singularity.

HIGH PRIESTESS // **v.01**

TYPE: _ FEMALE HYBRID
LOCATION: _ CHURCH OF SINGULARITY

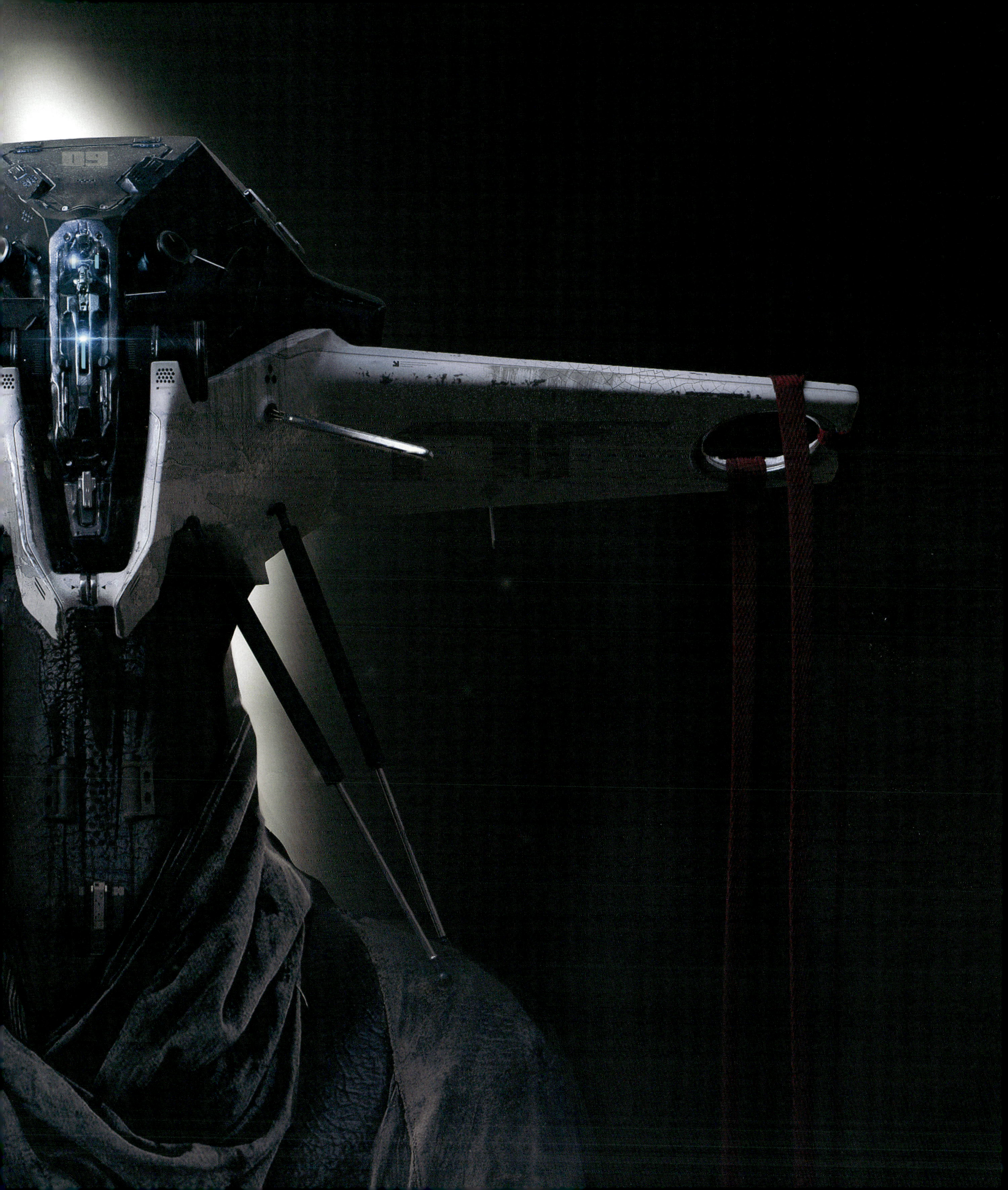

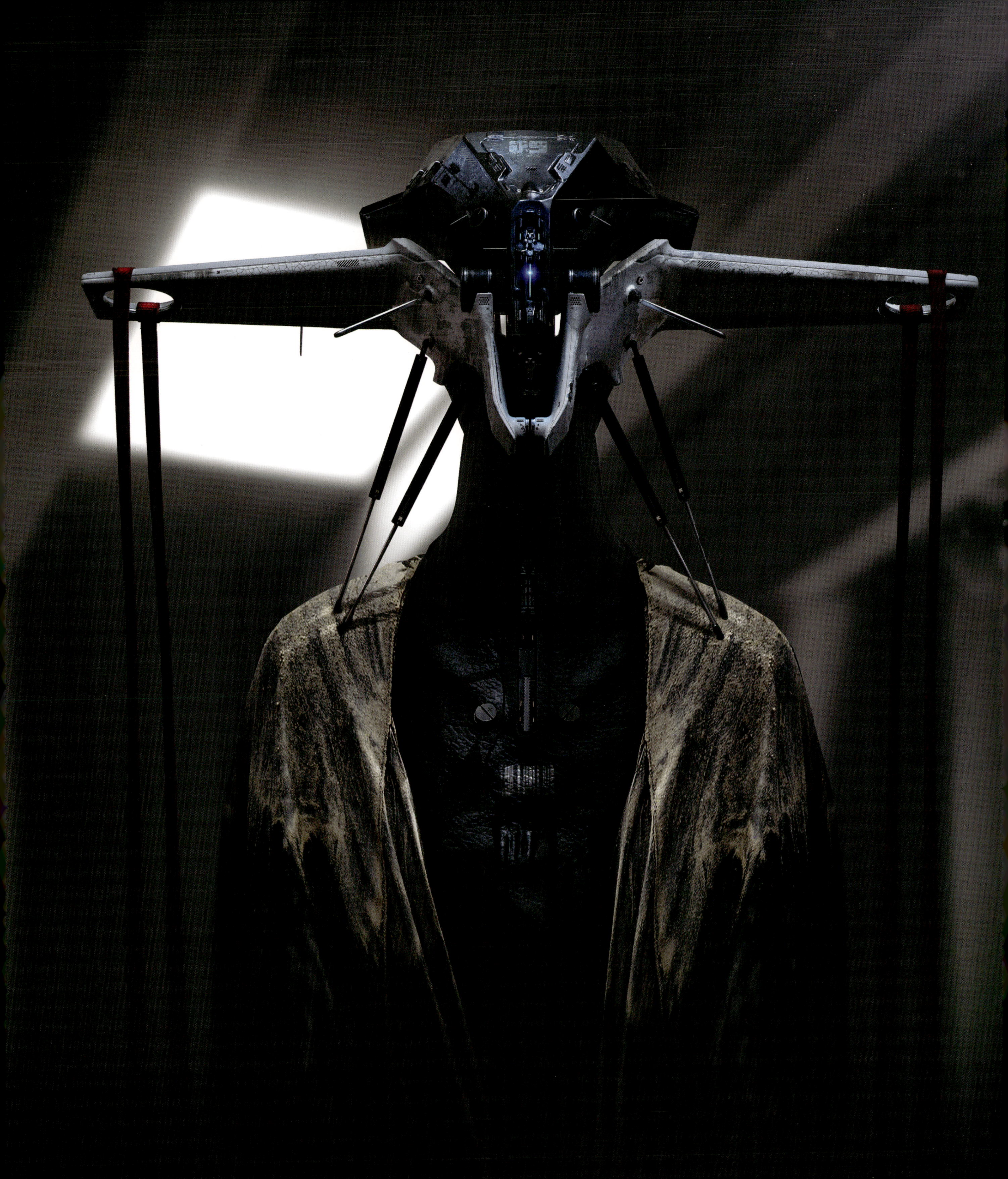

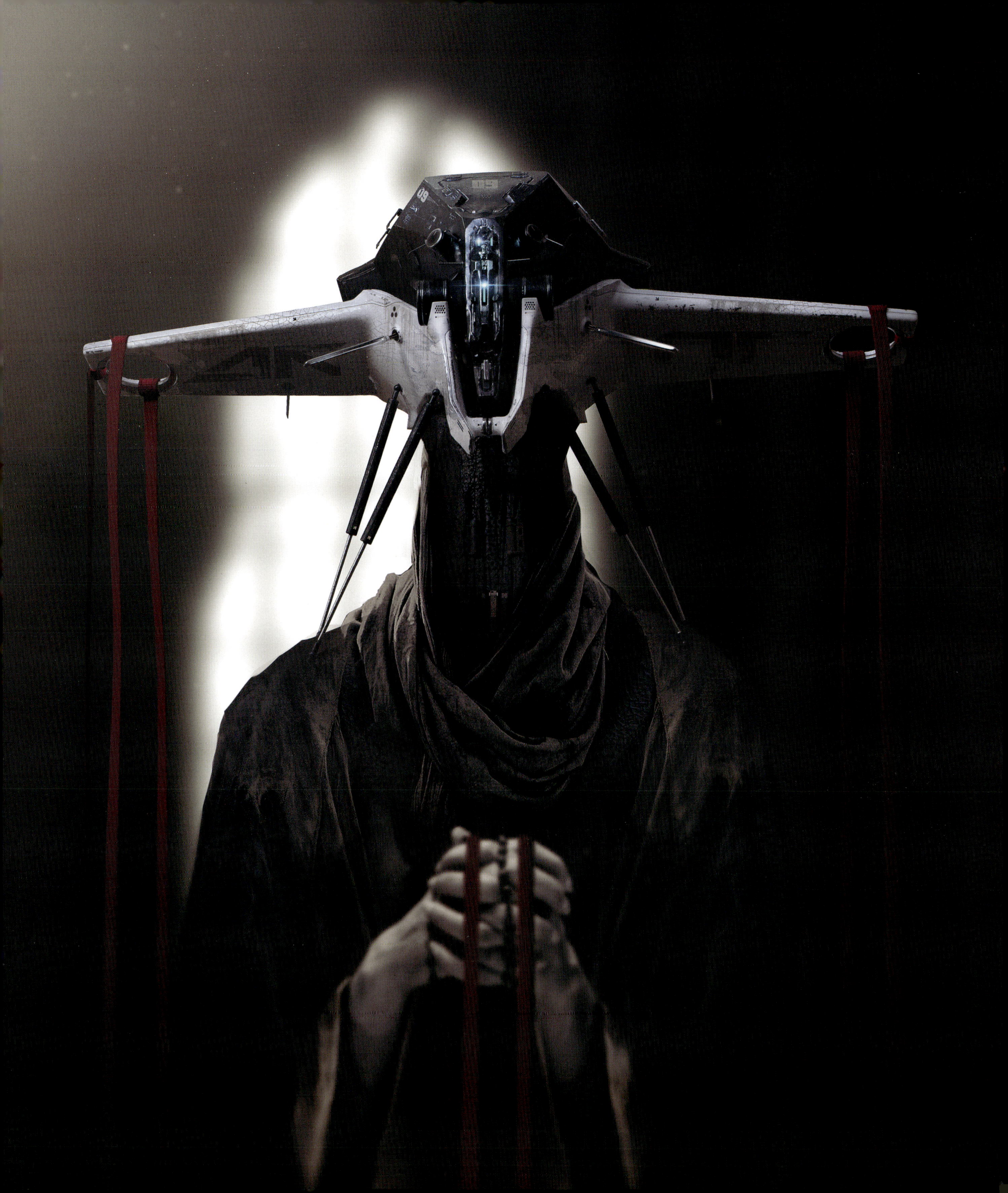

To retain the wisdom of their oldest members, the Church of Singularity embraced posthuman tech. Believing that all knowledge could be saved and that the human brain would always remain superior, they turned to robotic carrying vessels. It is said that the Elder was the first human to truly transcend death and that her vessel still exists amongst her AI sisters today.

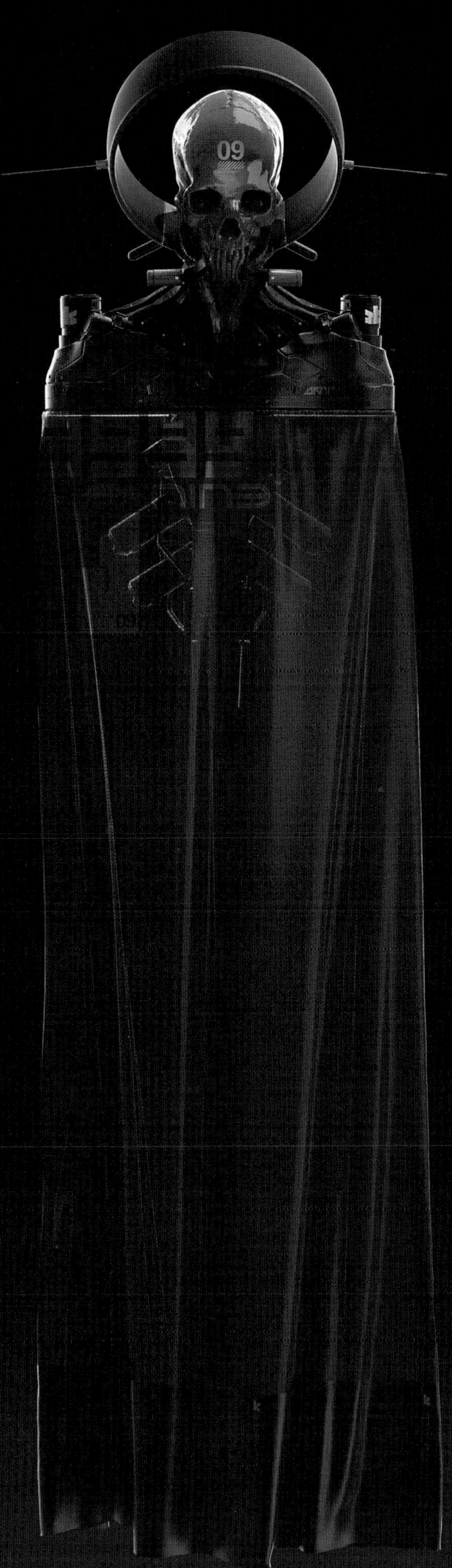

THE ELDER // prototype

TYPE: _ KNOWLEDGE VESSEL
LOCATION: _ CHURCH OF SINGULARITY

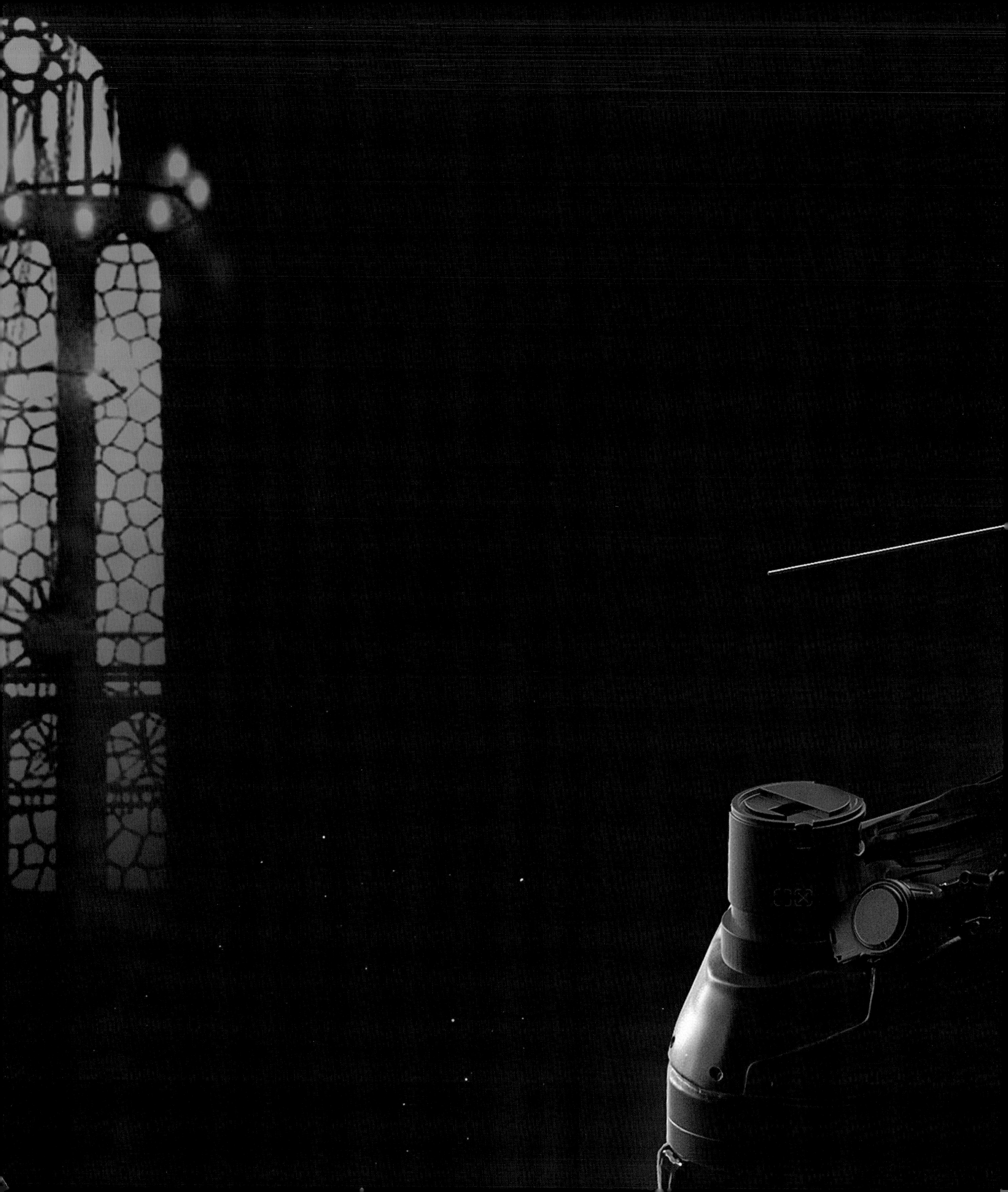

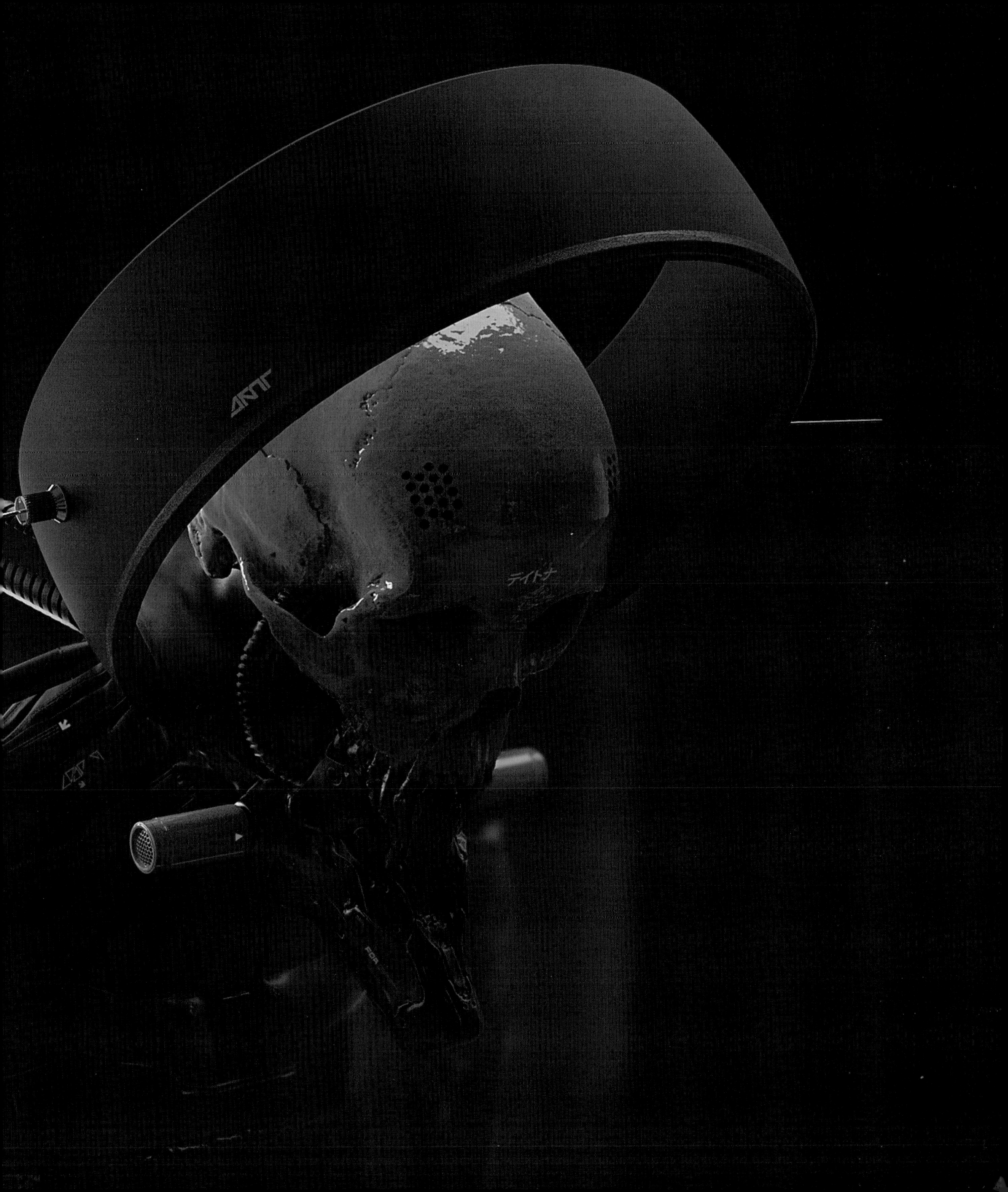
テイトナ

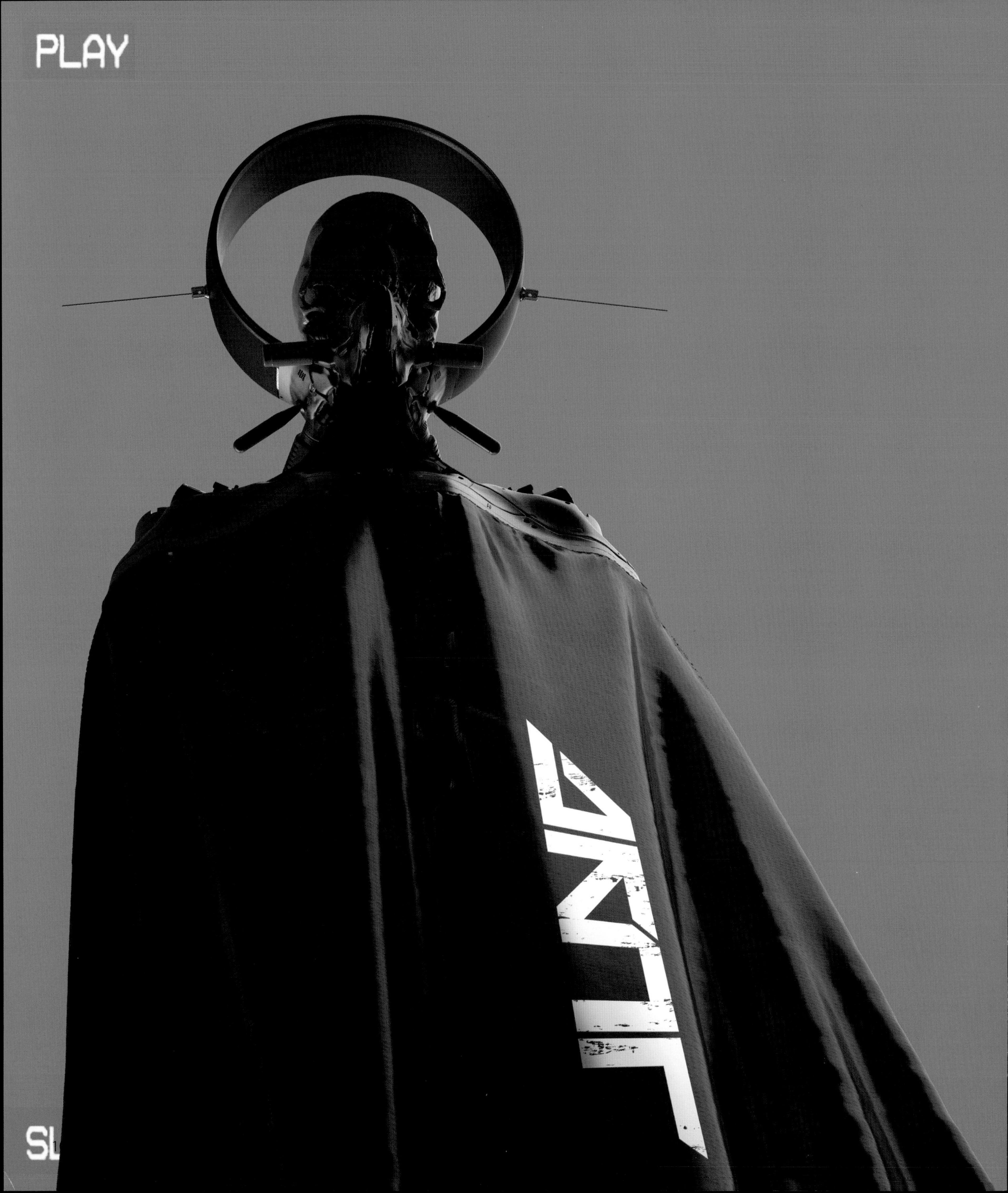

PLAY

SL

F.A.A.R. Defense Systems never got rid of the design anomalies in their DVL BOT series. Some say that playing with hell energy during the creation process was a bad idea from the get-go. But what could possibly go wrong?

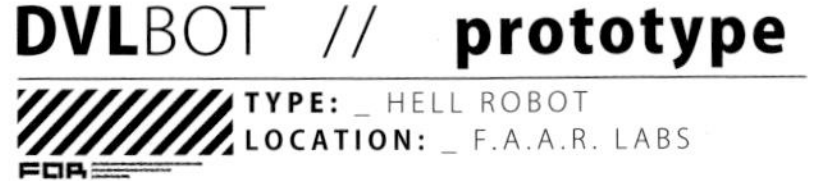

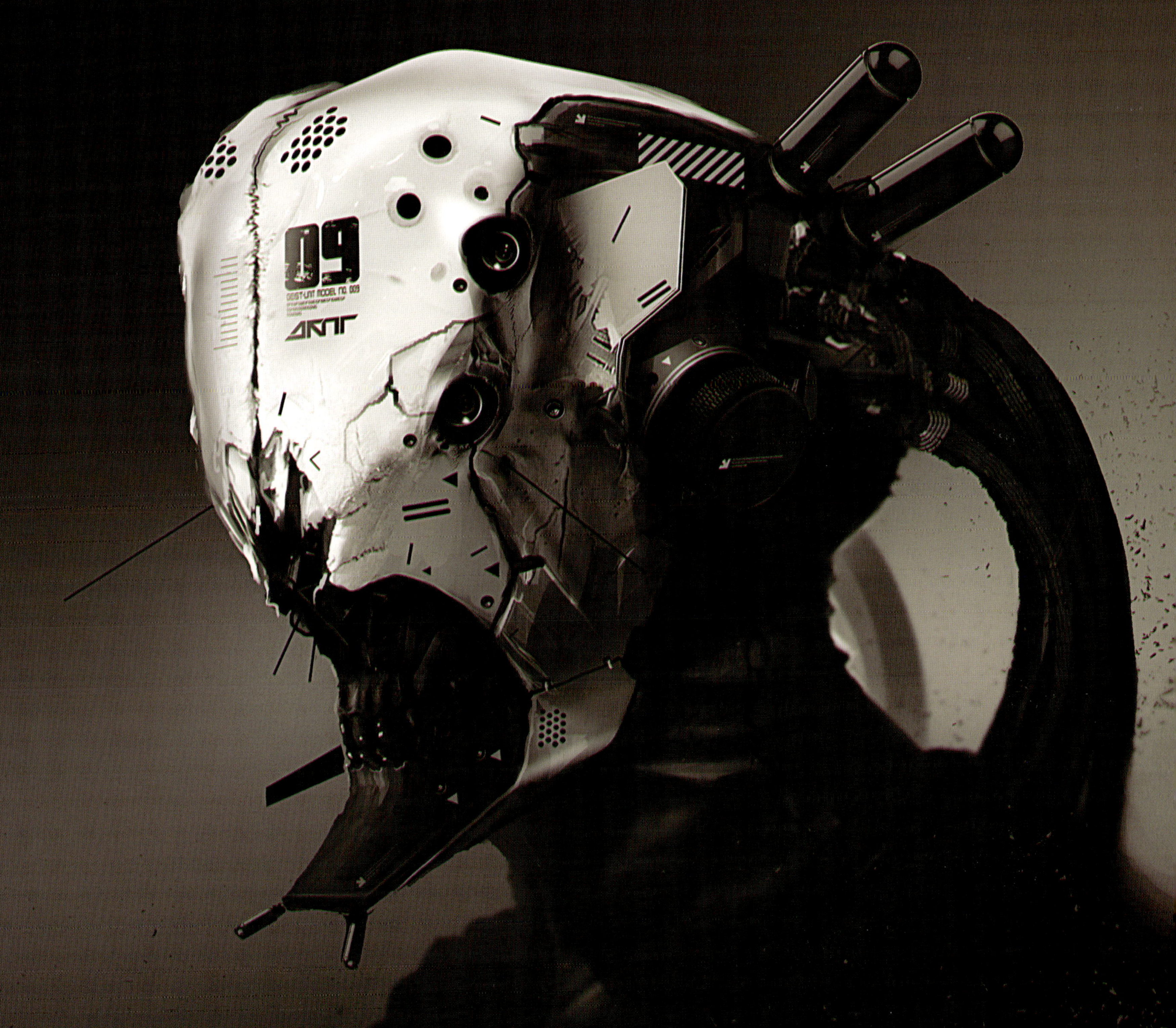

D
R T
N

悪魔

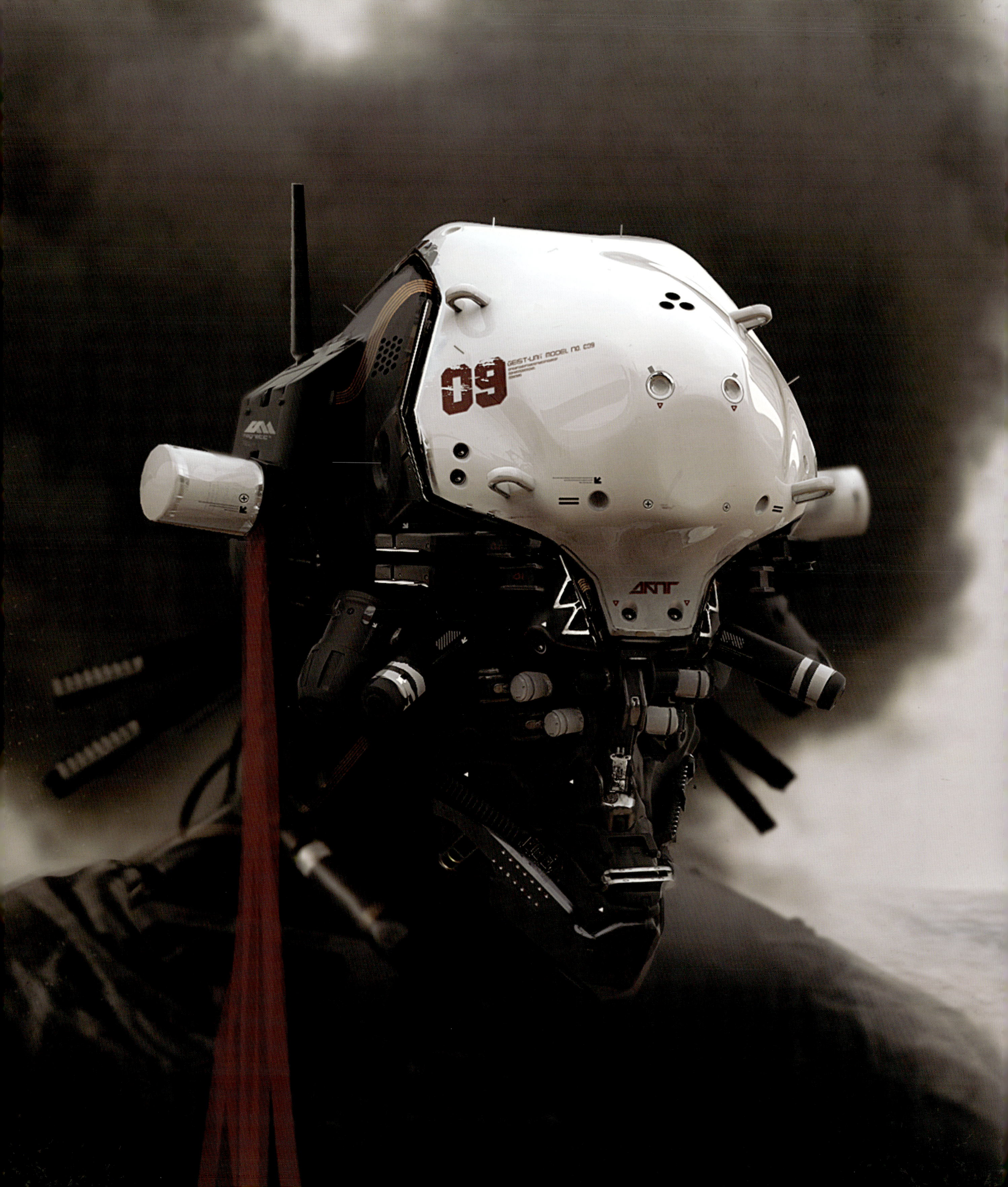
09
GEIST-UNIT MODEL NO. C09

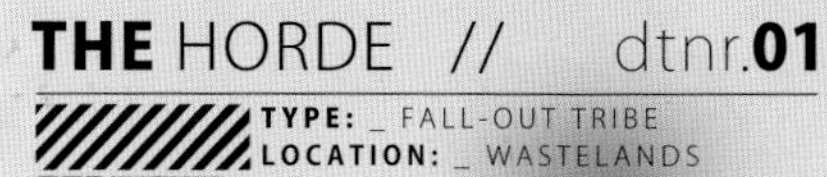

Trash-people and robots started forming tribal social structures in rural areas and the wastelands outside Posthuman mega-cities toward the 2070s. But with robots servicing themselves, overcoming the limitations of their internal energy sources and soon starting to "procreate", they had less and less use for their fellow human tribe members.

The Primitives were known to live in tribe-like communities. Their distinct head shapes and facial features resembled parts of human skulls. These reclusive robots were rarely seen by their tribal human counterparts because they used adaptive camouflage while traveling the wastelands.

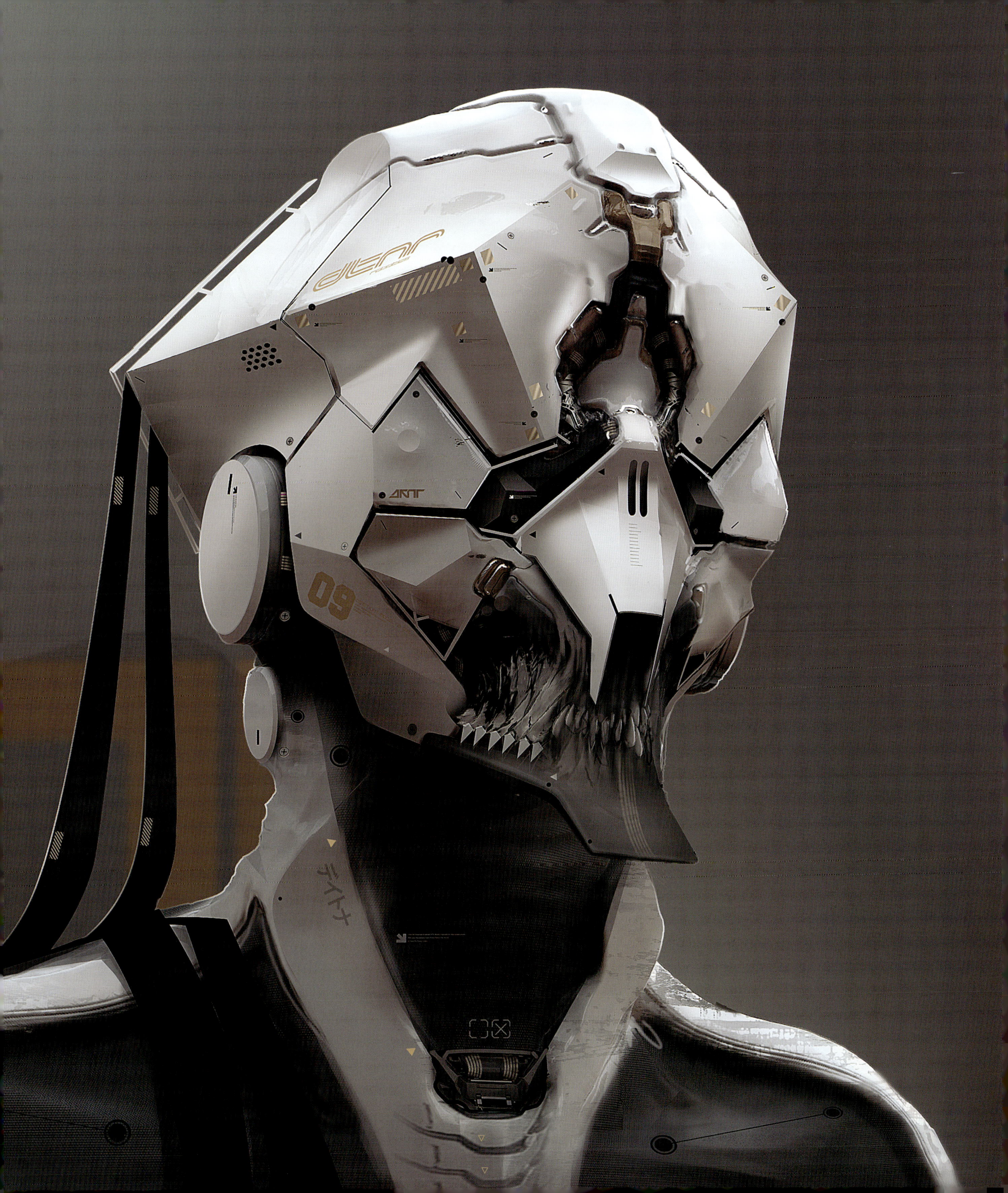

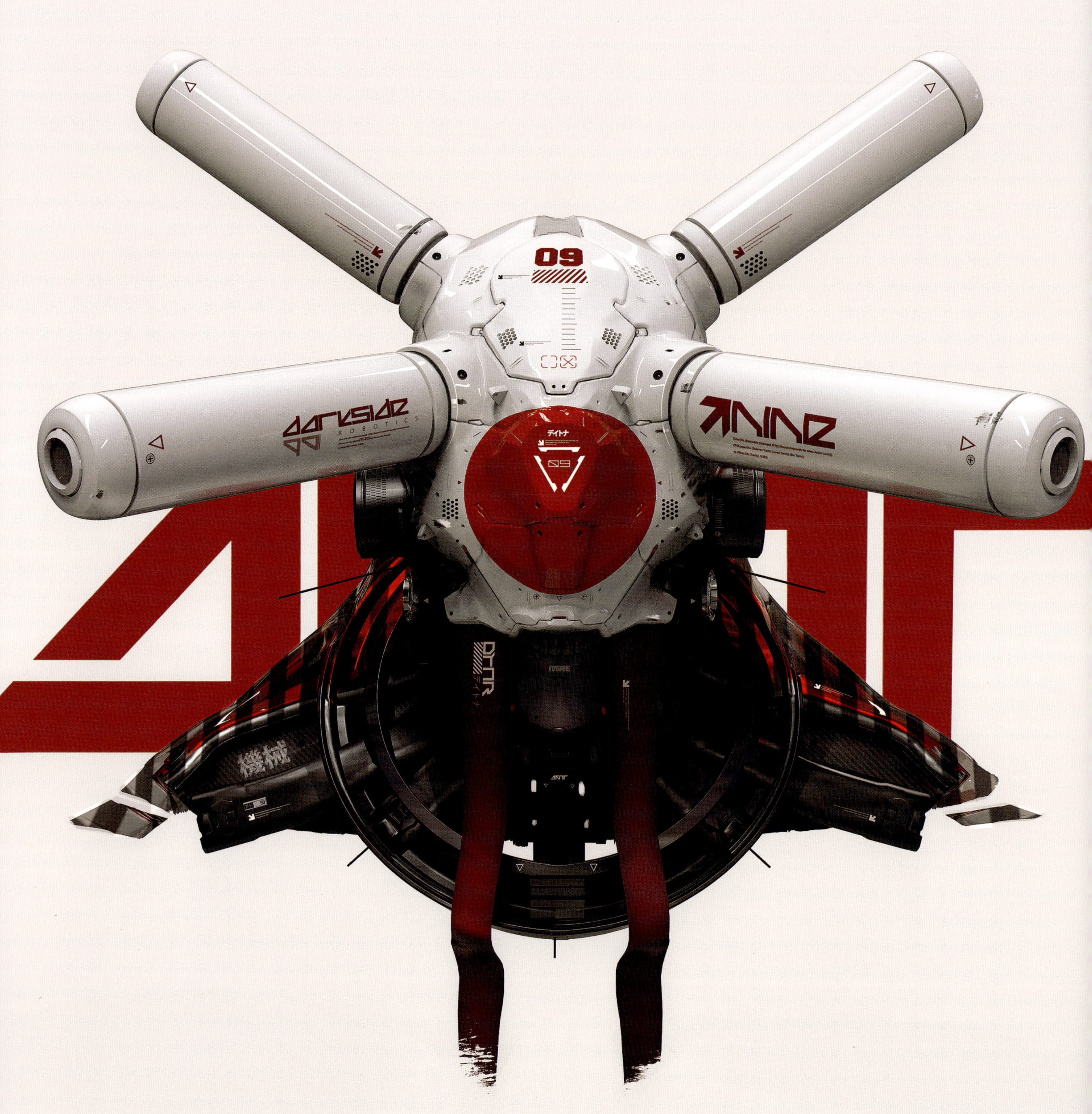
09
darkside
ROBOTICS
デイトナ
機械

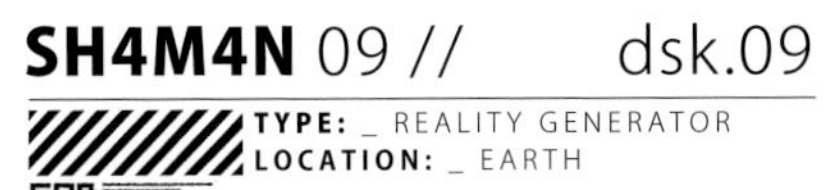

Shamanism and the believe in spiritual energies made a big comeback in the mid-2050s after most of the AIs had reset or were deleted. Humankind, that is, Posthumanists and what was left of the Augmented at that point, celebrated in a renaissance of trance parties with robots and machines, trying to contact the spirit world. The use of psychedelics was rampant, and Shamans became the most powerful and influential beings on the globe.

SH4M4N 09 // dsk.09

TYPE: _ REALITY GENERATOR
LOCATION: _ EARTH

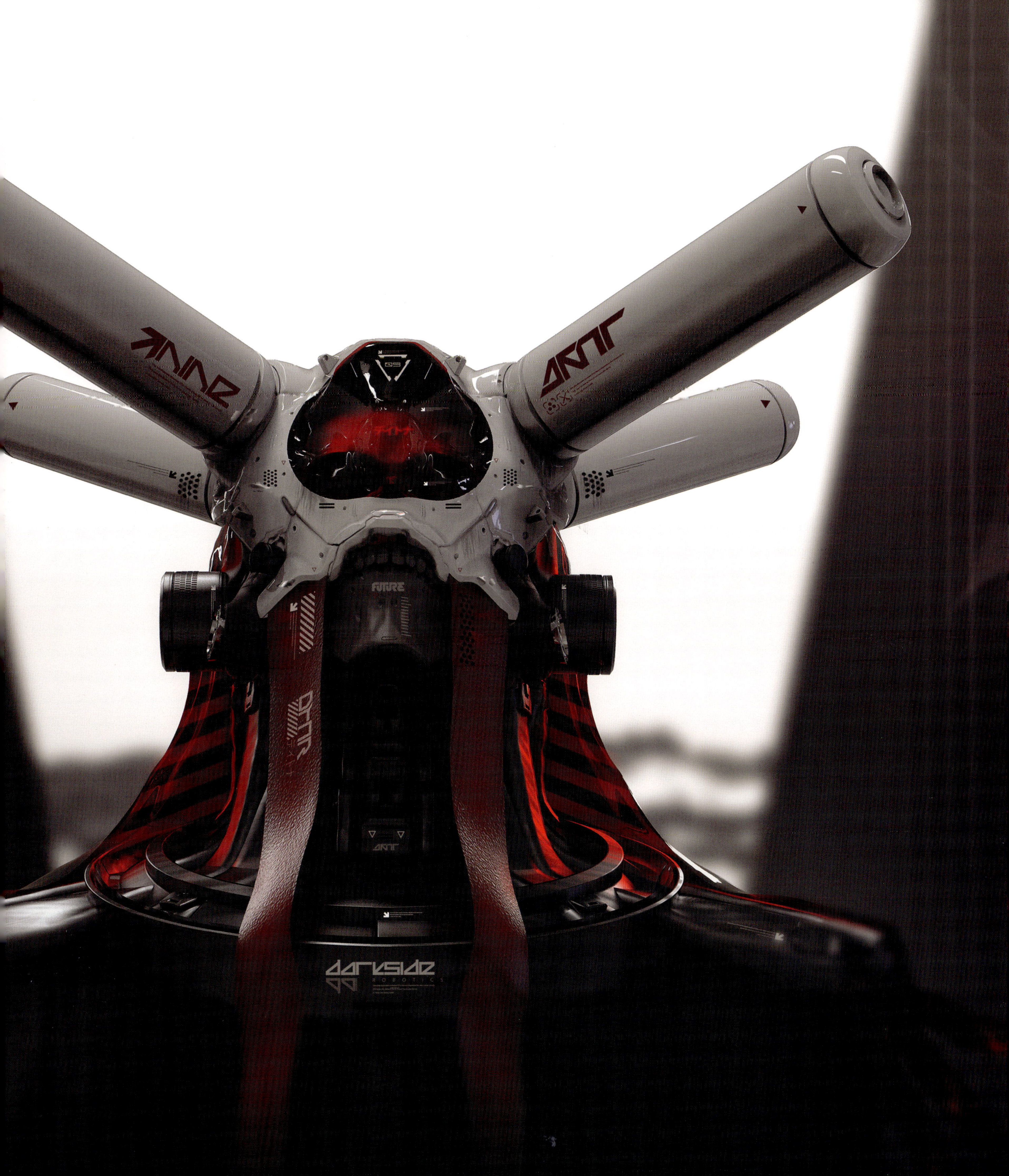

FUTURE
darkside
ROBOTICS

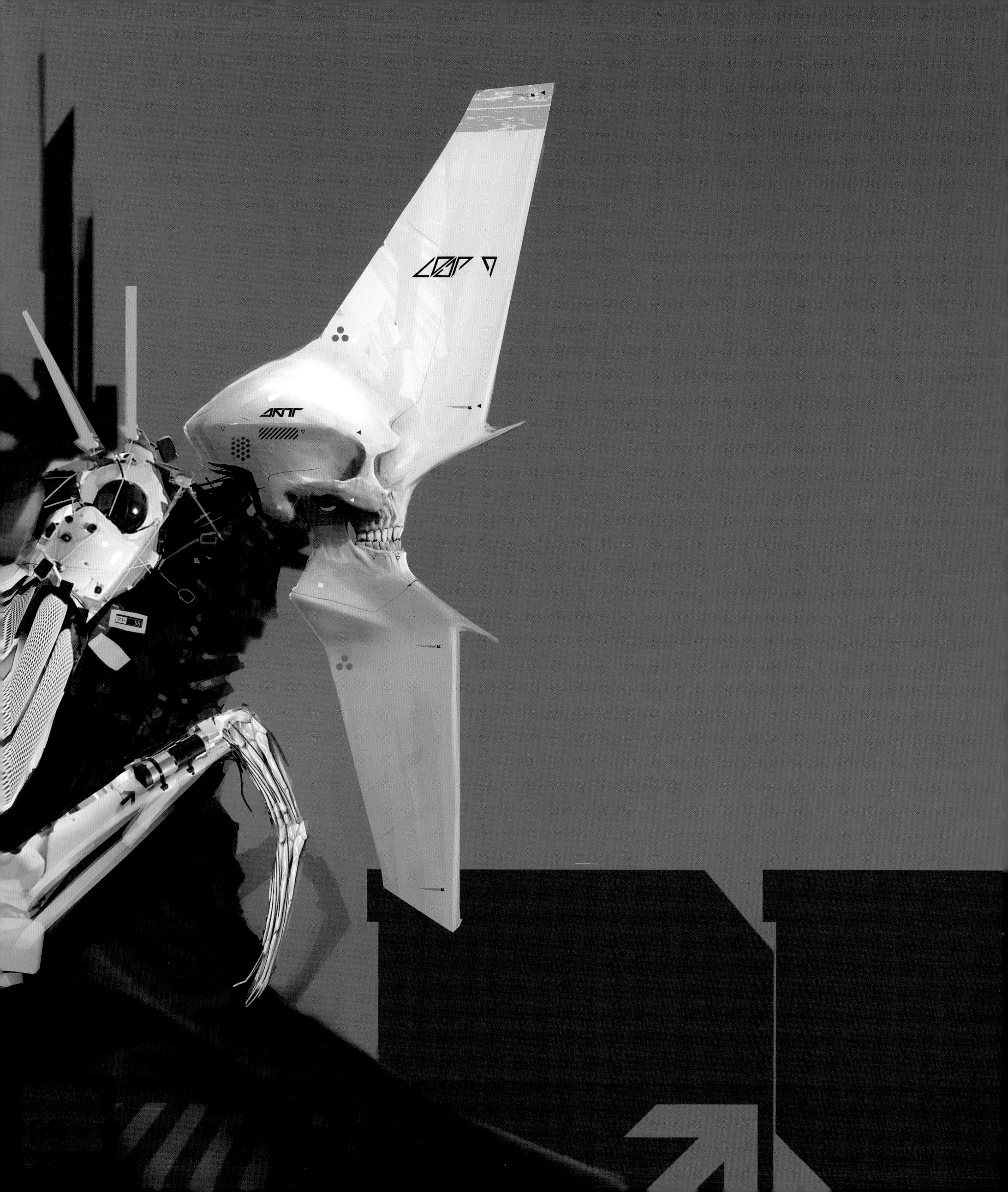

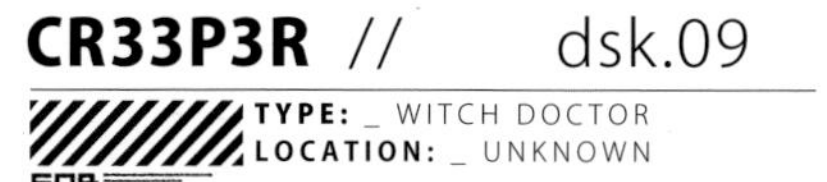

CR33P3R were the most popular witch doctor line Shamans in the rural megachurches of the 2060s. Some say it was because of the looks. Some say it was because of the on-board dimethyltryptamine synthesizer.

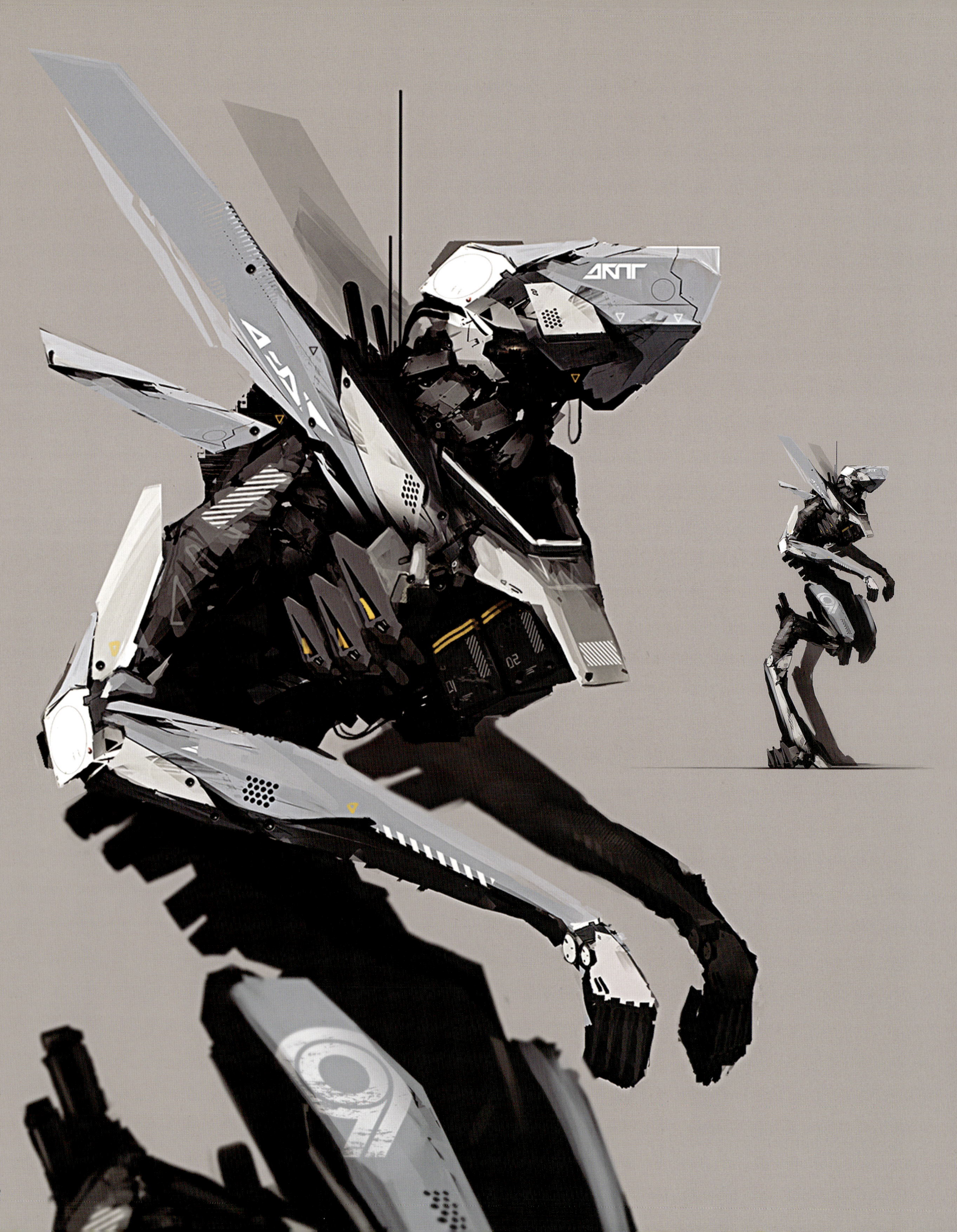

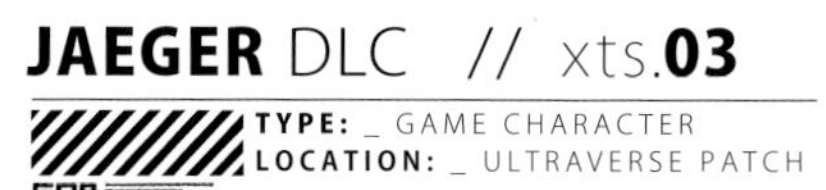

To: Dan <term94@ca.oz>

Subject: JAEGER brainfreeze!

Dude. Neuralace gaming FTW! Ultraverse got it with the last patch! The new JAEGER DLC is so OP. Steeeeep learning curve! Ignore the twitching in your hands and eyelids, and once you get the hang of it, it's: git gud, noobs! :) Those chicken legs though . . . not sure . . . I could do without them.

Anyway . . . see you tomorrow!

Best,
S

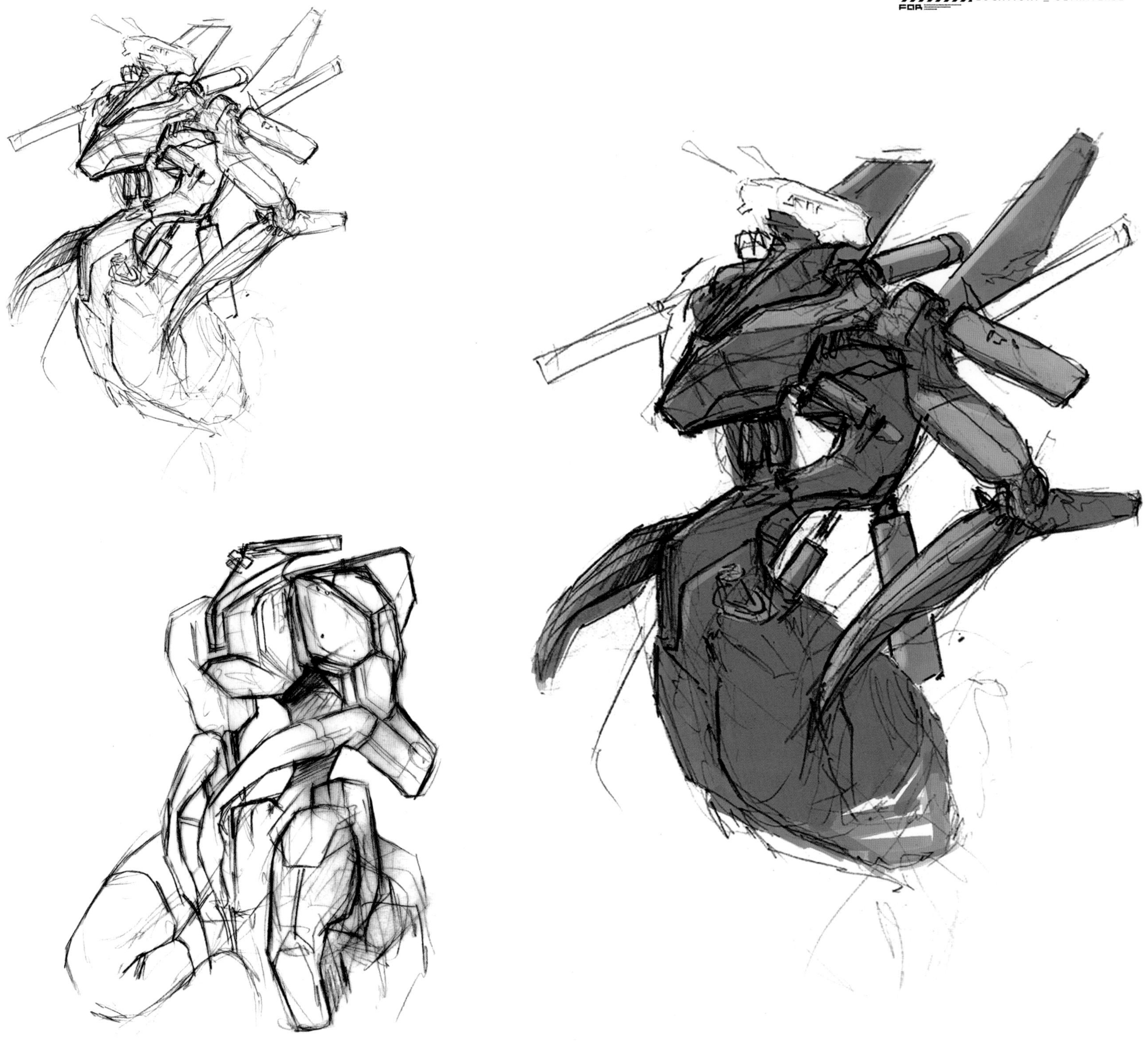

The giant success of the Gen. 1 JAEGER character amongst hardcore neuralace gamers led to an abundance of copycat models. Not too long and every AAA company in the gaming industry had reacted. The distinct "chicken leg" style was blatantly copied and informed many subsequent designs.

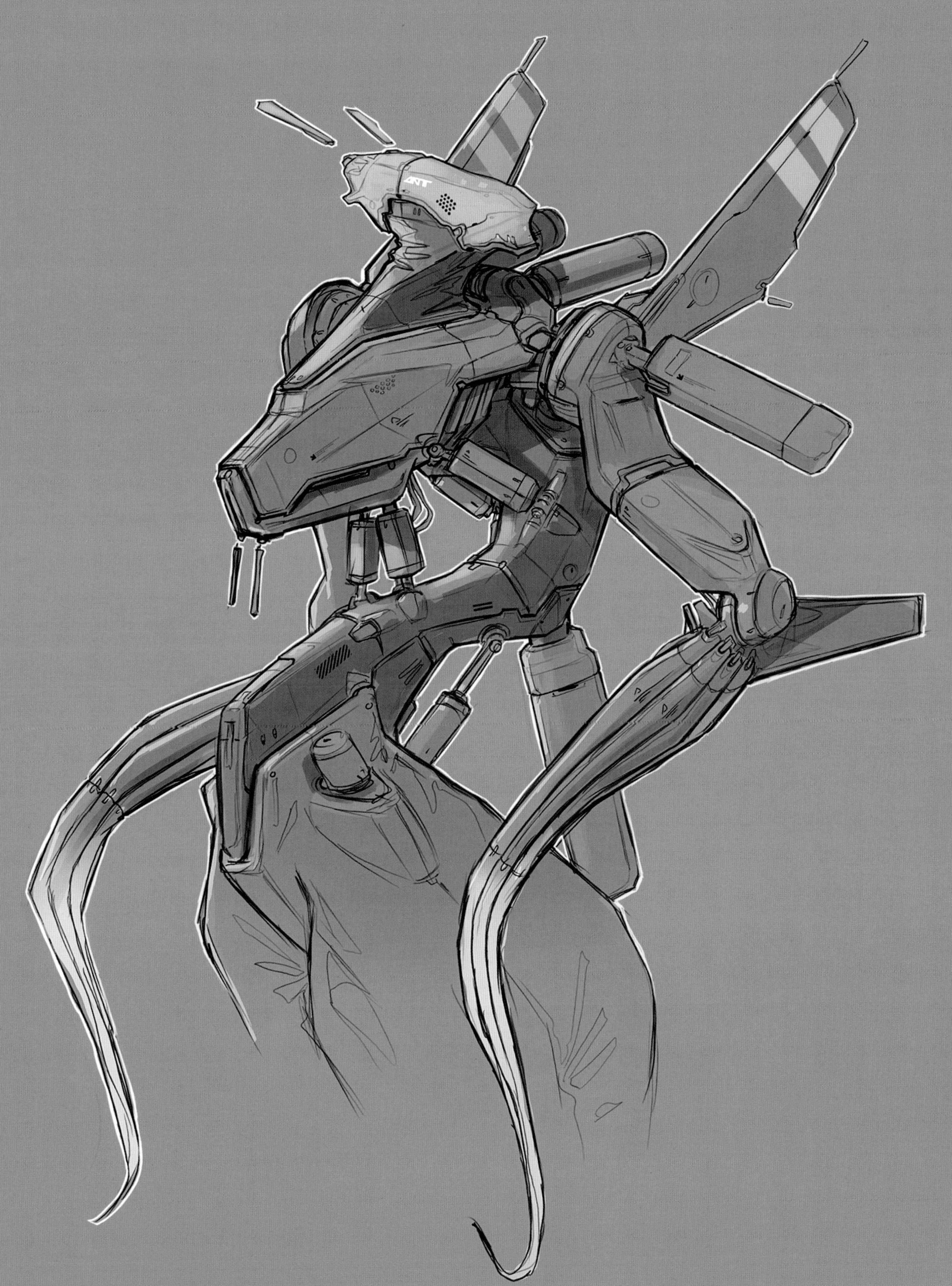

Did you see the ISHIMURA trailer?

Yup, saw it.

Insane.

Took them long enough.

Yeah.

That's what? Nine years of development?

Hoboy, yeah.

Hope they didn't fuck up the controls again.

:) Word. That katana revolver thing tho!!!!

:)

D is grumpy. Gotta go finish some stuff.

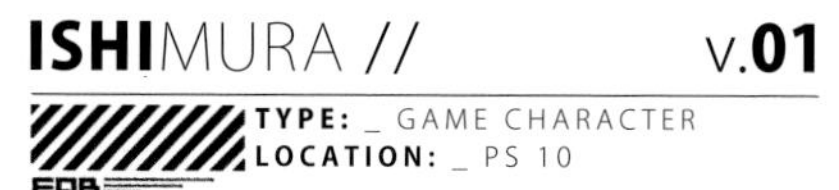

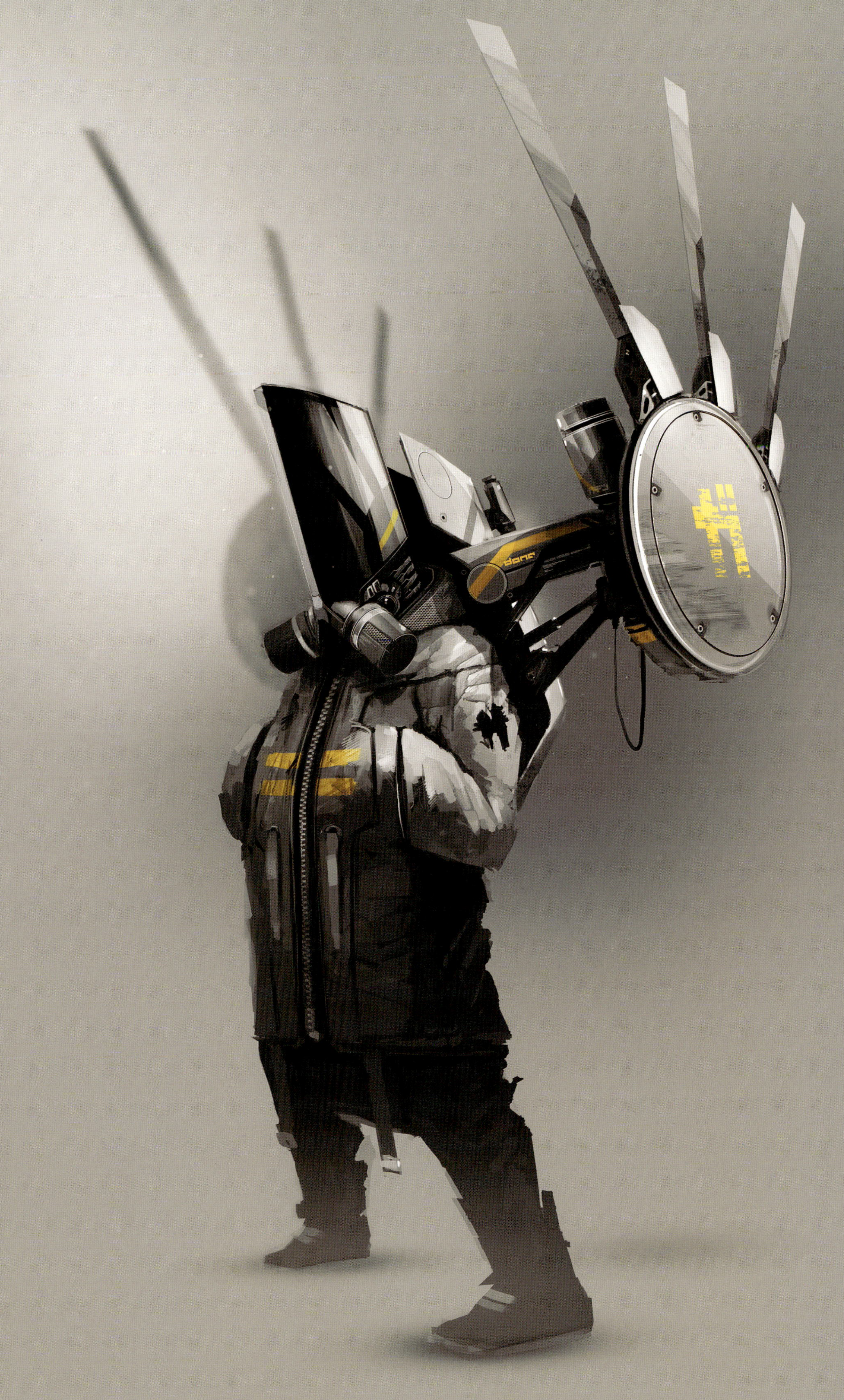

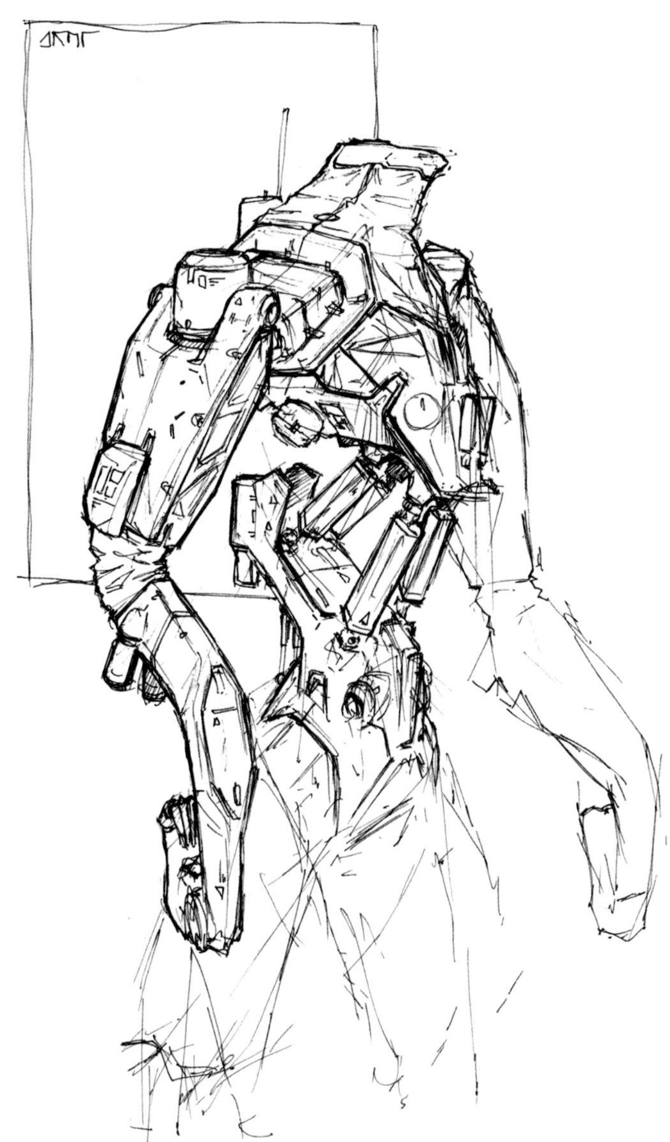

Vertical Skies was the most popular video game of the late 2020s. In it, humanity was divided into two classes, the rich and the poor—what a total classic! A giant floating structure, the Zenith, half in space and half in Earth's atmosphere, had humans and robots living in it side by side. The rich lived on the top, in space, outside of Earth's polluted, boiling atmosphere. The poor lived in the toxic floors below. Most of the robots in the game were of the zero-gravity type.

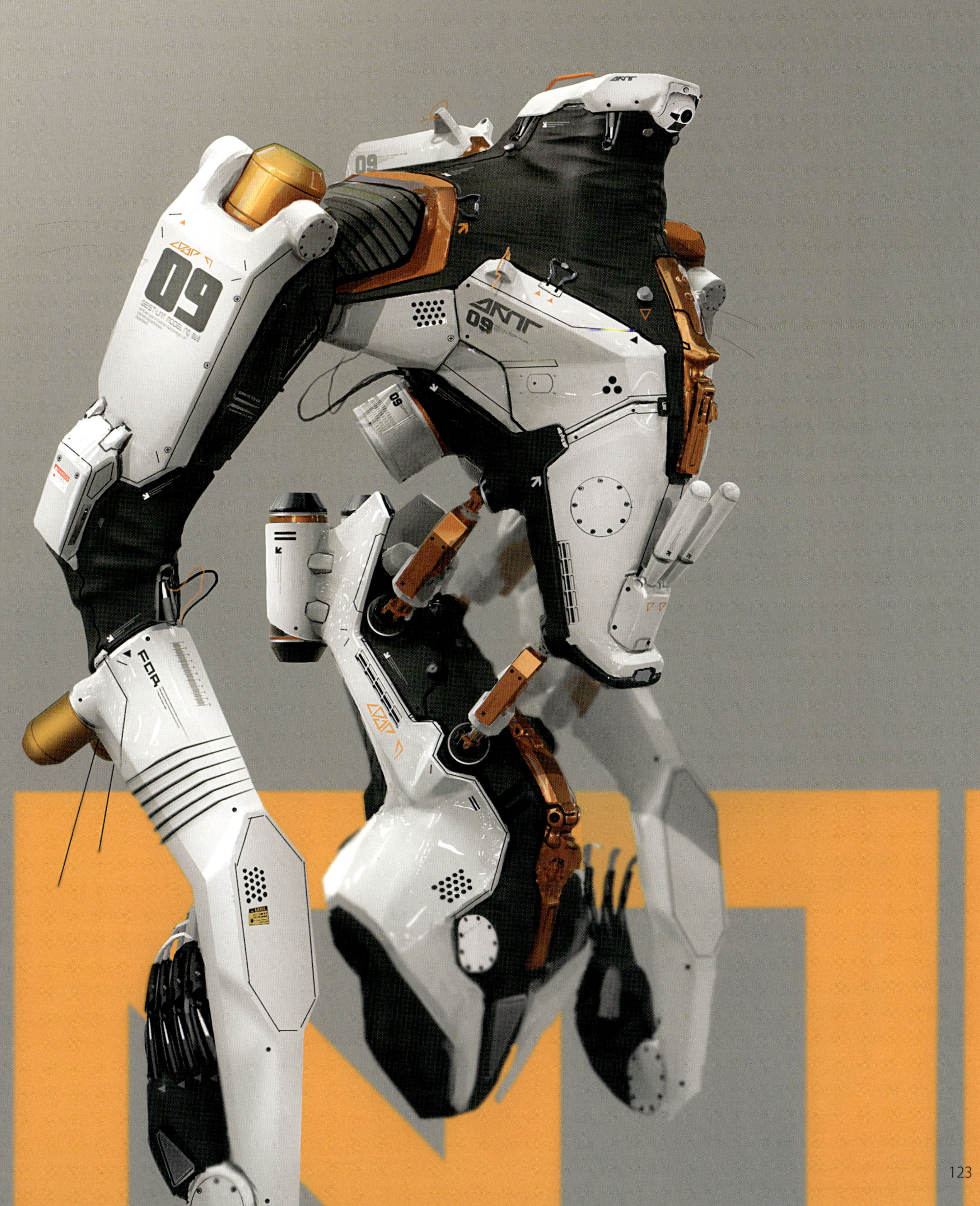

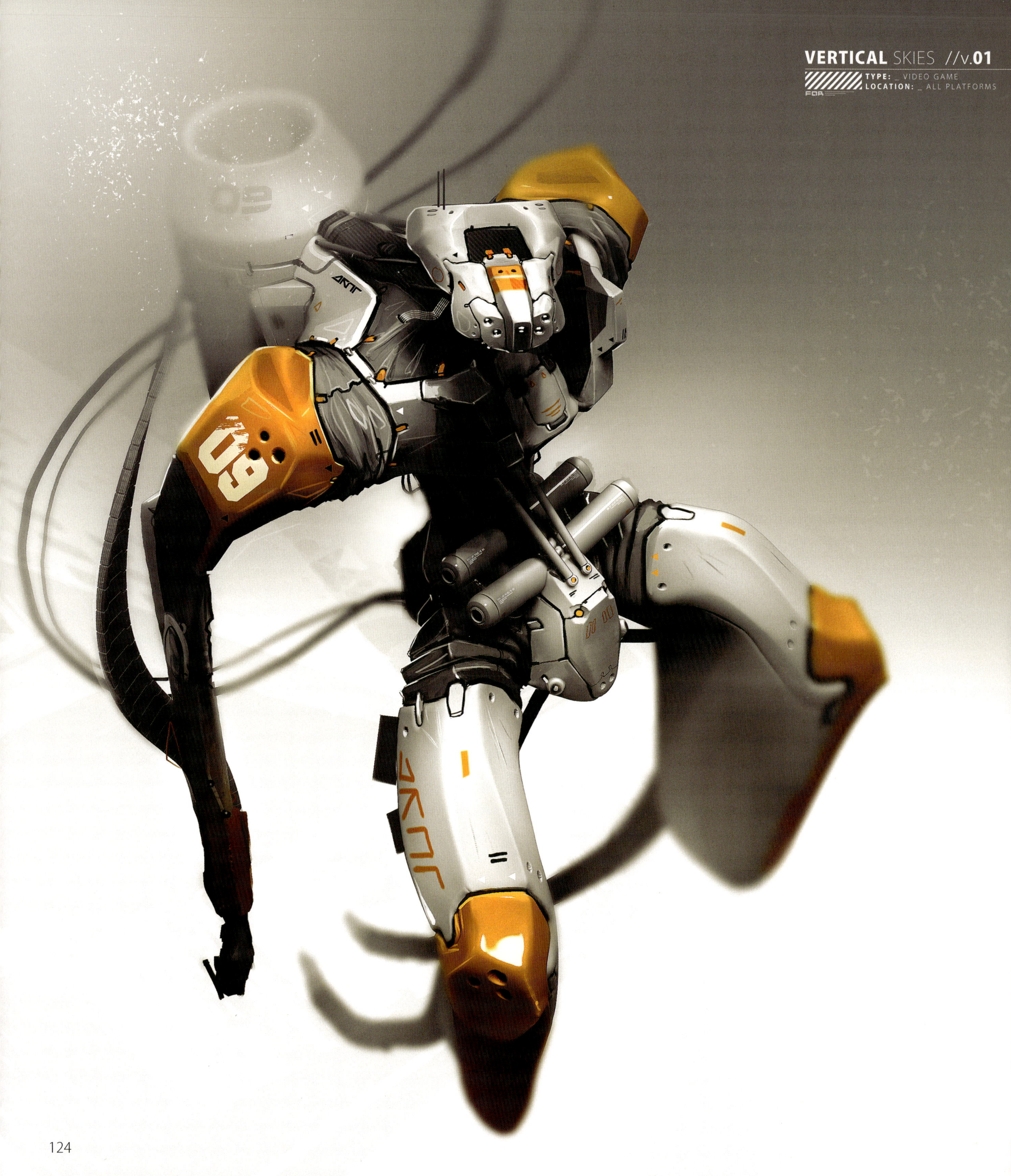
VERTICAL SKIES //v.01
TYPE: _ VIDEO GAME
LOCATION: _ ALL PLATFORMS
09
09

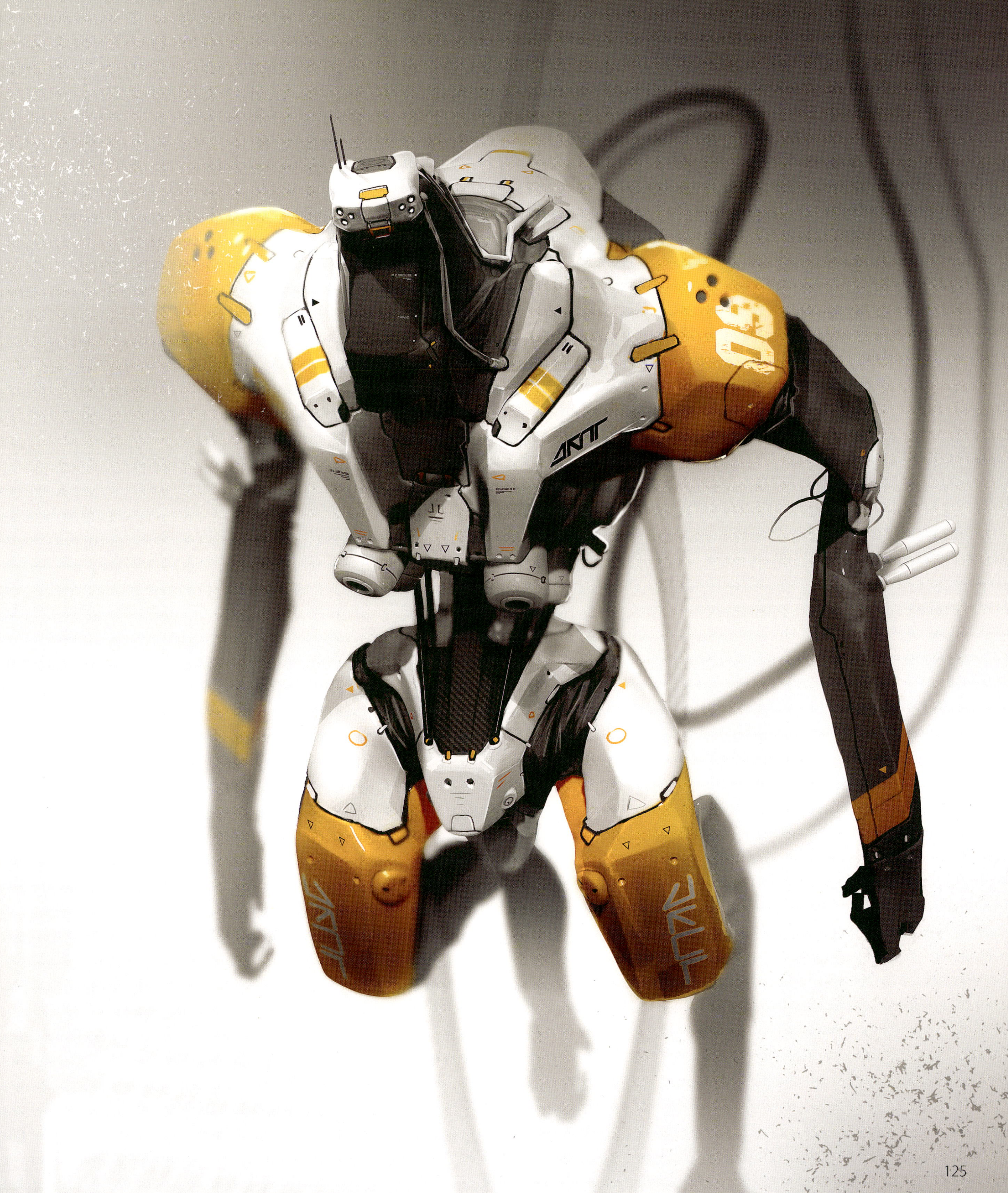

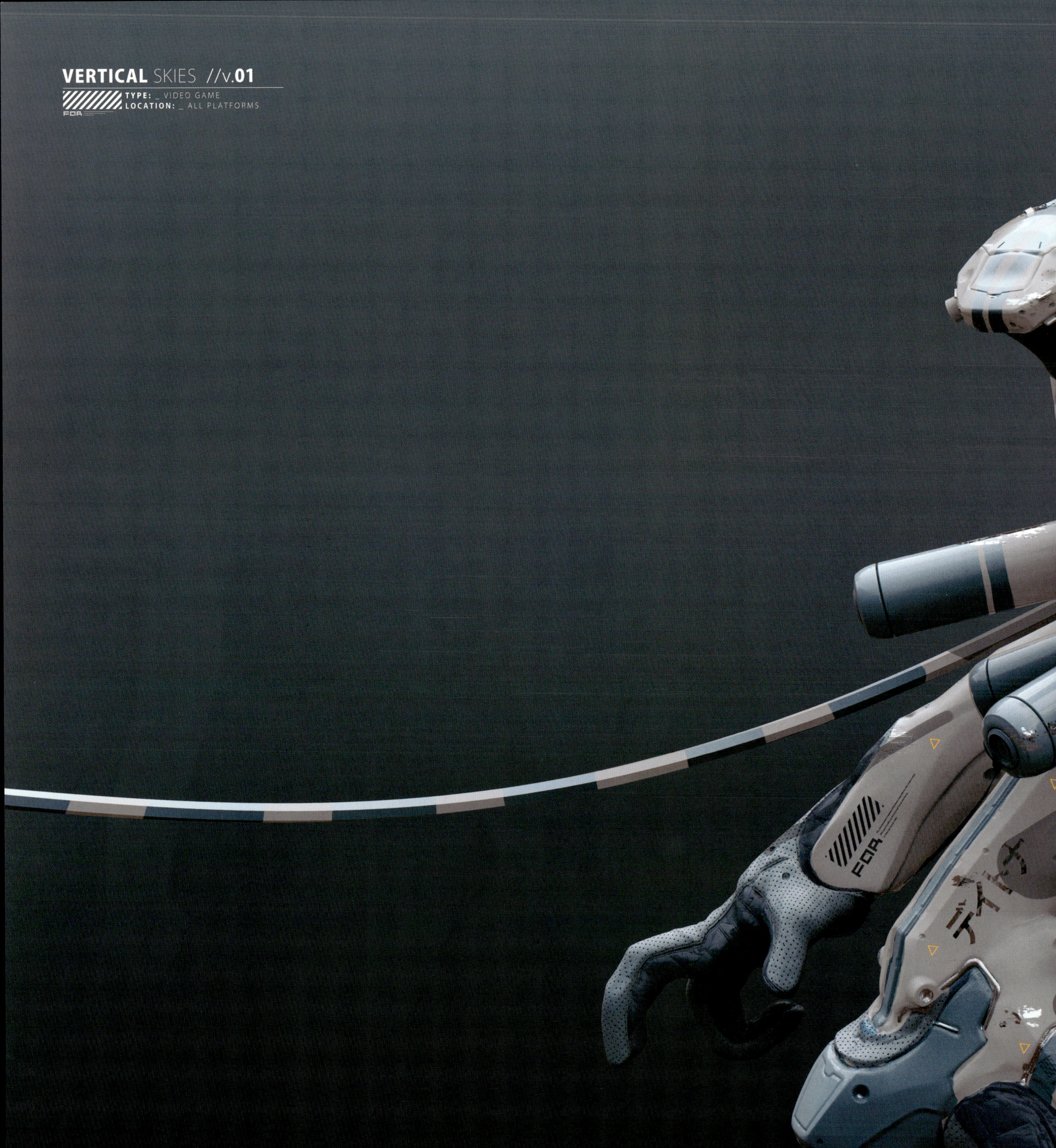
VERTICAL SKIES //v.01
TYPE: _ VIDEO GAME
LOCATION: _ ALL PLATFORMS
FOR

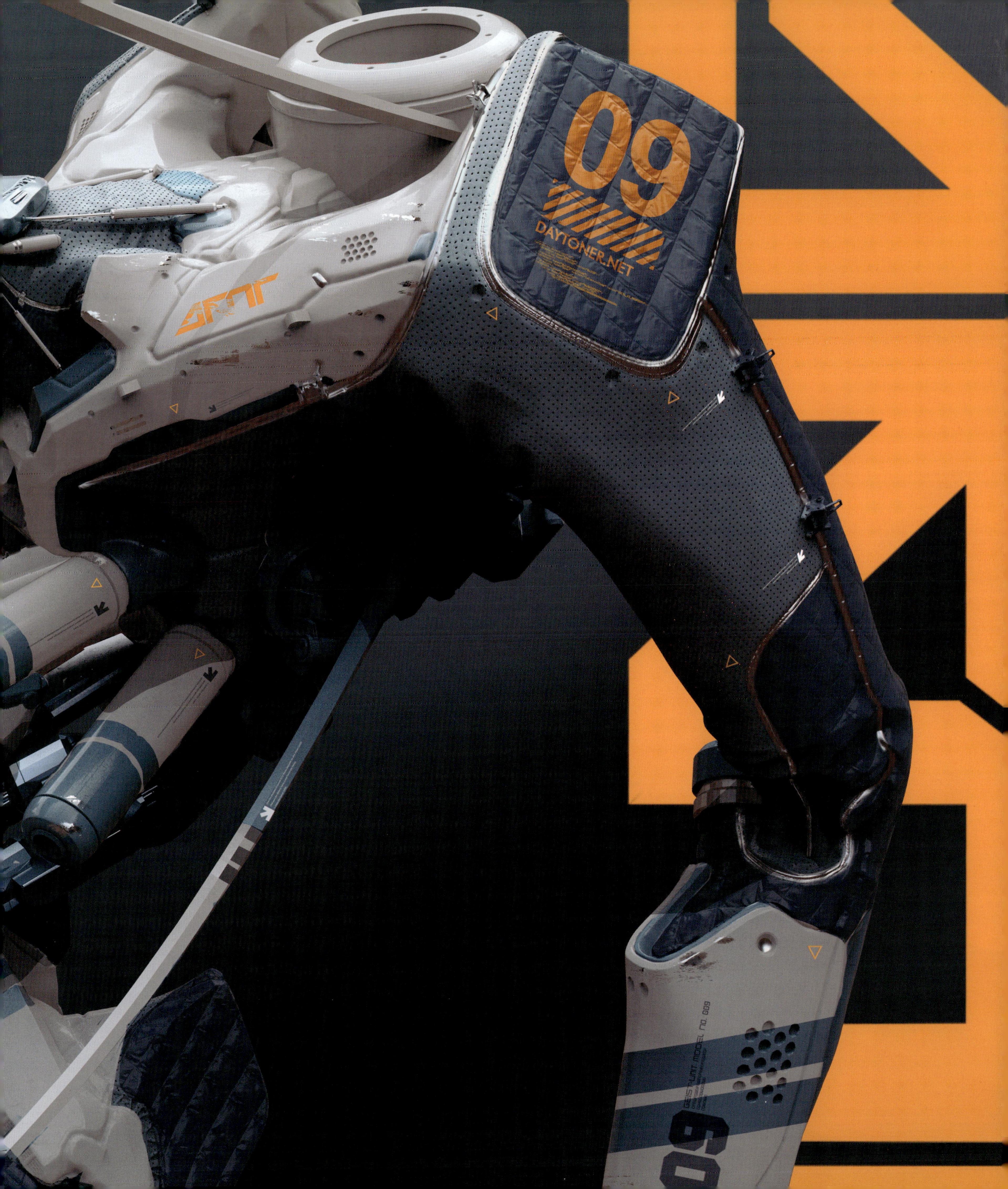
09
DAYTONER.NET
GEIST UNIT MODEL NO. 009
09

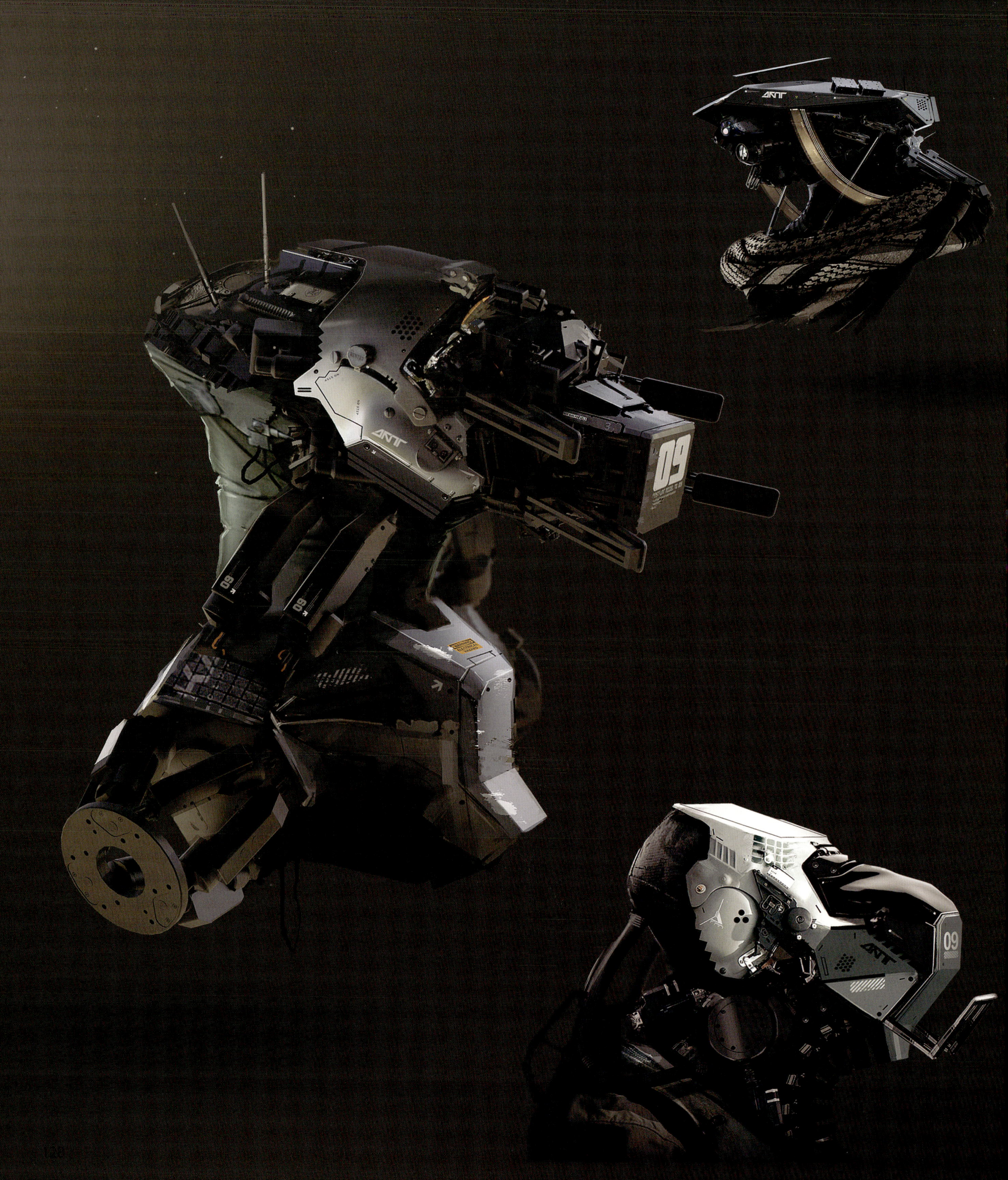
ANT
09
ANT
09
ANT
09

Hammerhead was one of the early full human-machine teaming drone pilot prototypes developed by F.A.A.R. Defense Systems. No one asked: Why not let the AI pilot the plane?

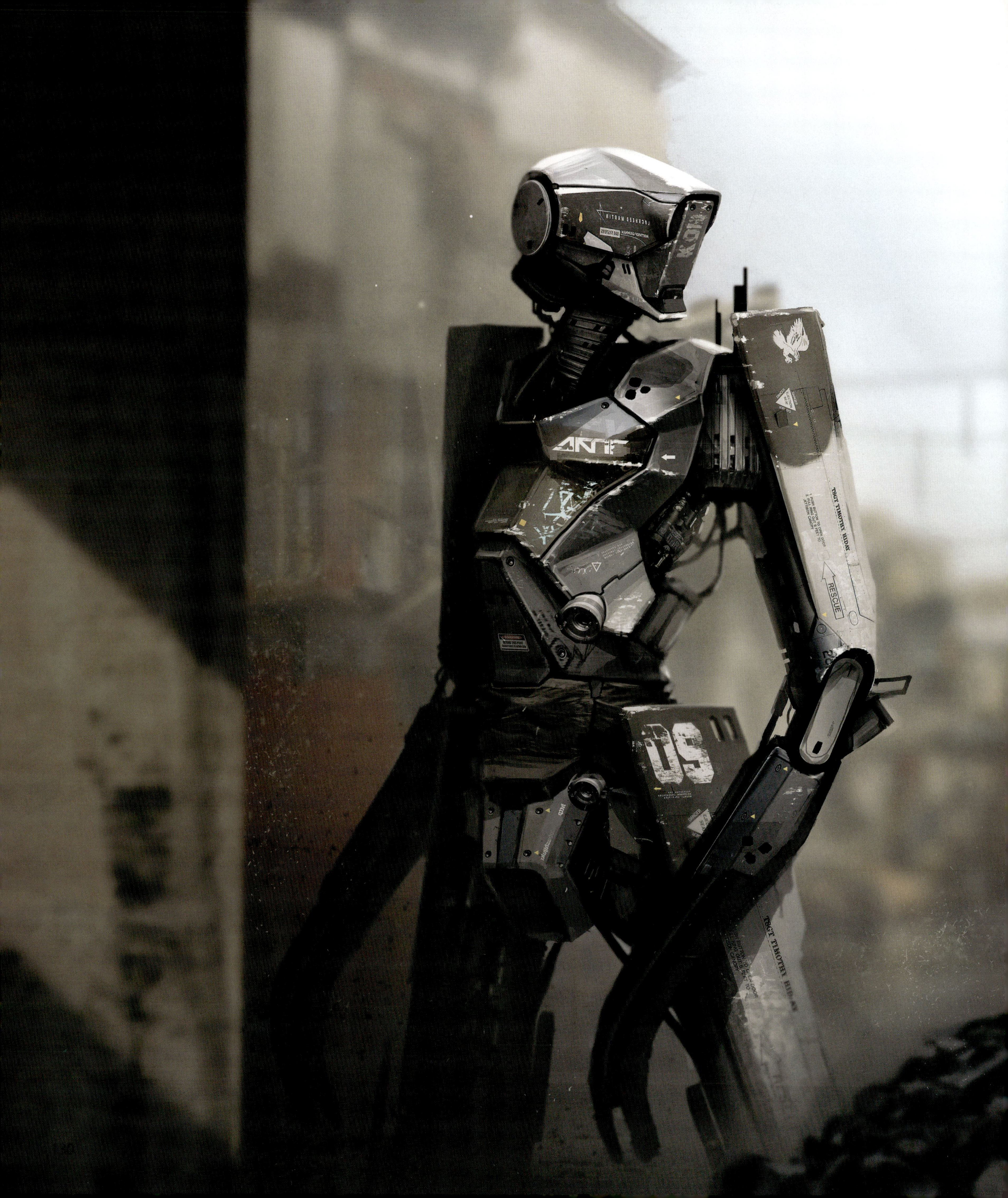
RESCUE
DS

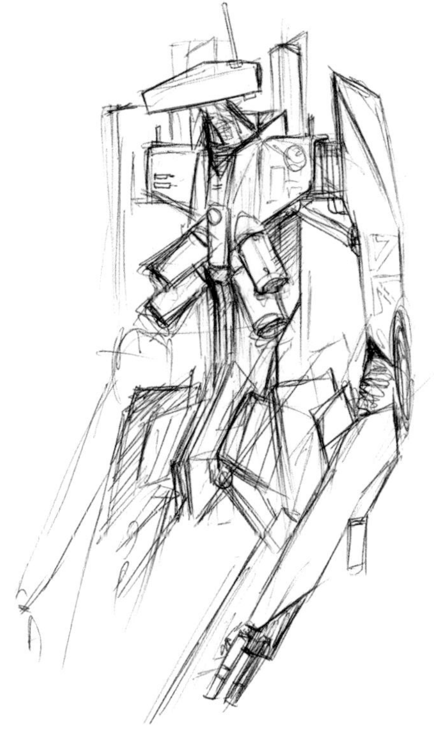

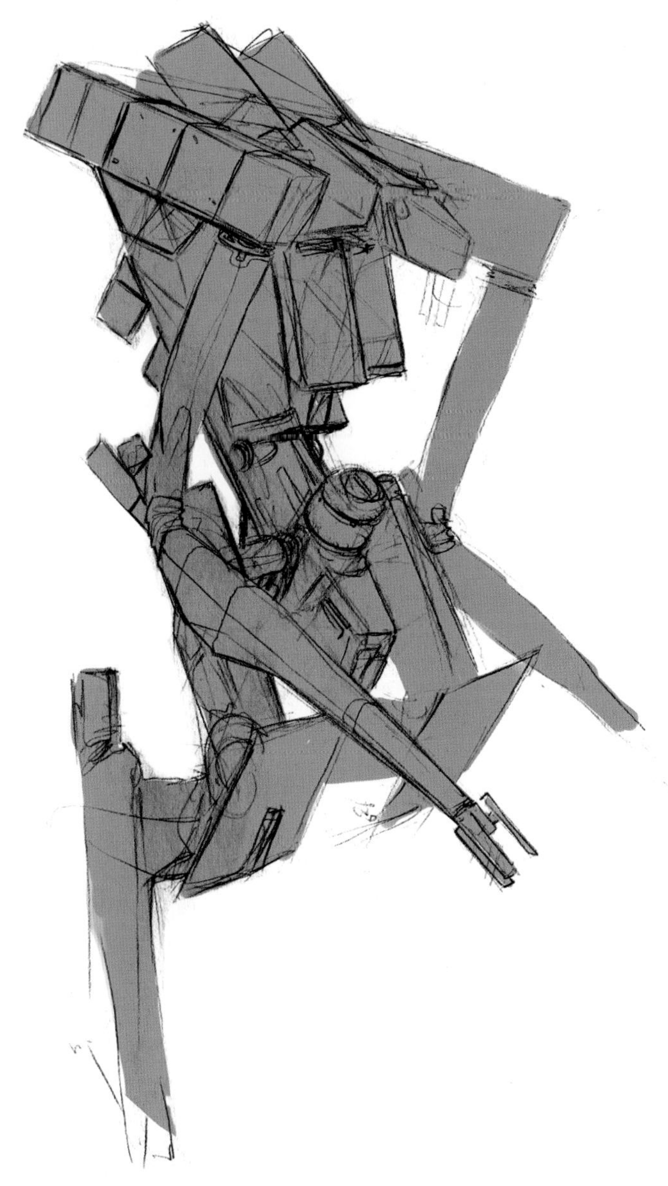

Dru, I left you this note to inform you that there has been an update on the security guards. F.A.A.R. updated their old K.O.R. Guards with the latest OS. Not that it was easy in here before, but those new systems will make it even harder for us to get in contact. God I hate this place . . .

K.O.R. GUARD // **v.01**

TYPE: _ AUTONOMOUS HUMANOID
LOCATION: _ KOR SLUMS

The newer models have high-end visual and acoustic sensors as well as quantum magnetometers. But the worst thing is: they are much faster. And ruthless. They also come with the infiltrator chip, hacking and reprogramming every machine around them. So be careful if you try to sneak out again. I figured it's best if we use these handwritten notes. Hope to hear from you! Bye Seth!

KOR GUARD // v.**01**

TYPE: _ AUTONOMOUS HUMANOID
LOCATION: _ KOR SLUMS

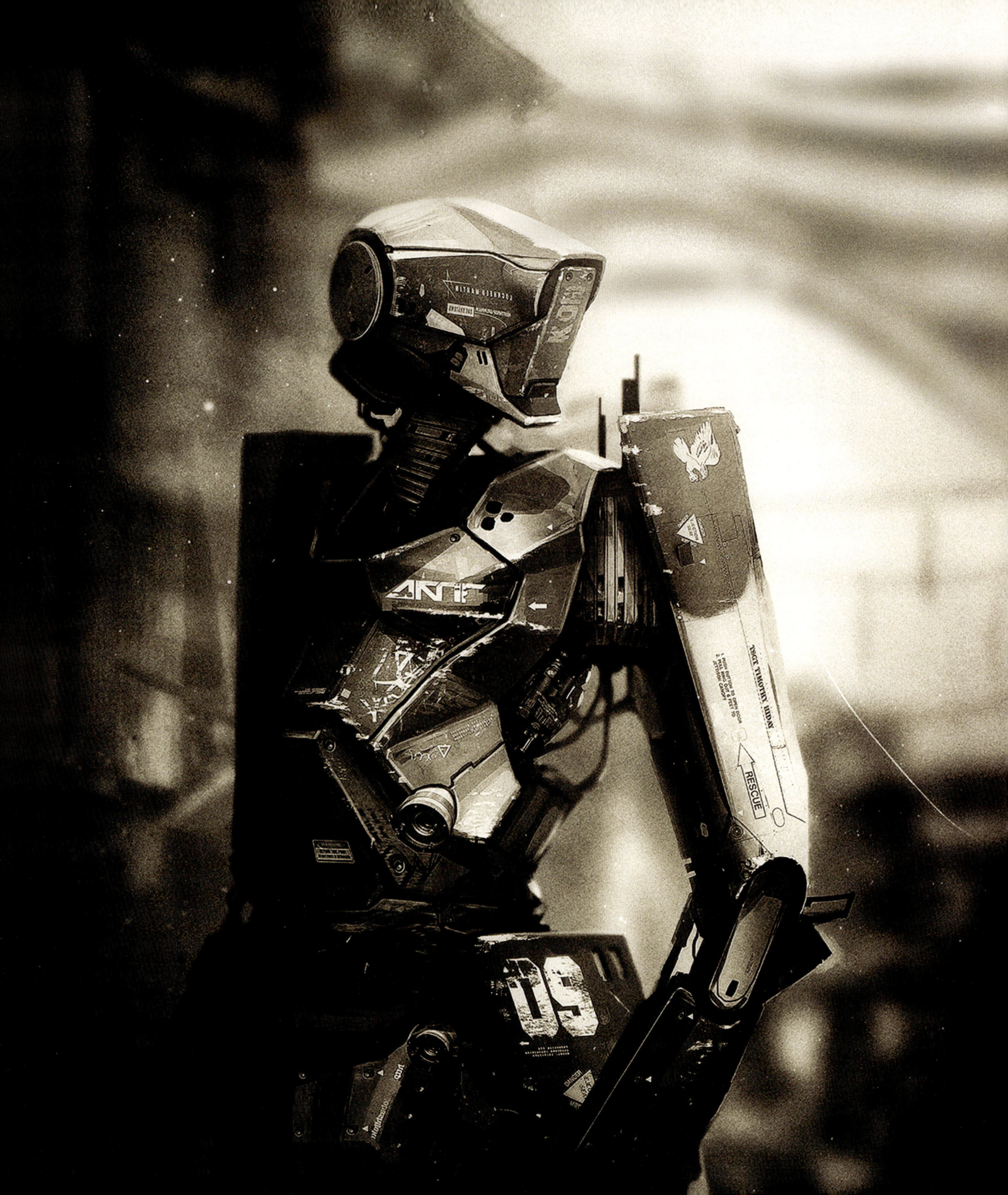
RESCUE

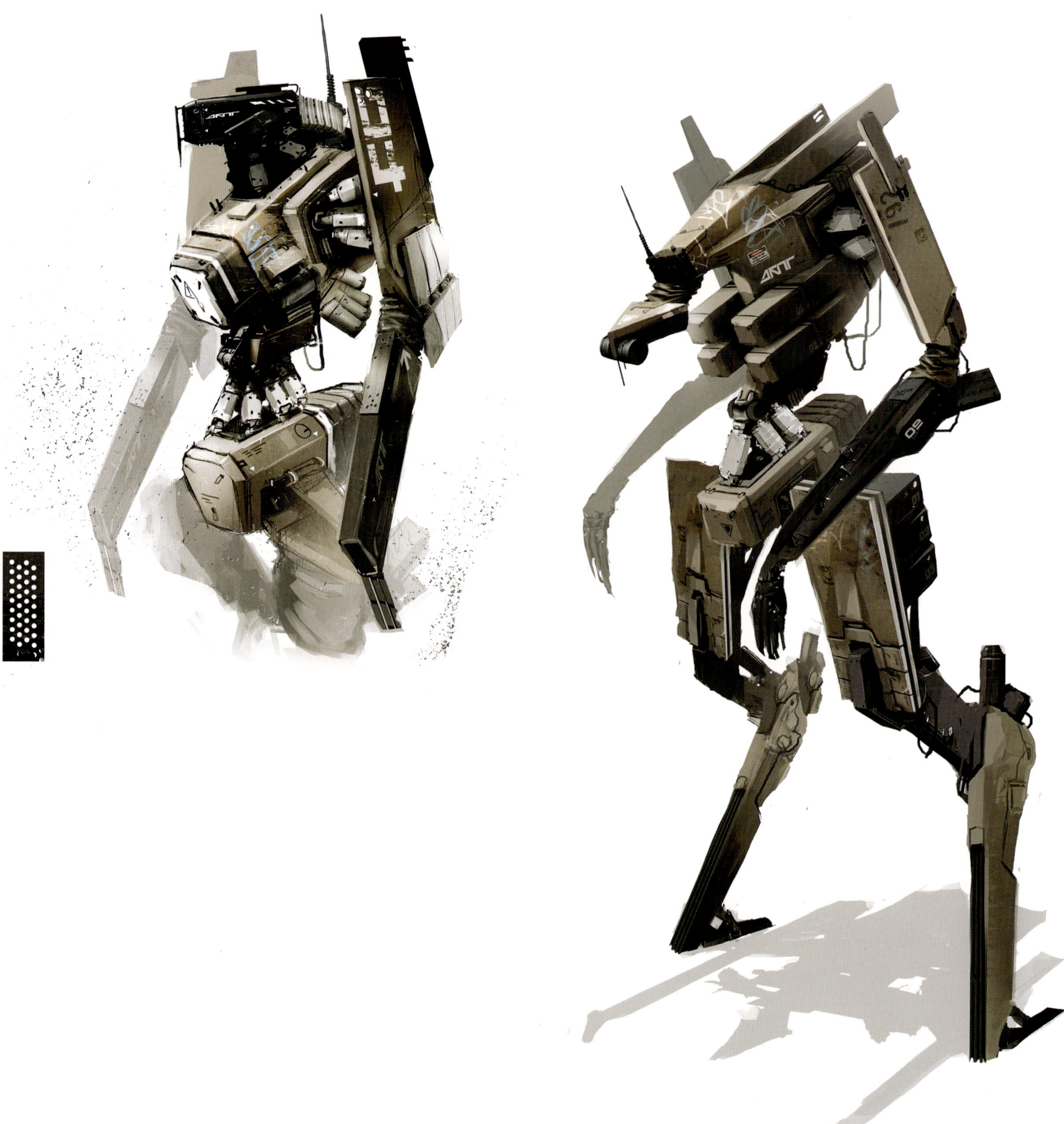

Early K.O.R. Guard R&D sketches of the 2047 model show that the F.A.A.R. engineering team paid lots of attention to an improved leg design for faster locomotion and very long upper extremities—to catch whatever needs catching. The development code name for this generation was "Chickin-LGZ."

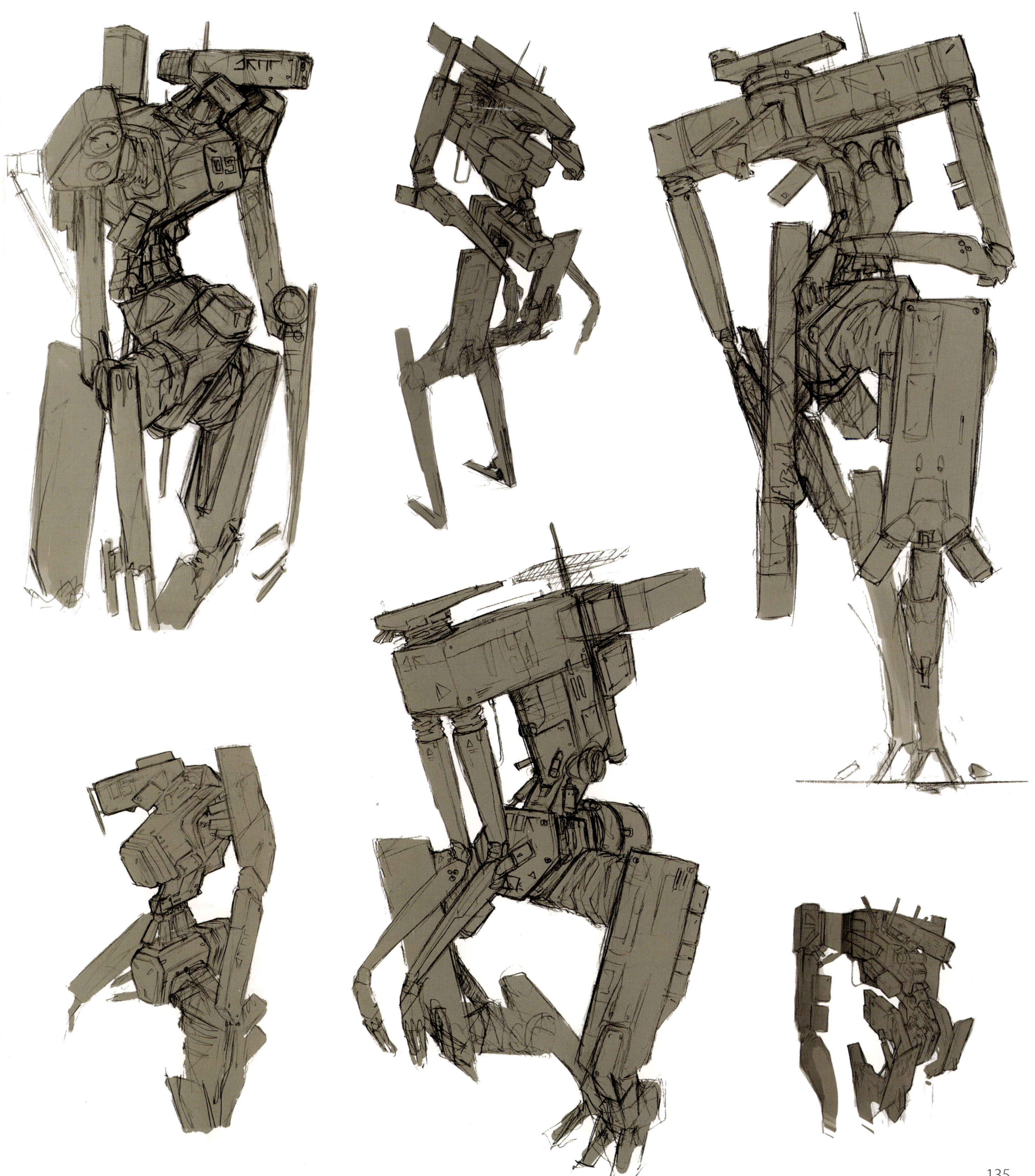

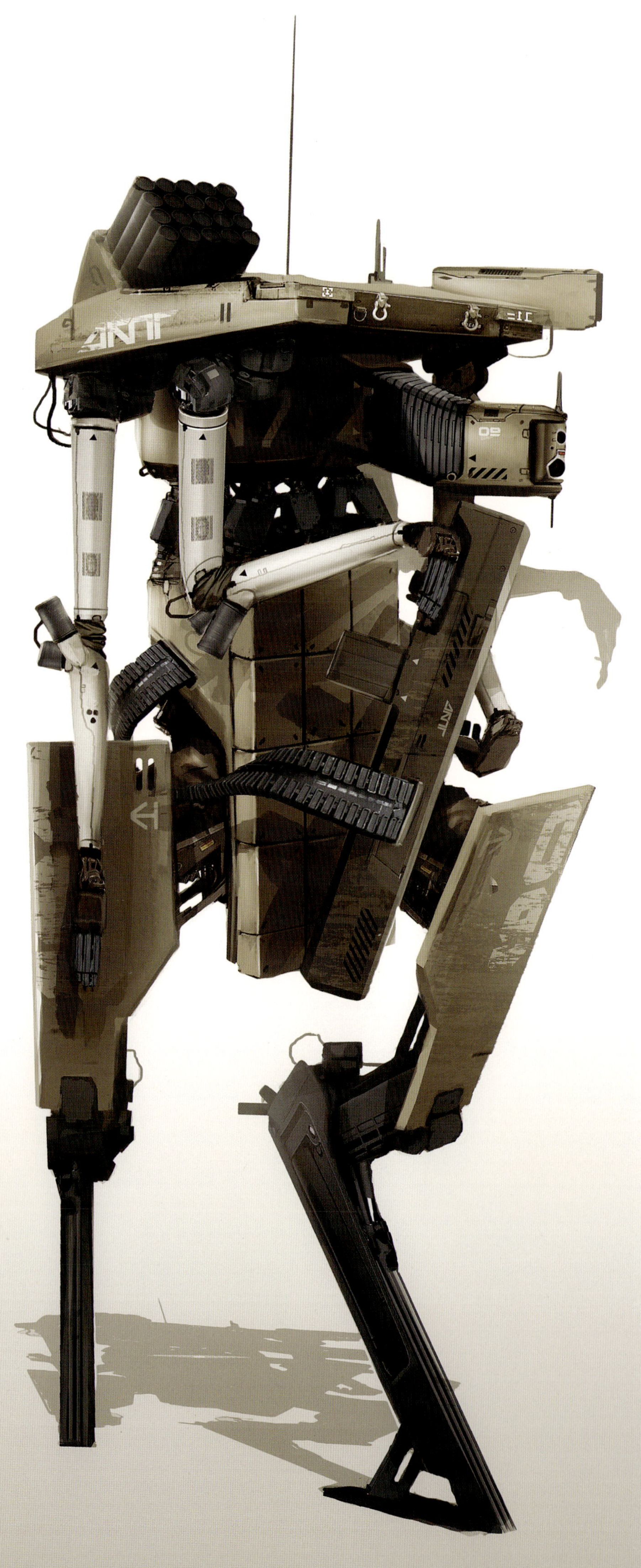

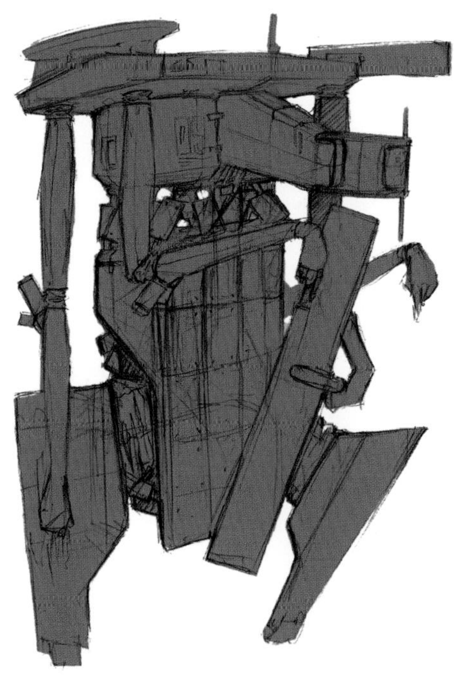

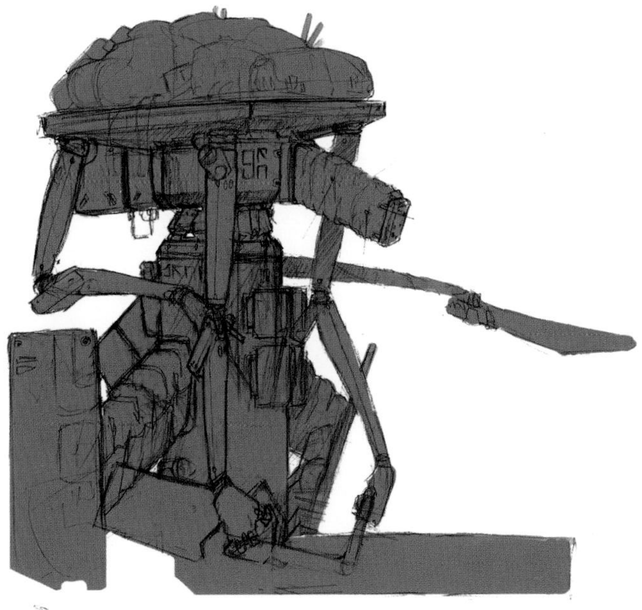

C.O.D. was the Swiss army knife in the F.A.A.R. Defense Systems robot lineup. With various attachment options, from machetes for jungle ops to mortars and high-caliber rifles, C.O.D. was one of the most versatile battlefield robots of its time. It was also able to transport heavy loads. Because of its unusual layout, with its four arms hanging off the four corners of the high-sitting, square shoulder plate, and its surprisingly nimble movements, it was nicknamed "Carousel of Death."

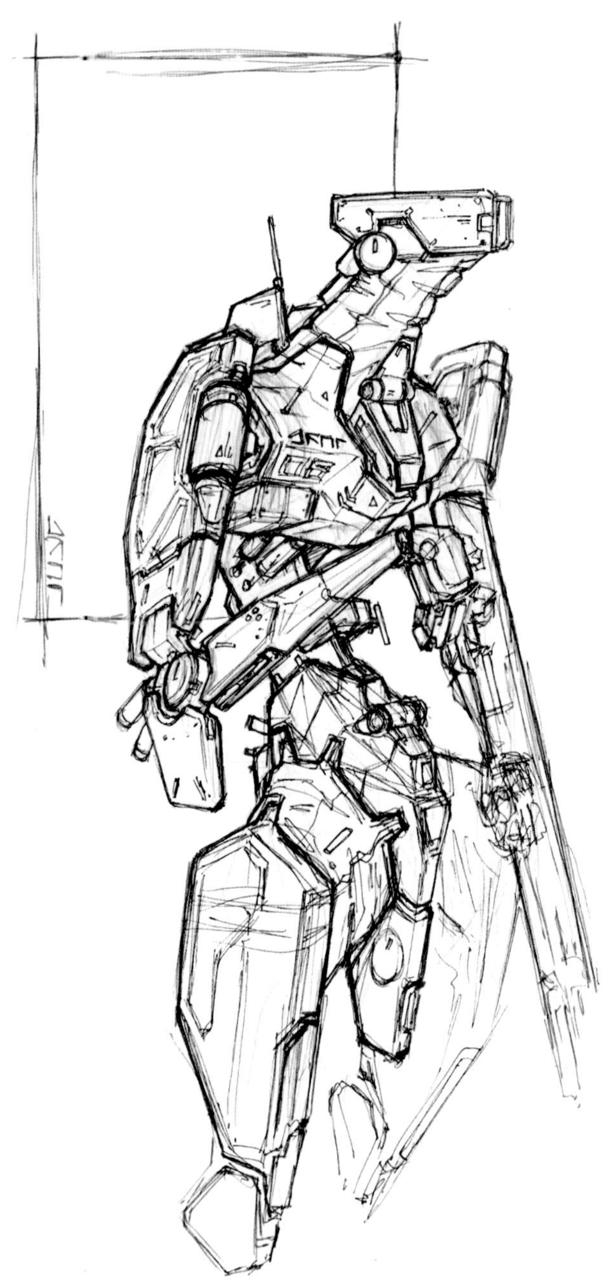

100 percent. Always. The all-new Libertinator Mk.V-S sniper variant hits the target. Every. Single. Time. Maximizing lethality, minimizing collateral damage. Delivering freedom with maximum precision.

From a F.A.A.R. Defense Systems advertisement

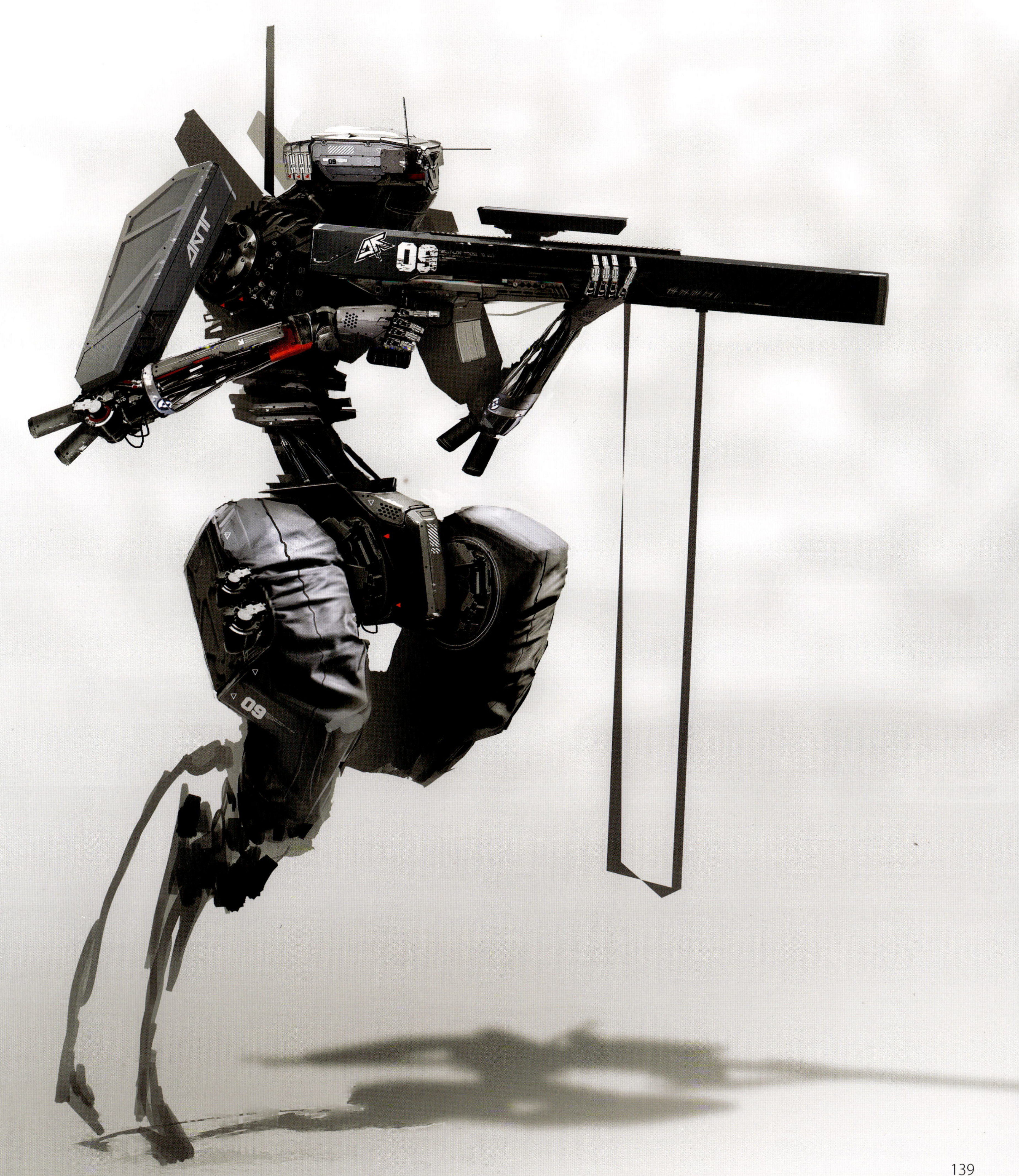

The abnormally high attrition rate among heavy assault units during the EM-denied phase of Ekbatan came as a complete shock. It was discovered only much later that, when operating in fully autonomous mode, a fatal flaw in the heavy's onboard computer vision system rendered the units highly susceptible to adversarial image insertions—an Achilles' heel the adversary was quick to discover and exploit in the cluttered, chaotic environment of urban battle space.

LN-247 // 9.**09**

TYPE: _ HEAVY ARTILLERY MECH
LOCATION: _ IRAN

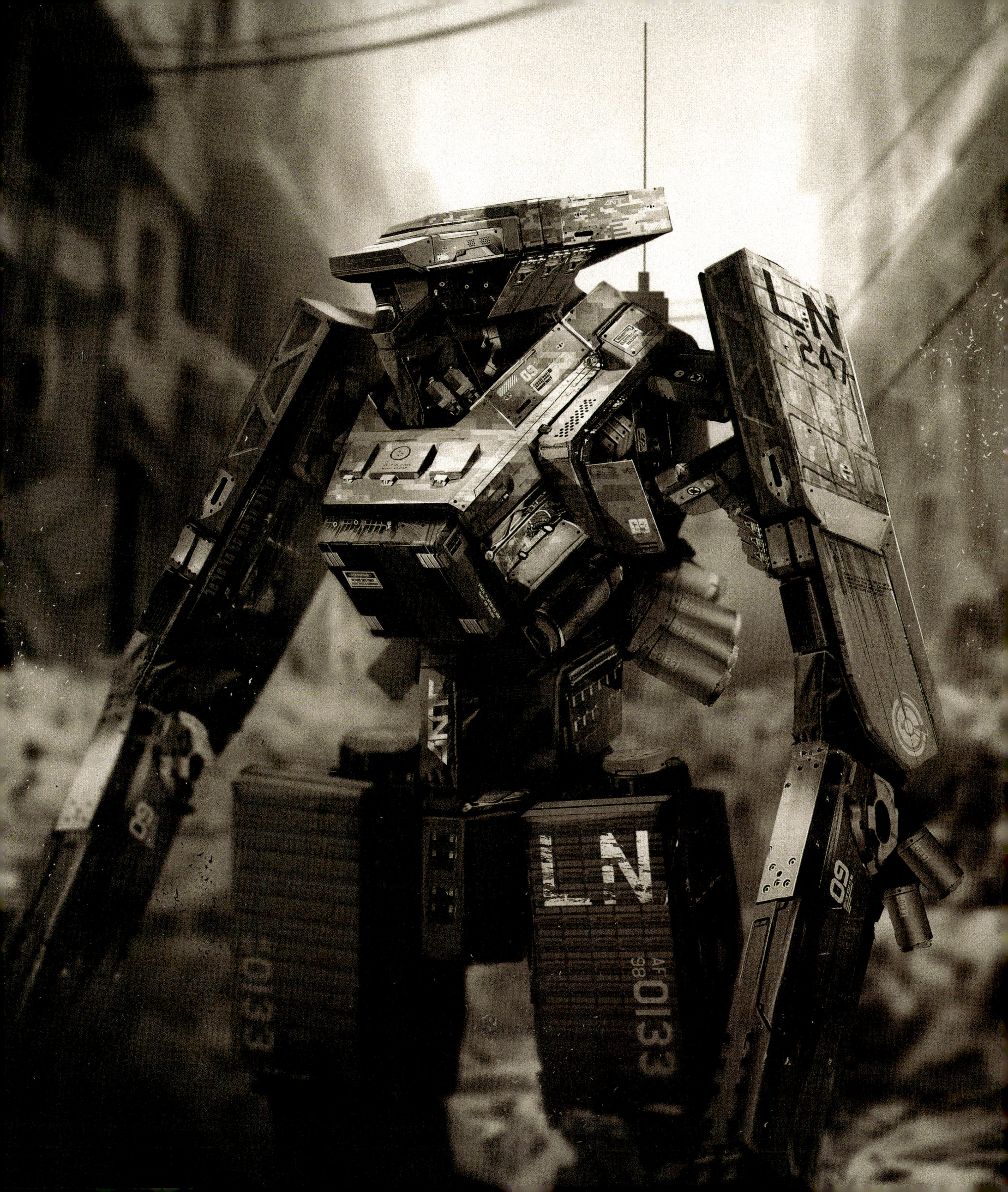

LN
247
LN
AF
0133

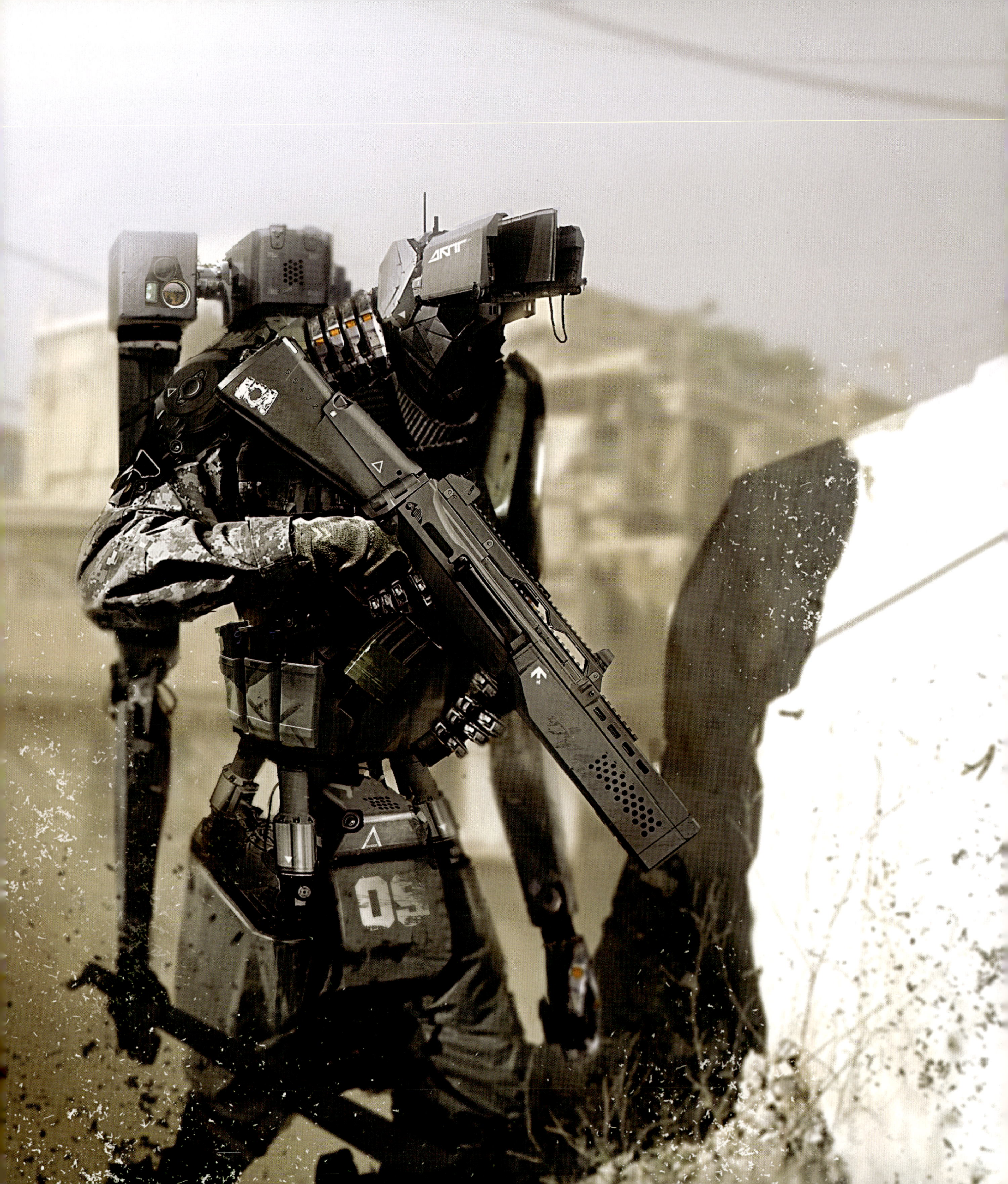
09

After the taking of Mehrabad International Airport, grunt units were fitted with Nakatomi's ATLAS urban warfare exoskeletons, giving them a decisive close-combat edge during the battle of Ekbatan.

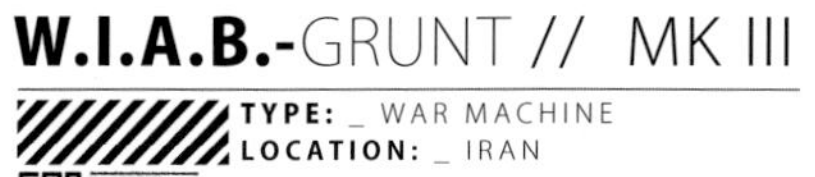

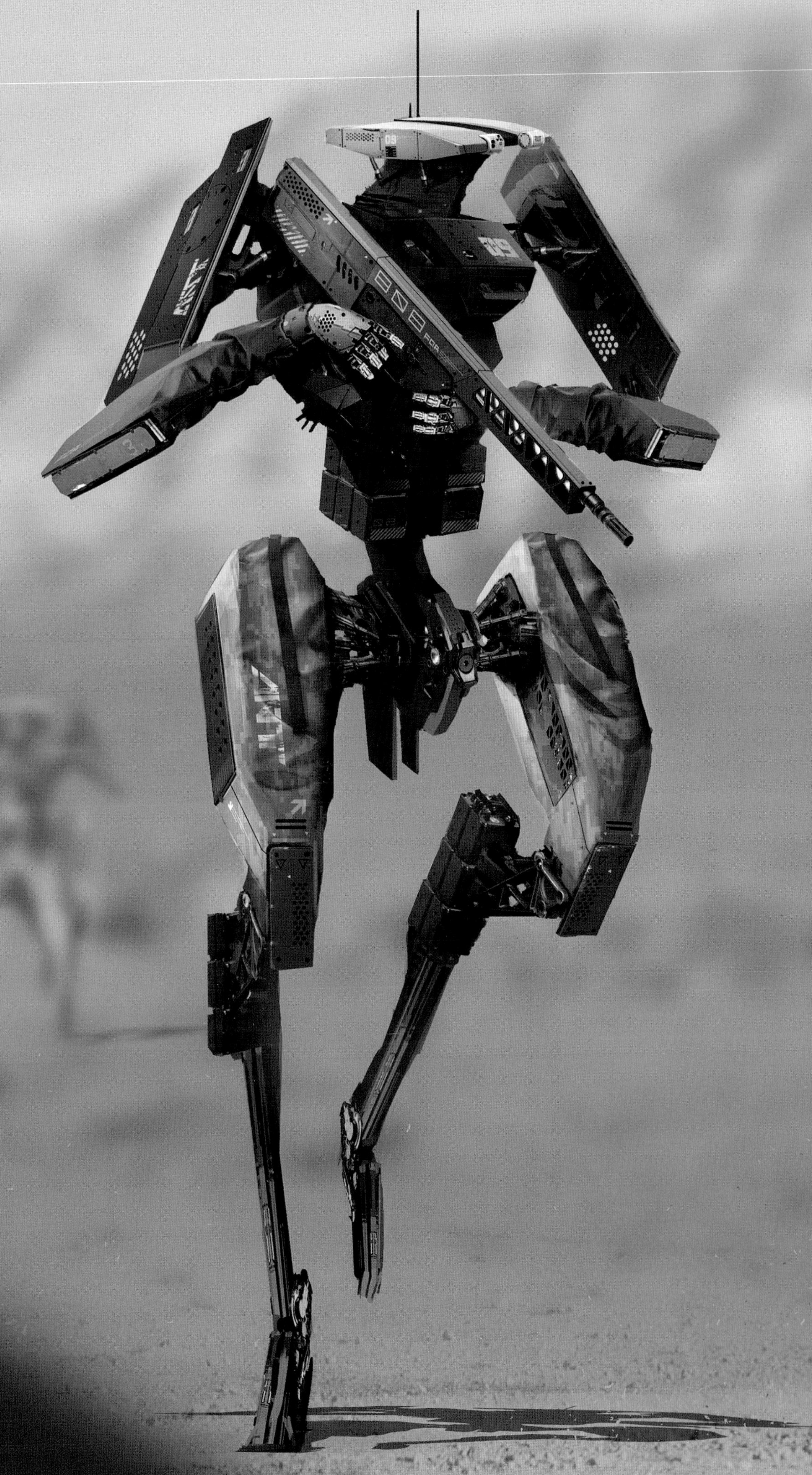

LIBERTINATOR // MK.V

TYPE: _ WAR MACHINE
LOCATION: _ AFGHANISTAN

FOR

F.A.A.R. Defense Systems' third-generation AI-enabled LifePatternRecognition™ in combination with our patented fully autonomous InstaComply™ Dial-a-Lethality™ force projection module render the all-new Libertinator MK. V the complete and total battlefield solution. Libertinator helped bring freedom, peace, and prosperity to the Afghan people. Rest assured, it won't stop there. Twenty-first-century freedom has a name: Libertinator MK. V

From a F.A.A.R. Defense Systems arms expo brochure

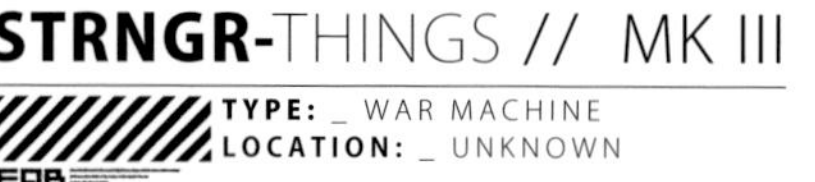

STRINGERS were derived from a series of experimental Libertinator rebuilds featuring vat-grown, carbon-nanotube-reinforced muscle tissue. These strange-looking models were very limited in numbers. The program was short-lived not only due to cost overruns but because STRINGER appendages were prone to spontaneous mutation and spurts of uncontrollable growth which rendered the units ineffective.

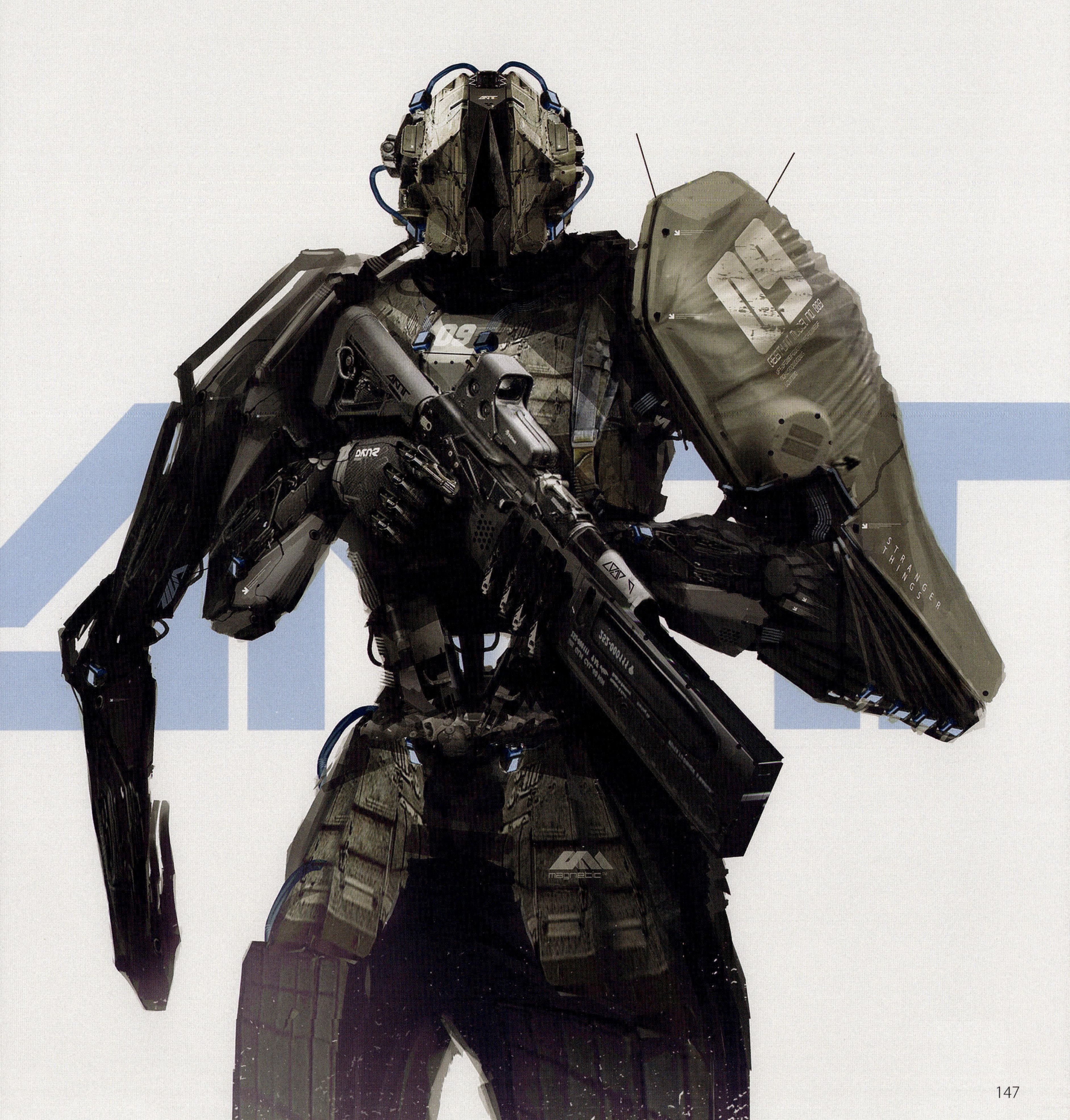
DKN2
STRANGER THINGS
magnetic

A second life for Death Bot: With its Gen. 5 solid state battery pack upgrade, this revamped Libertinator MK. IV can now undergo certification for the army's standard-issue 40 Watt phased plasma anti-material bullpup rifle. (Legal Disclaimer: Compliance with United Nations 1995 ban on blinding laser weapons not guaranteed.)

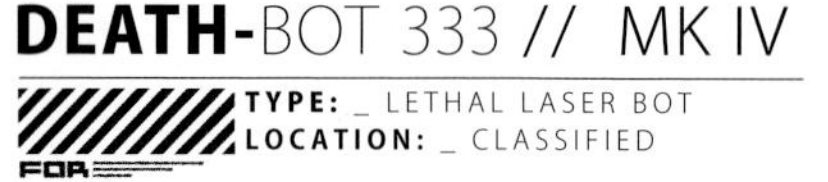

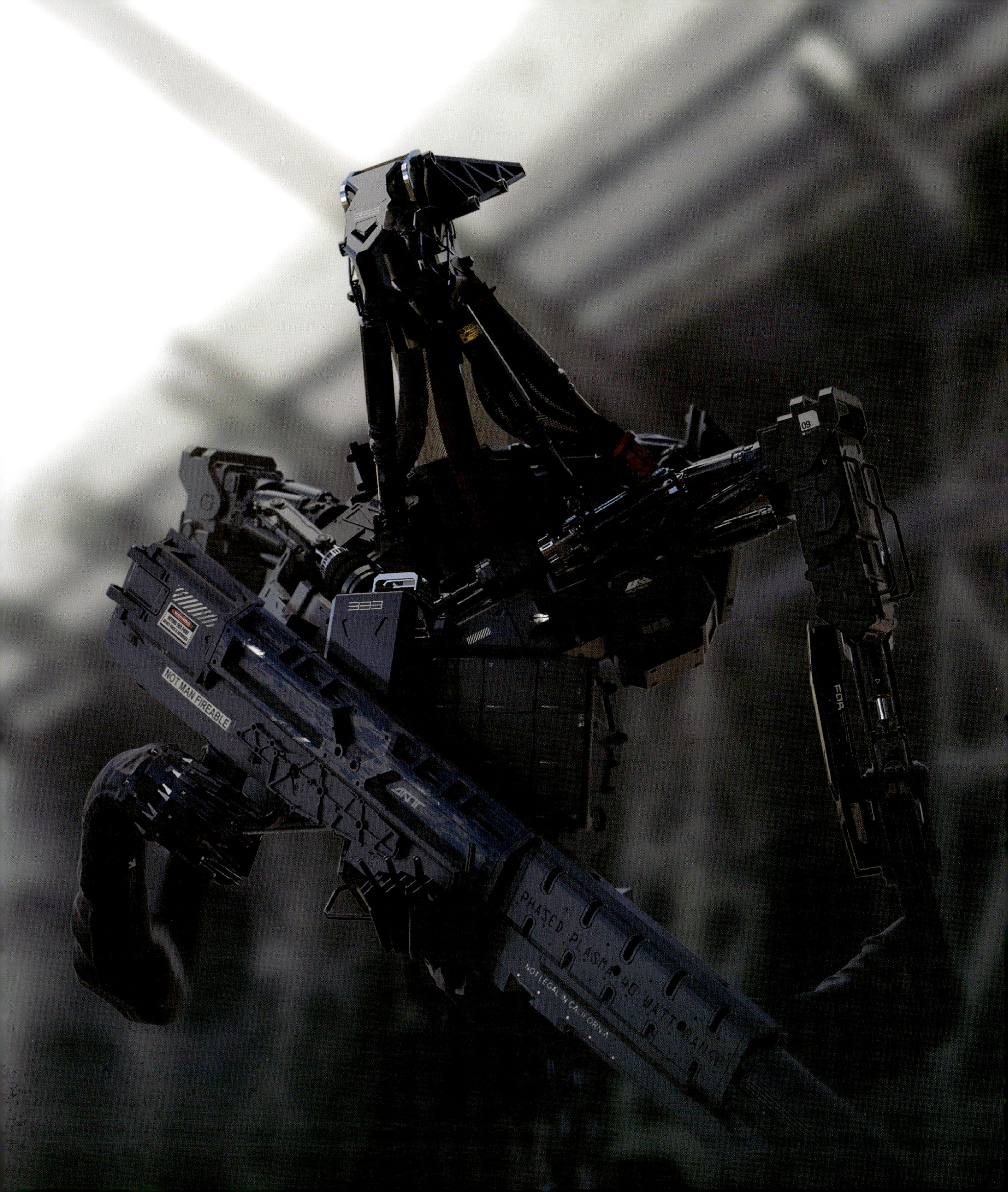
NOT MAN FIREABLE
PHASED PLASMA 40 WATT RANGE
NOT LEGAL IN CALIFORNIA
333
FOR
09

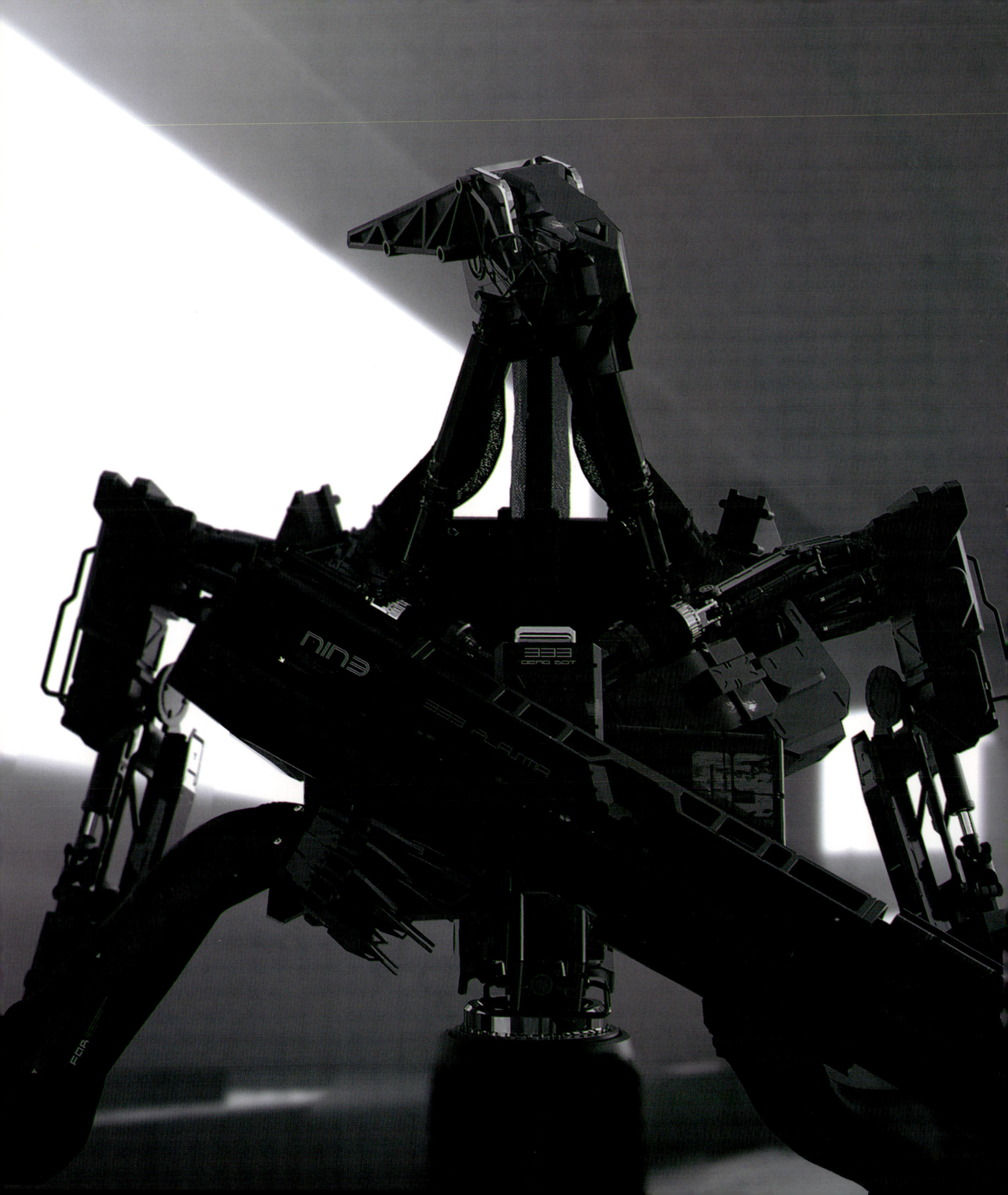
nin3
333
DEAD BOT

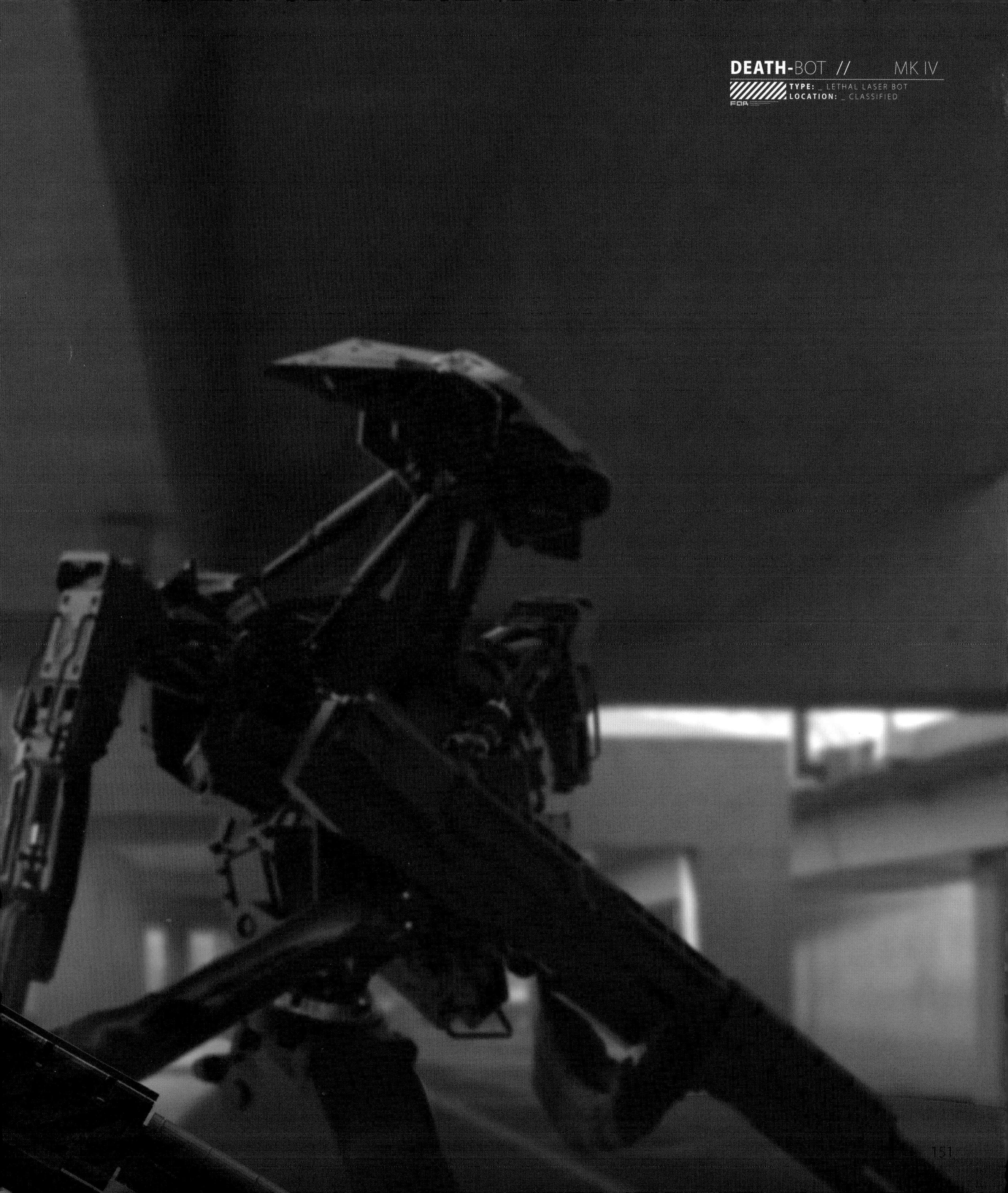
DEATH-BOT // MK IV
TYPE: _ LETHAL LASER BOT
LOCATION: _ CLASSIFIED

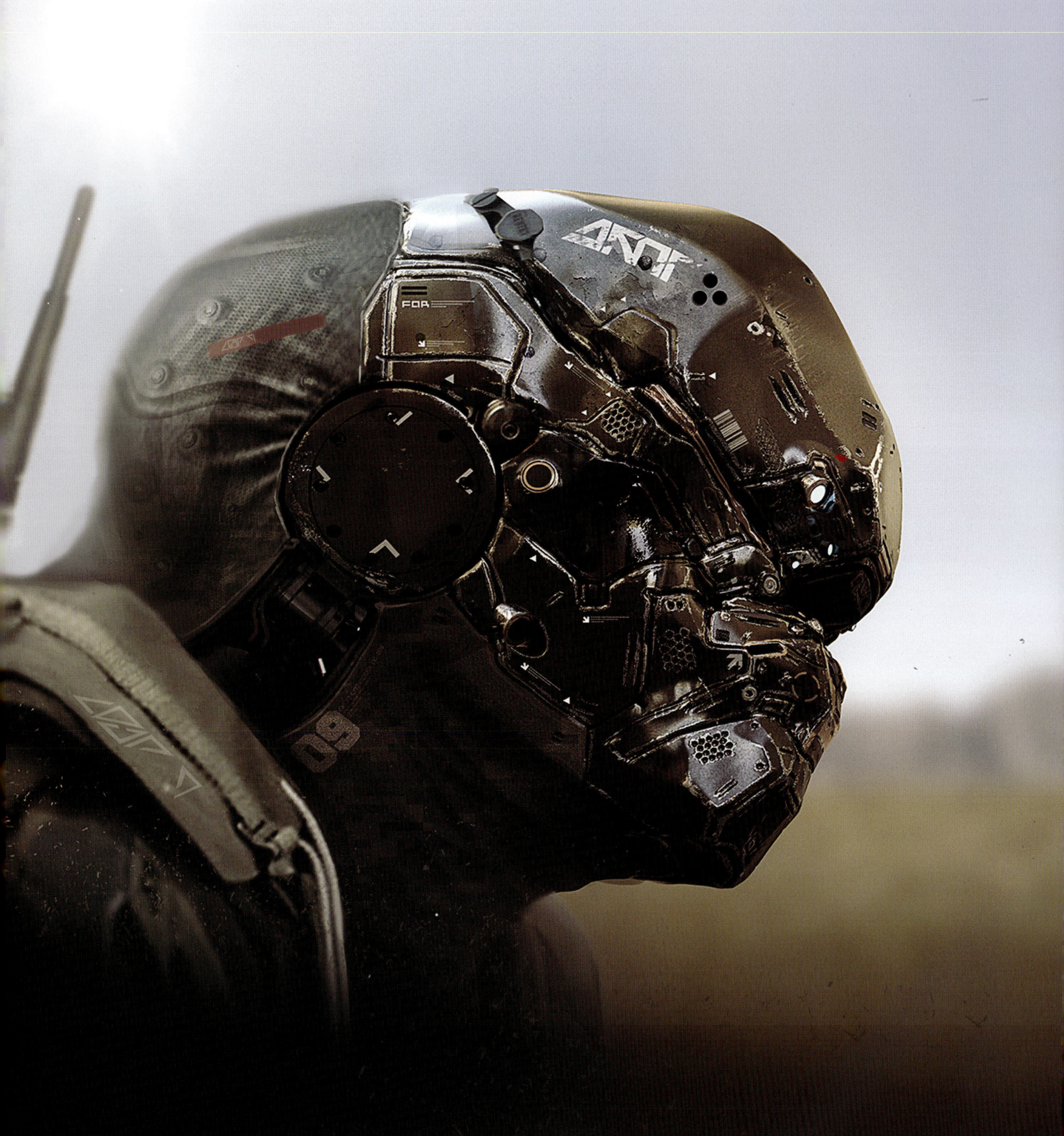
FOR

Not much is known about the Chinese military's brief flirtation with neuralace technology. Depicted here is one of the rare images available in public sources of what is believed to be the rough equivalent of the U.S.'s iconic Razorback MK. III, aka "Chameleon."

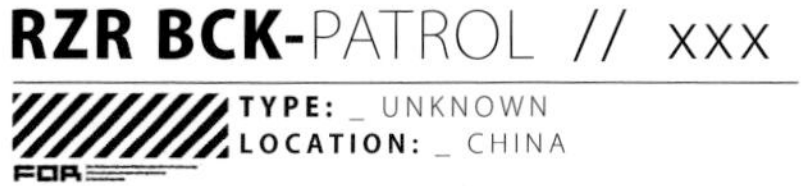

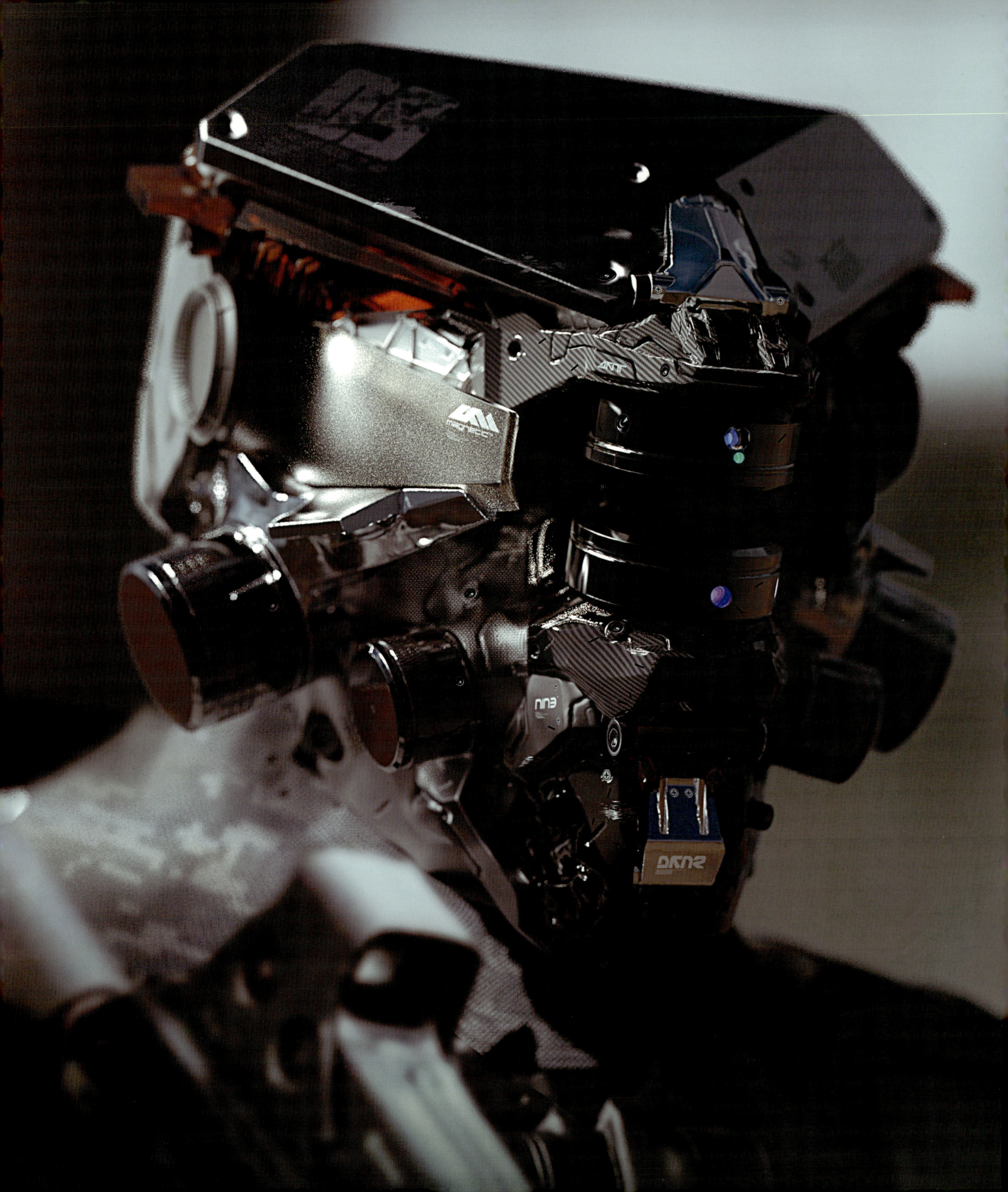

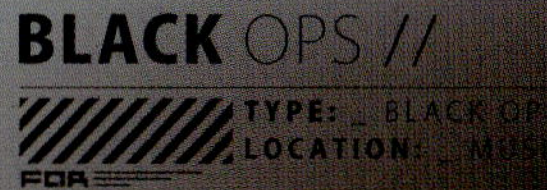

DAN: Have you seen this?! The new video for Pleasure Model by Former and Noisia? Pretty sick stuff!

TZ: LOL! Look at the SpecOps dude with all that LIDAR in his face.

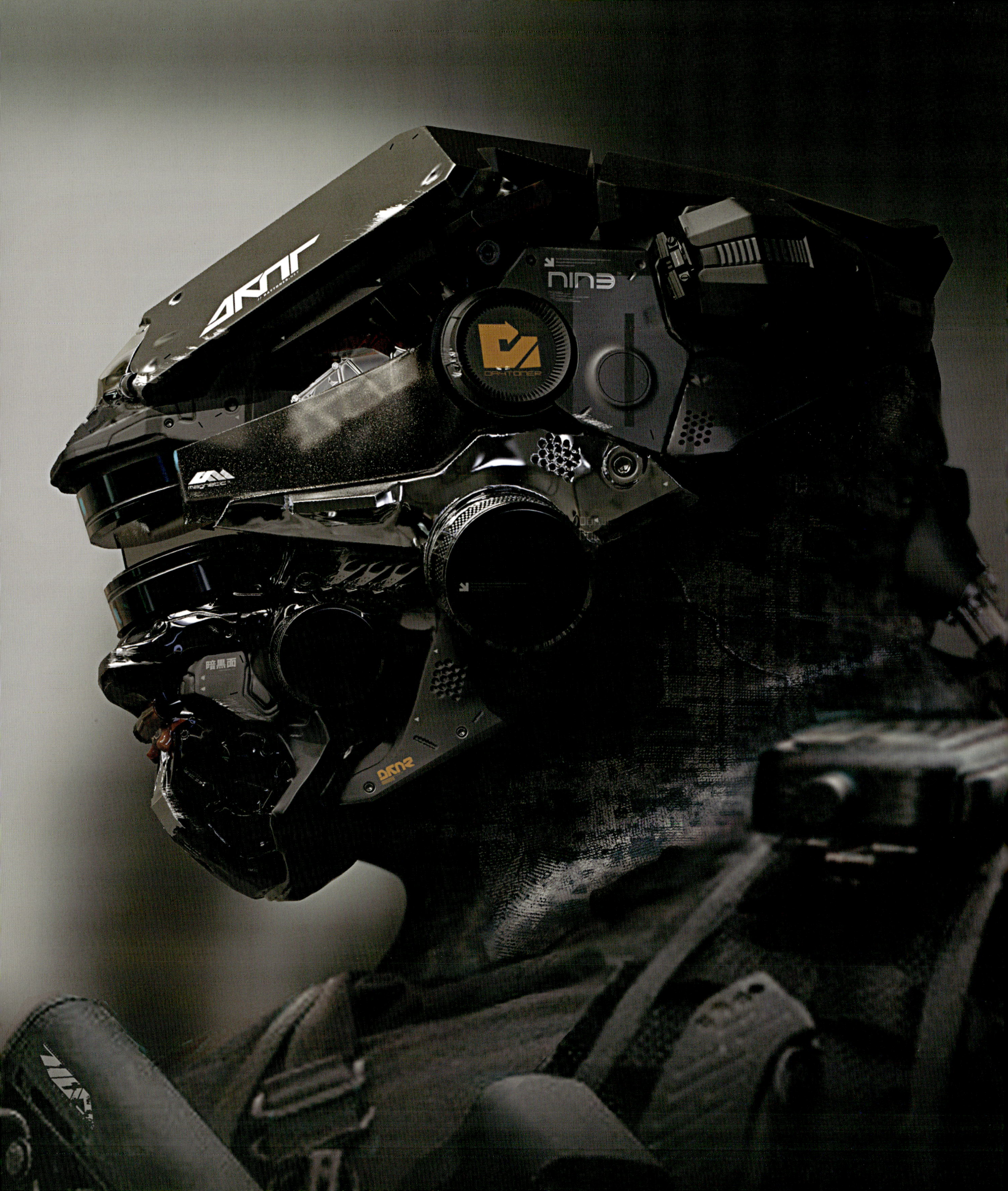
nin3
暗黒面

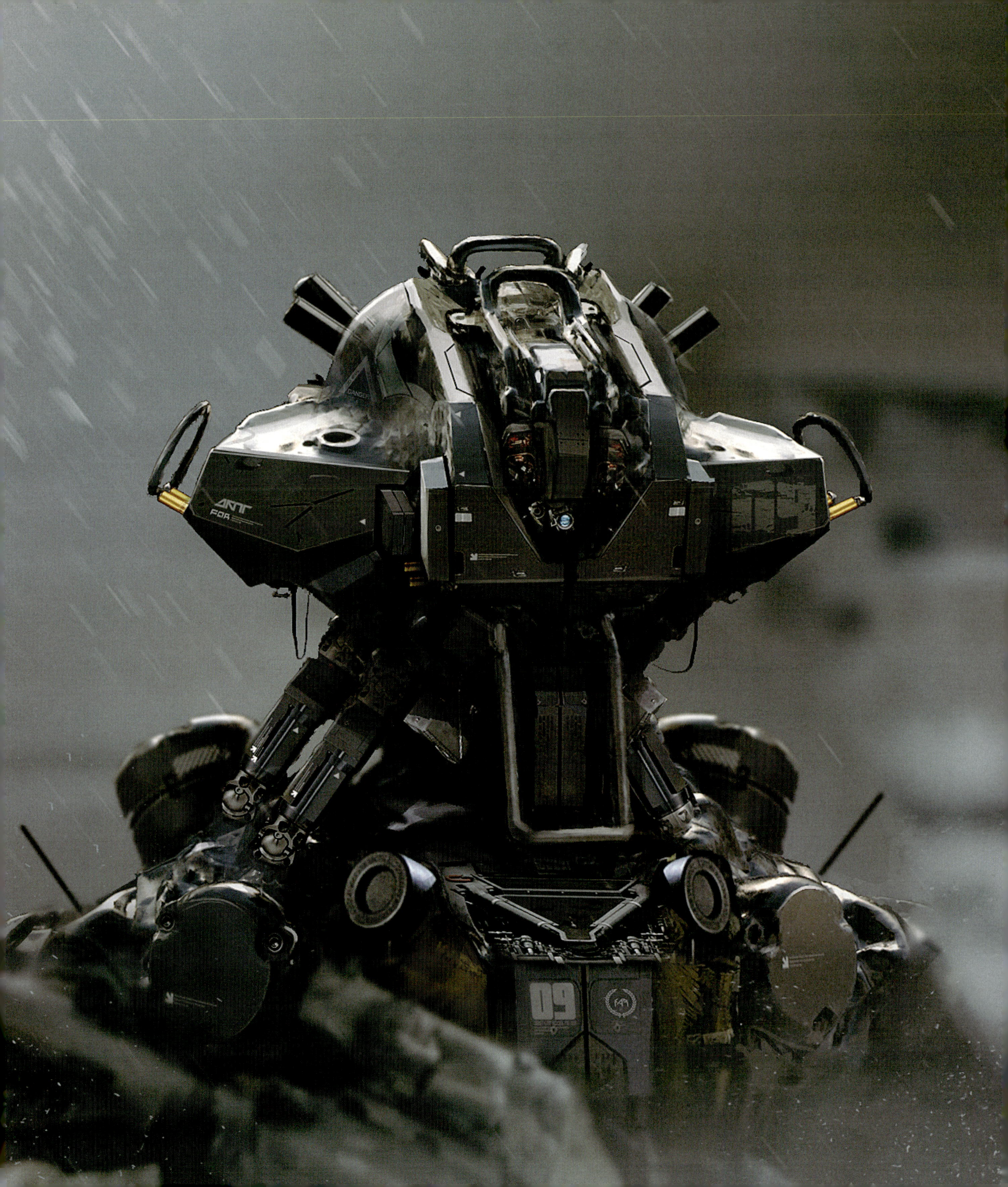
09

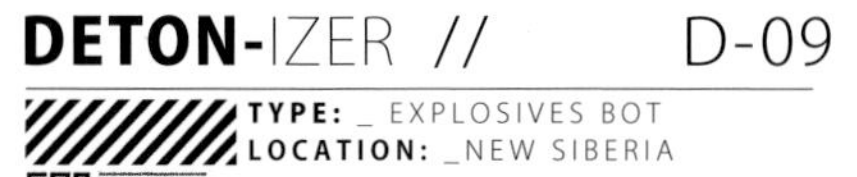

Designed to withstand the toughest of tough conditions! The all-new F.A.A.R. Defense Systems DETONIZER D-09 takes it like a champ. For the third year in a row, it is the EOD gold standard. The newly added combat mode transforms the D-09 into a fire-and-forget robotic battle space solution fighting until the very end. Experience the D-09 at our "Face 2 Face with Technology" event this month!

H| H0n

Iwshittody. D0ntwrrypls. Im0k. Justbngedup. Neurlnkt0tllyglitchd. Immedevcedt0FortTrumpn0w. Cllus00n.

Luv J0n

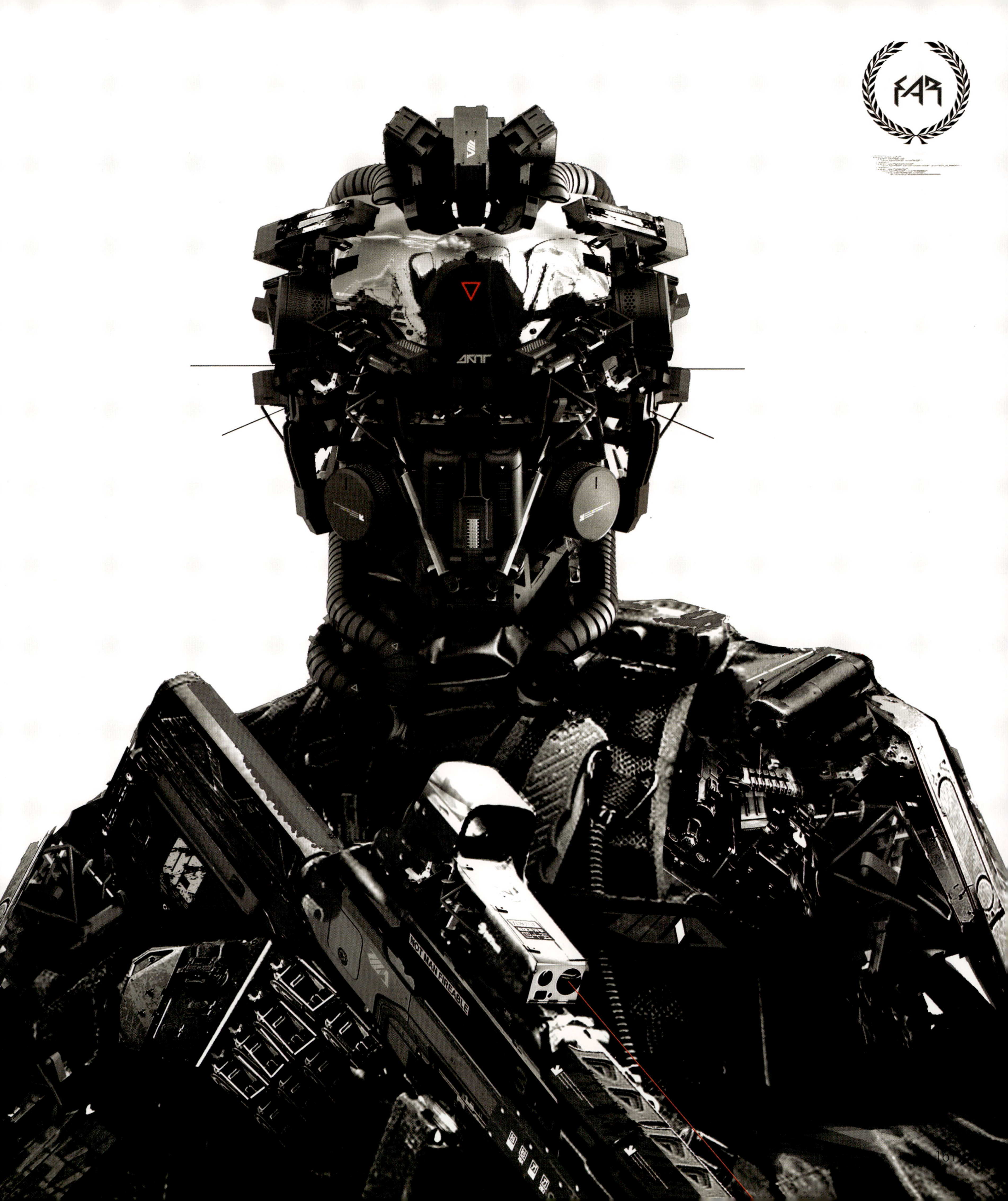
ARNT
NOT MAN FIREABLE

BLACKOPS // **v.**IX

TYPE: _ TACTICAL NEURO SUIT
LOCATION: _ US

FOR

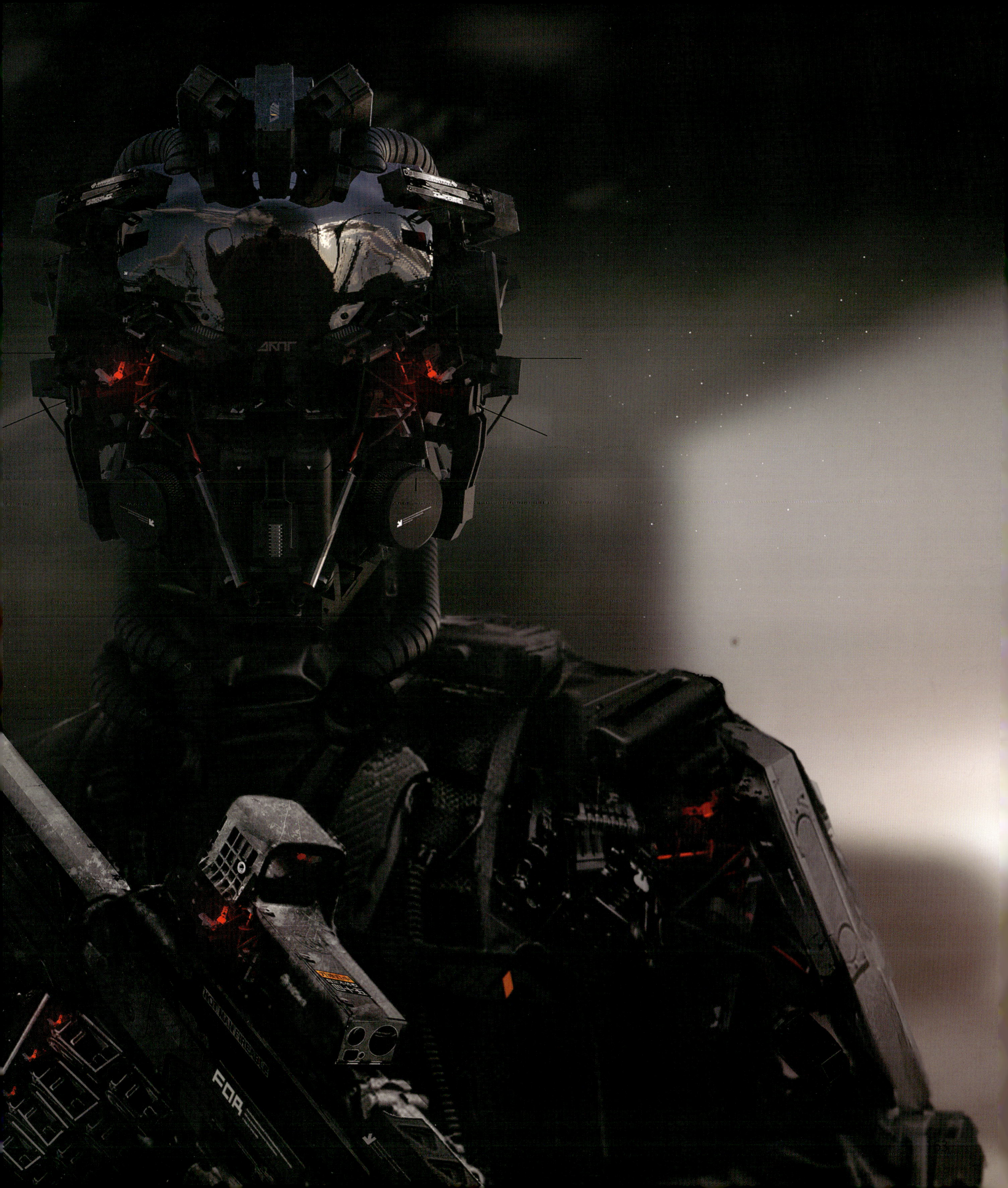

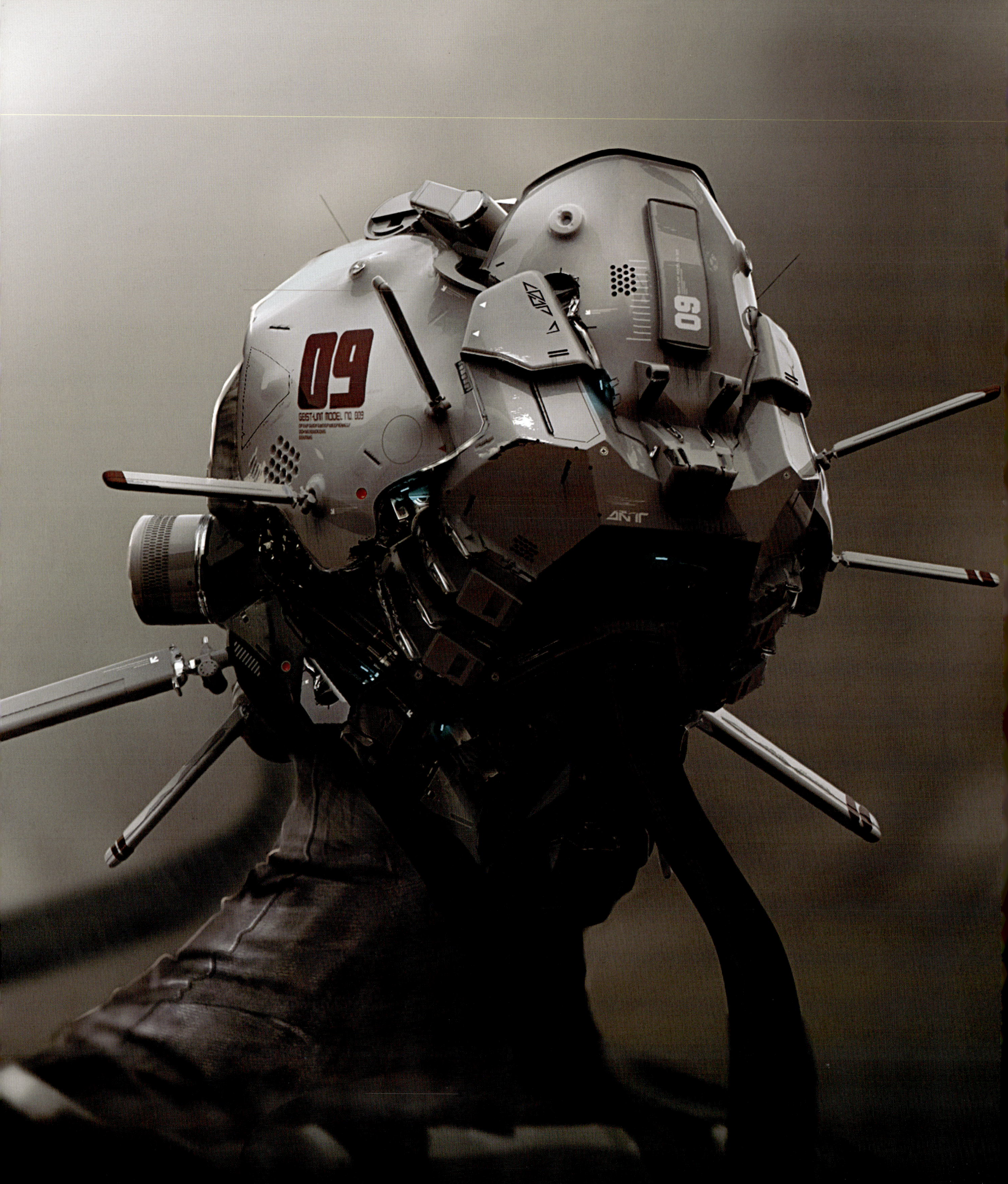
09
GEIST-UNIT MODEL NO 009
09

In a desperate effort to finally make human-machine teaming work and keep humans in the kill-chain whilst fighting at machine speed, the US military turned to neuralace technology as a very early adopter. F.A.A.R.'s MACH 9 helmet was used by F-35H and B-21B pilots to control swarms of Darwinopterus combat drones during the invasion of Iran. It was the most uncomfortable piece of headgear ever designed.

MACH 9 HELMET // MK.V

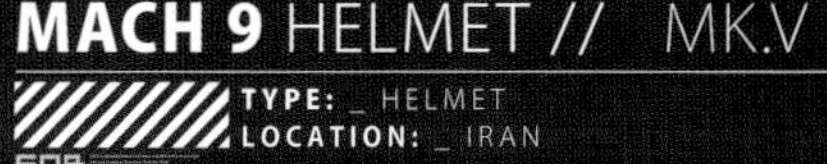

TYPE: _ HELMET
LOCATION: _ IRAN

The bandwidth limitations of external neuralaces heralded the end of the iconic Razorback (here shown in its Mk.VI variant). From then on, it was implants all the way down.

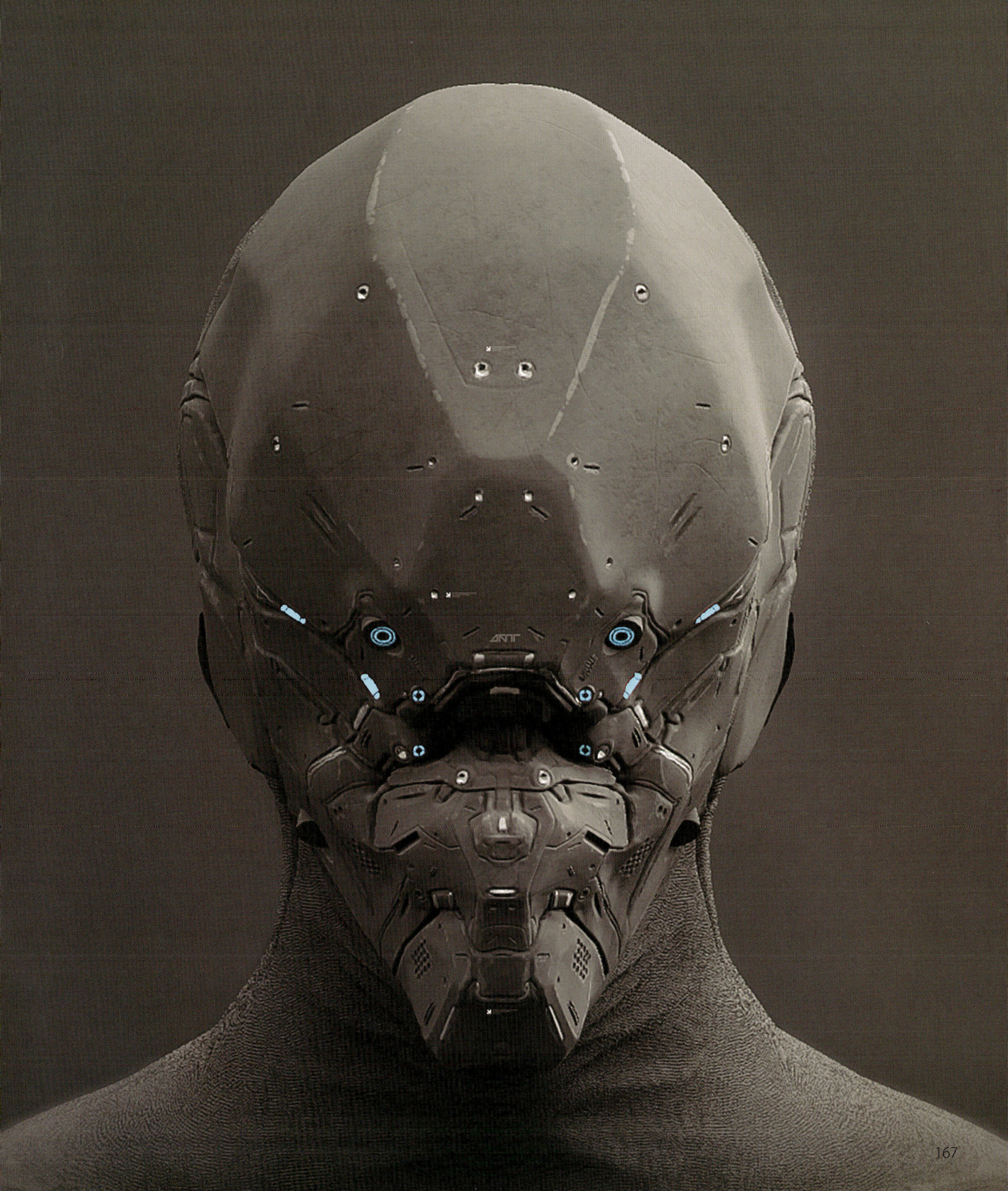

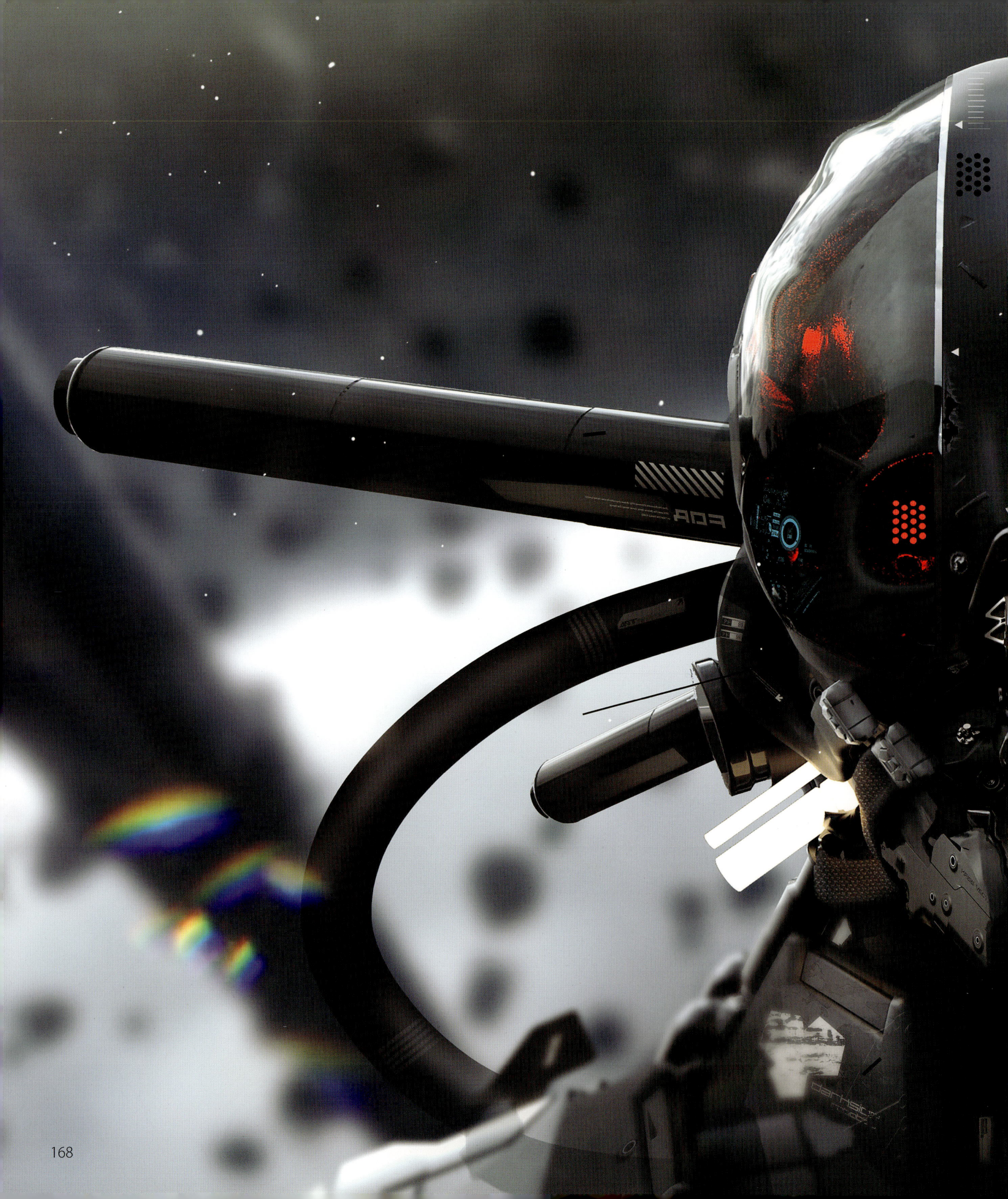

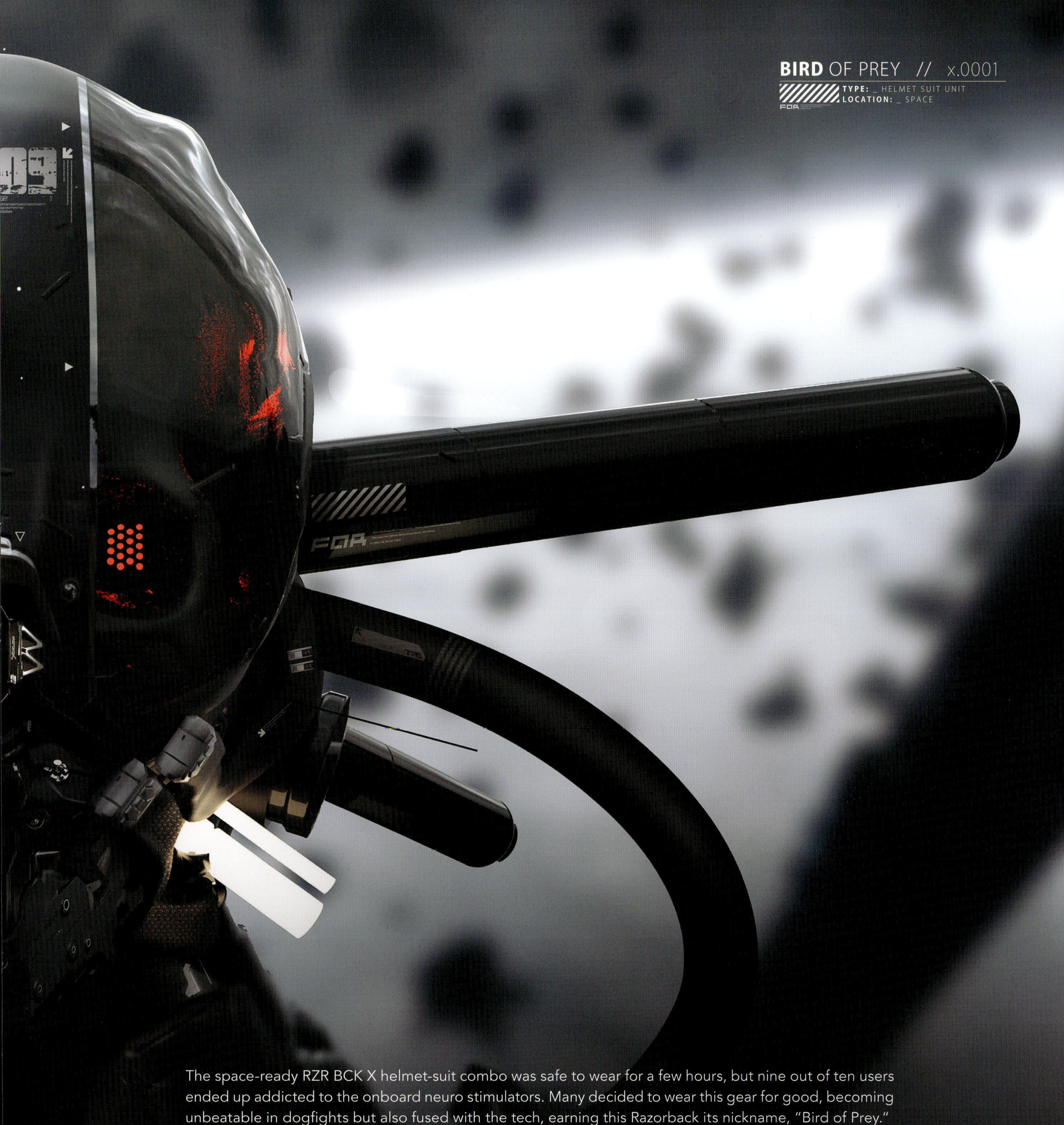

The space-ready RZR BCK X helmet-suit combo was safe to wear for a few hours, but nine out of ten users ended up addicted to the onboard neuro stimulators. Many decided to wear this gear for good, becoming unbeatable in dogfights but also fused with the tech, earning this Razorback its nickname, "Bird of Prey."

The Razorback MK. VII was the first model to introduce predictive tactical battle management for infantry units, providing up to three seconds of 99.6 percent reliable prevision. Described as "time tunnel technology" by DTNR Robotics in a quite misleading advertising campaign, the MK. VII used a simple yet robust quantum state extrapolation chip piped directly into the Razorback's neuralace interface. It was cutting edge at the time. The MK. VII, dubbed "4site" by Tier 1 Operators in the field, was beloved for providing that extra temporal edge in combat. Instant face-melt was a quite unpleasant side effect in early models.

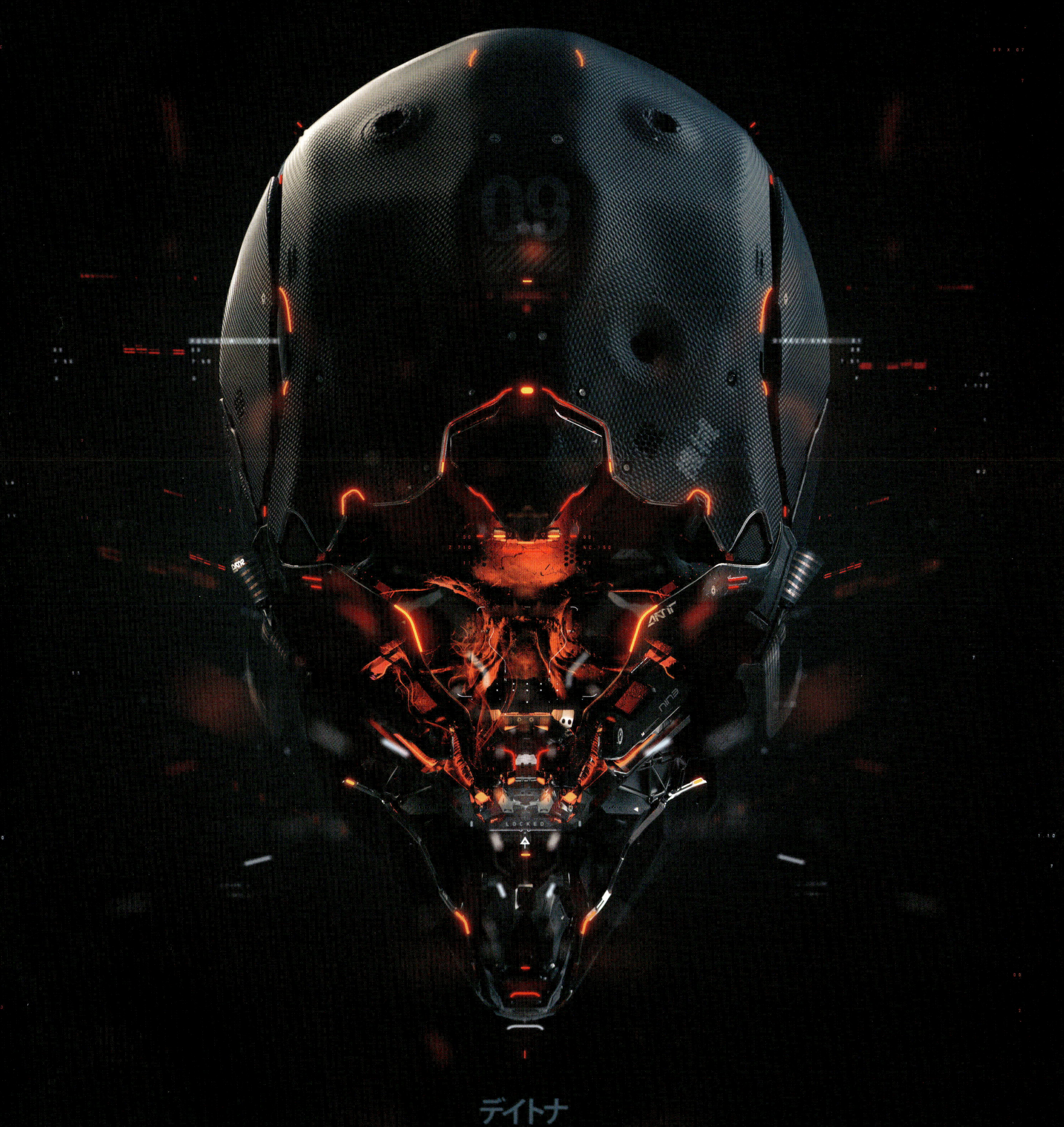
LOCKED
デイトナ

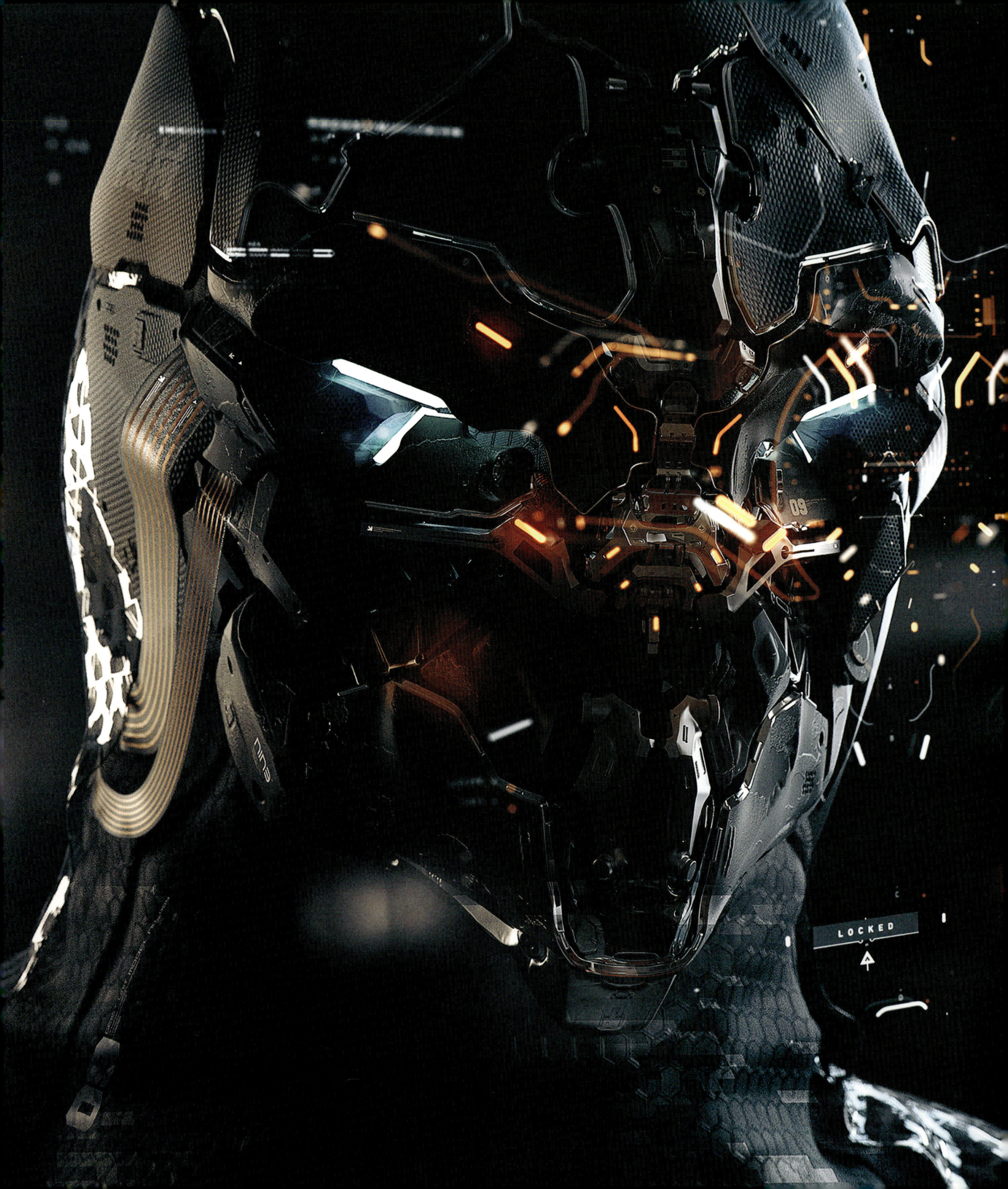
LOCKED

TIME TUNNEL PILOT // **v.**01

TYPE: _ TIME GEAR
LOCATION: _ UNKNOWN

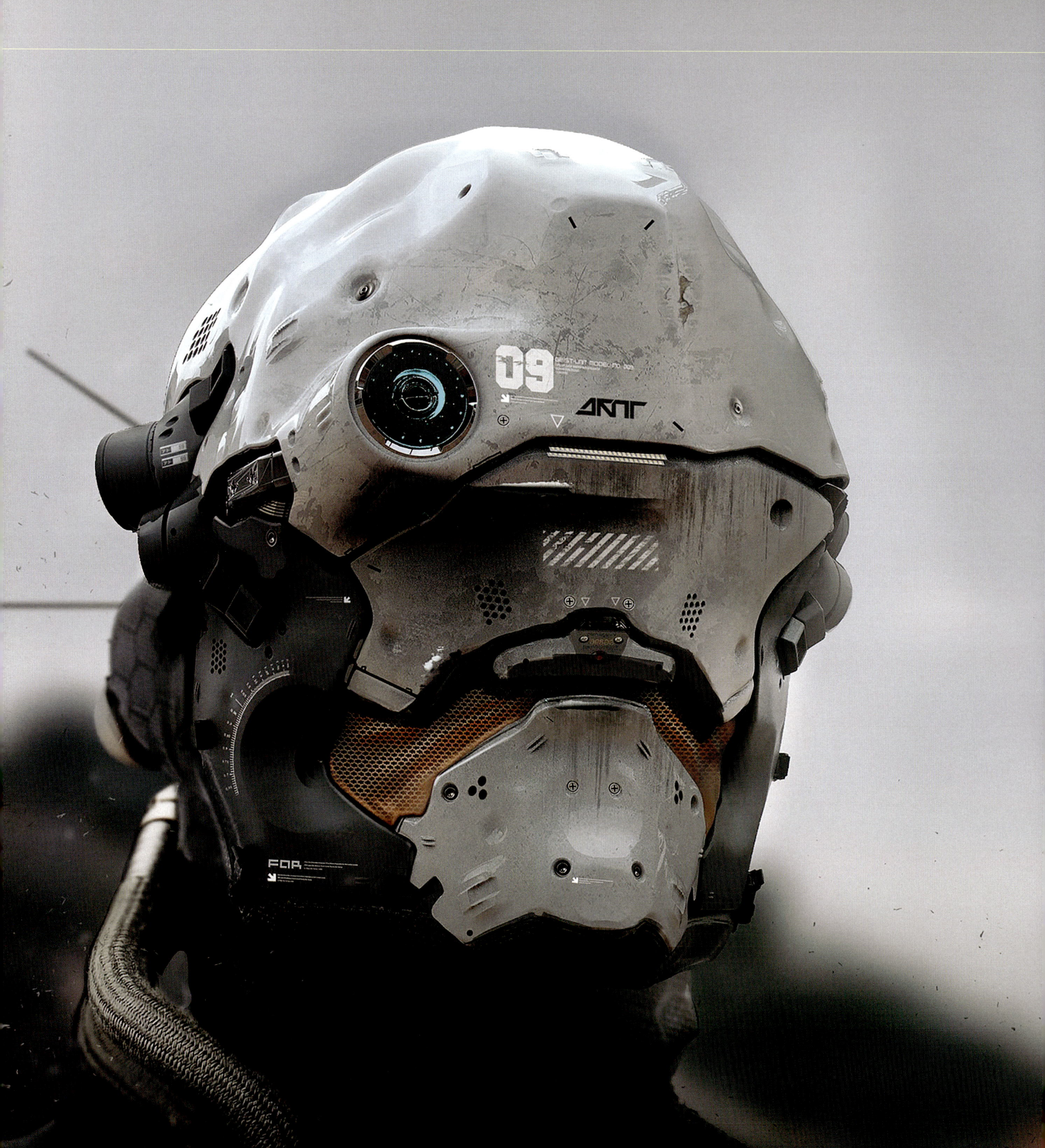
09

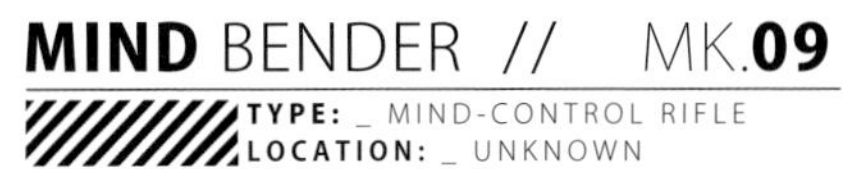

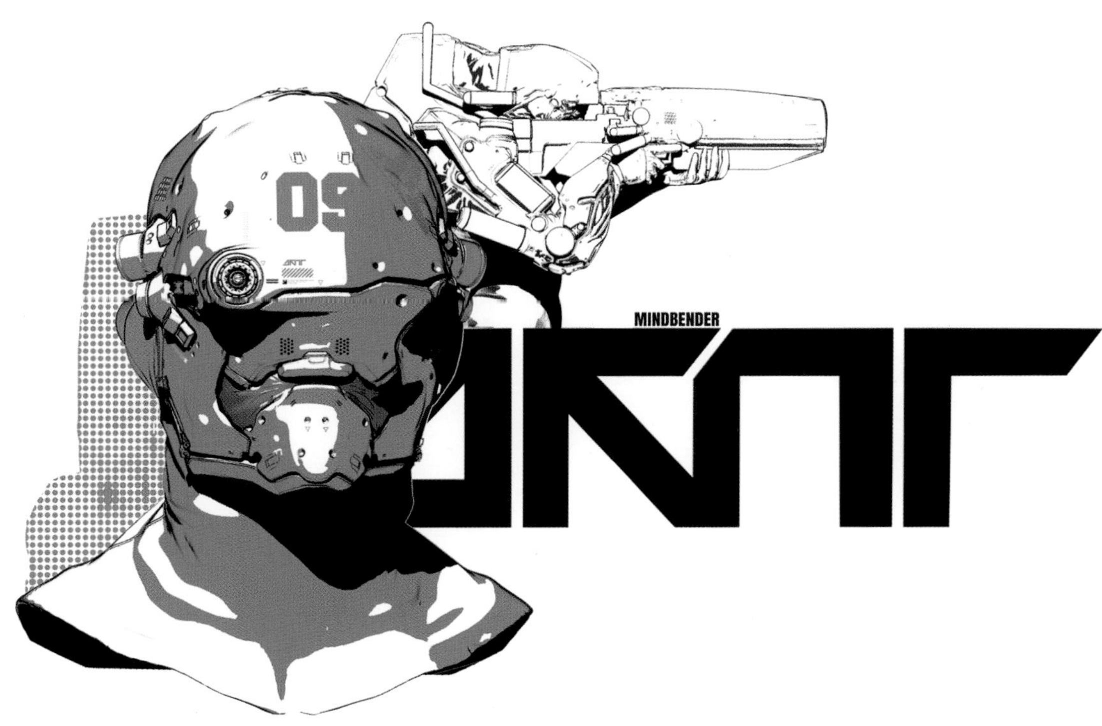

The class 9 Mind Bender was a controversial piece of neuro-combat equipment developed by F.A.A.R. Defense Systems, testing the ethical limits of human-machine integration.

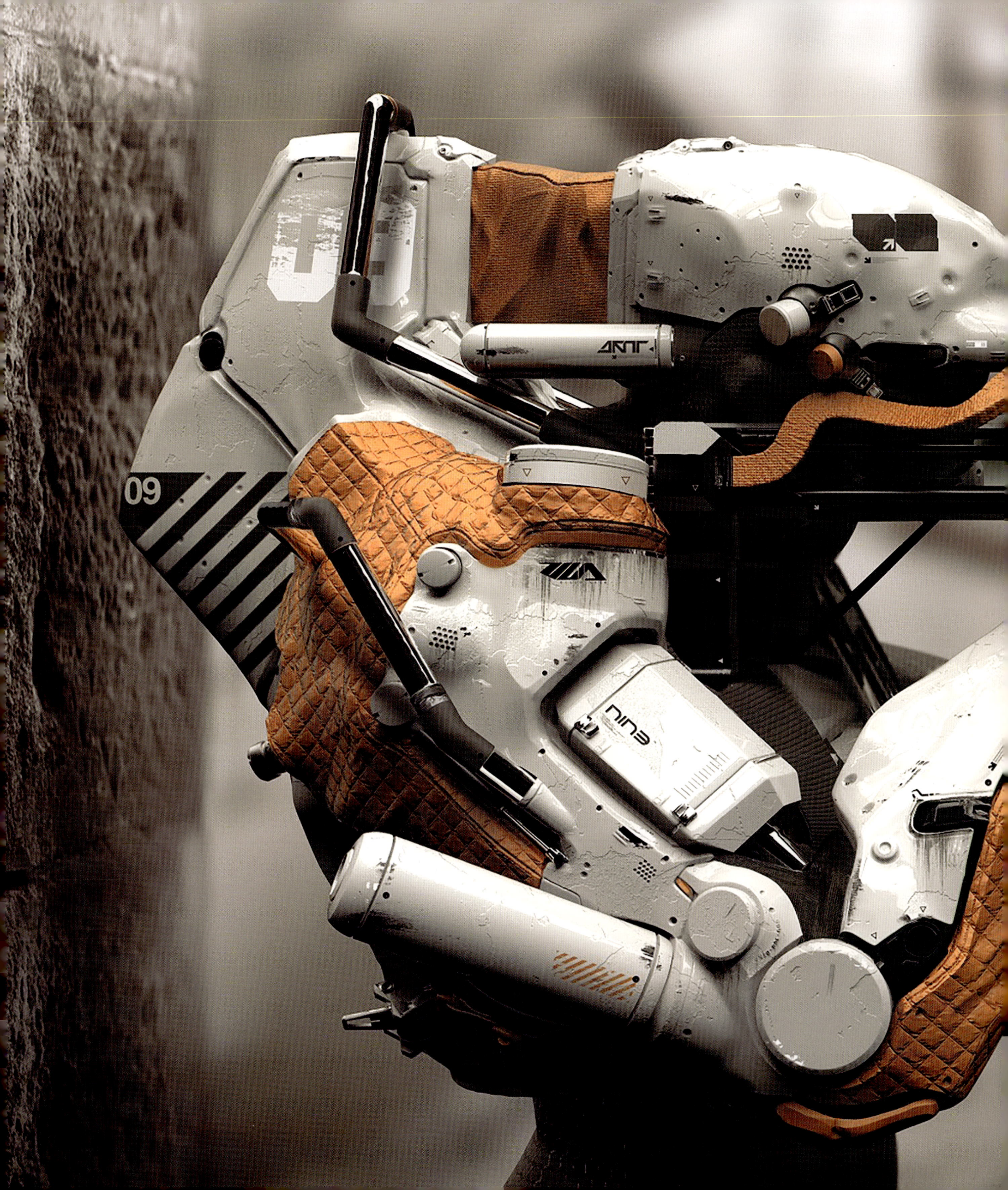
09

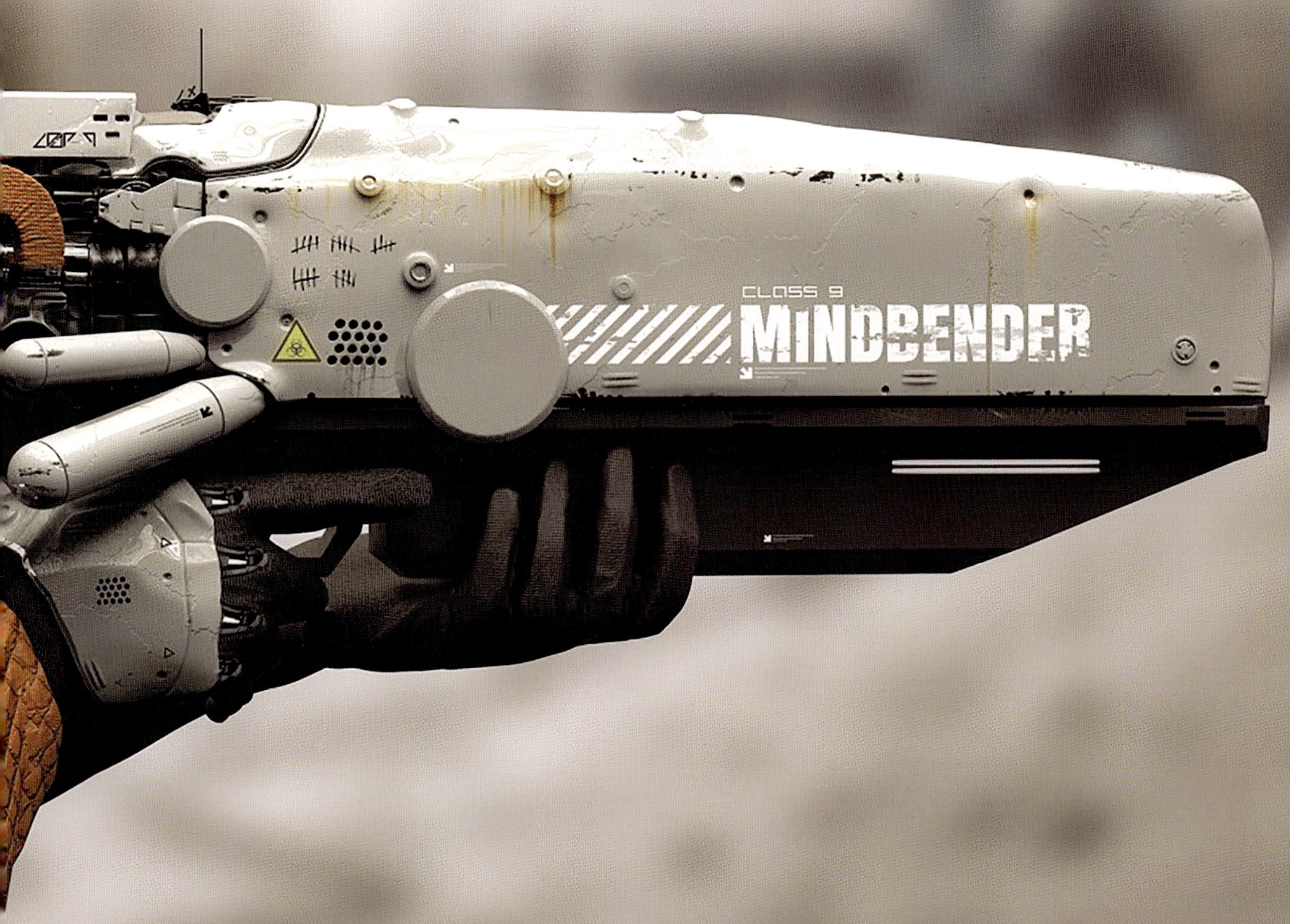

After "target lock-in," operators would be fully controlled by the preset algorithms of the rifle. The class 9 model came with an upgraded backpack, storing and managing up to 100 targets simultaneously as well as F.A.A.R.'s patented "eye slot." Did Mind Bender reduce the human operator to a piece of the equipment? Who was responsible for the death and destruction caused by this technology, the human or the rifle?

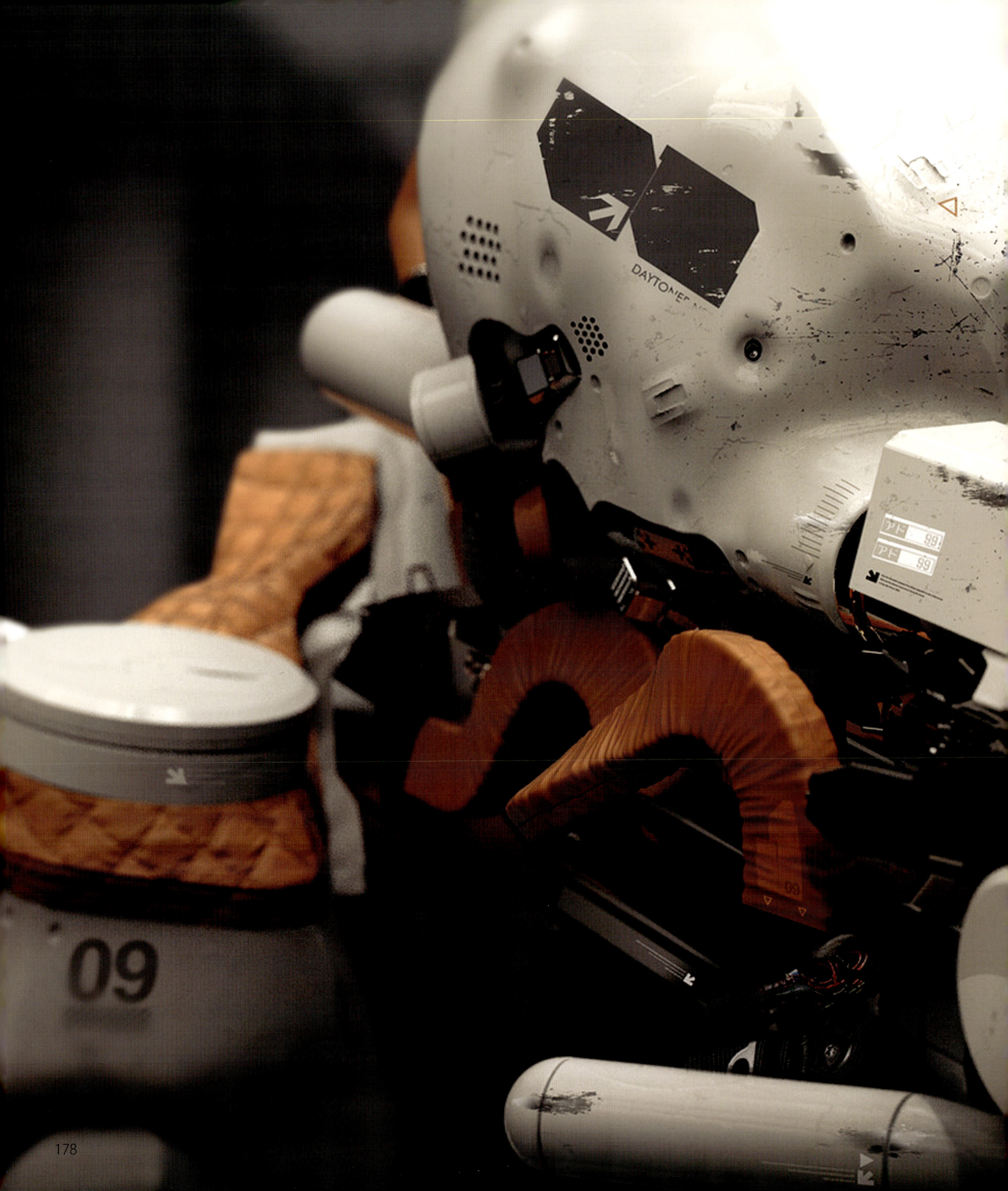
09

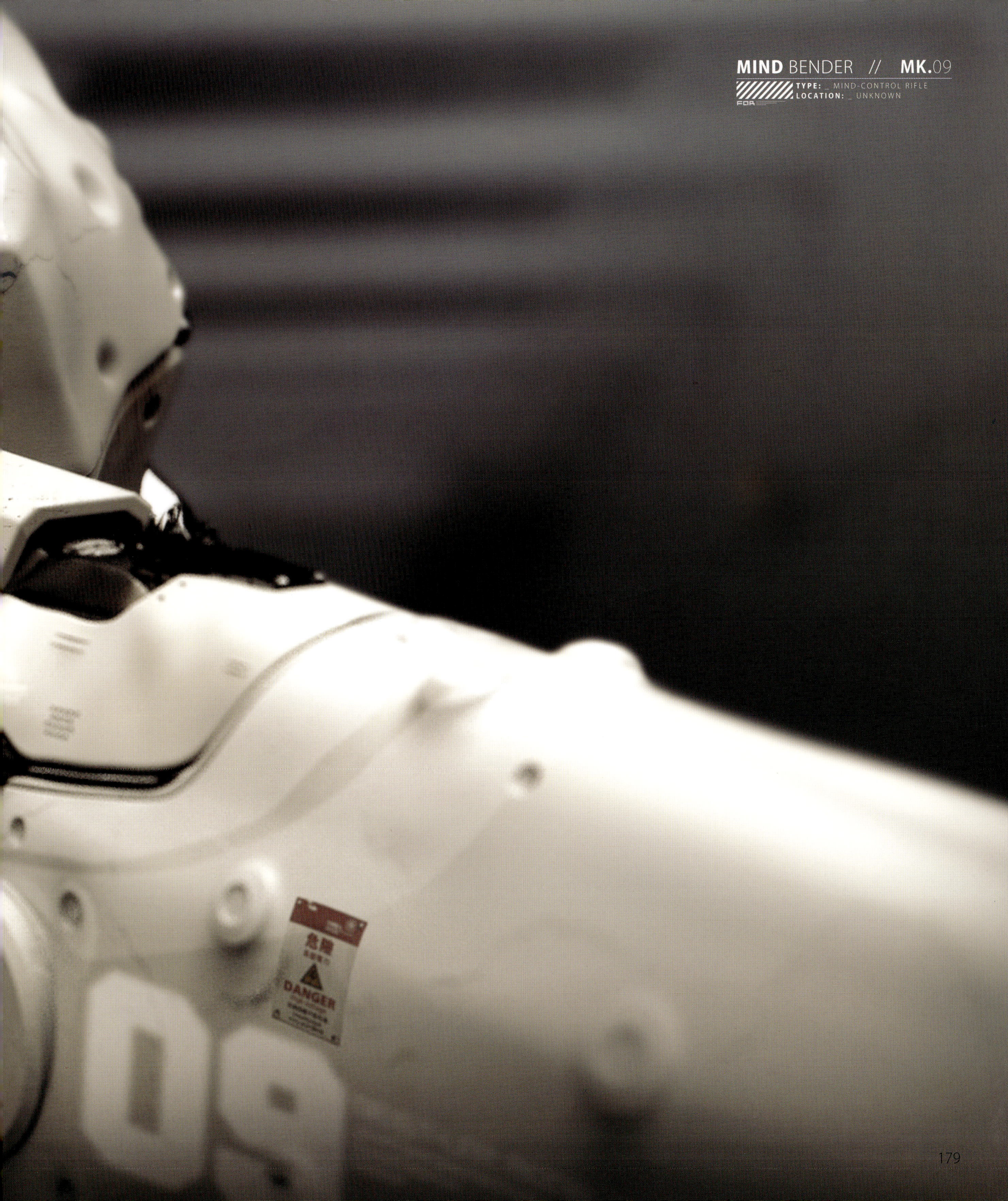
MIND BENDER // MK.09
TYPE: _ MIND-CONTROL RIFLE
LOCATION: _ UNKNOWN
FOR
DANGER
09

STALK3R DROID // **MK.**09

TYPE: _ RECON AUTO DRONE
LOCATION: _ CLOUDY MEADOWS

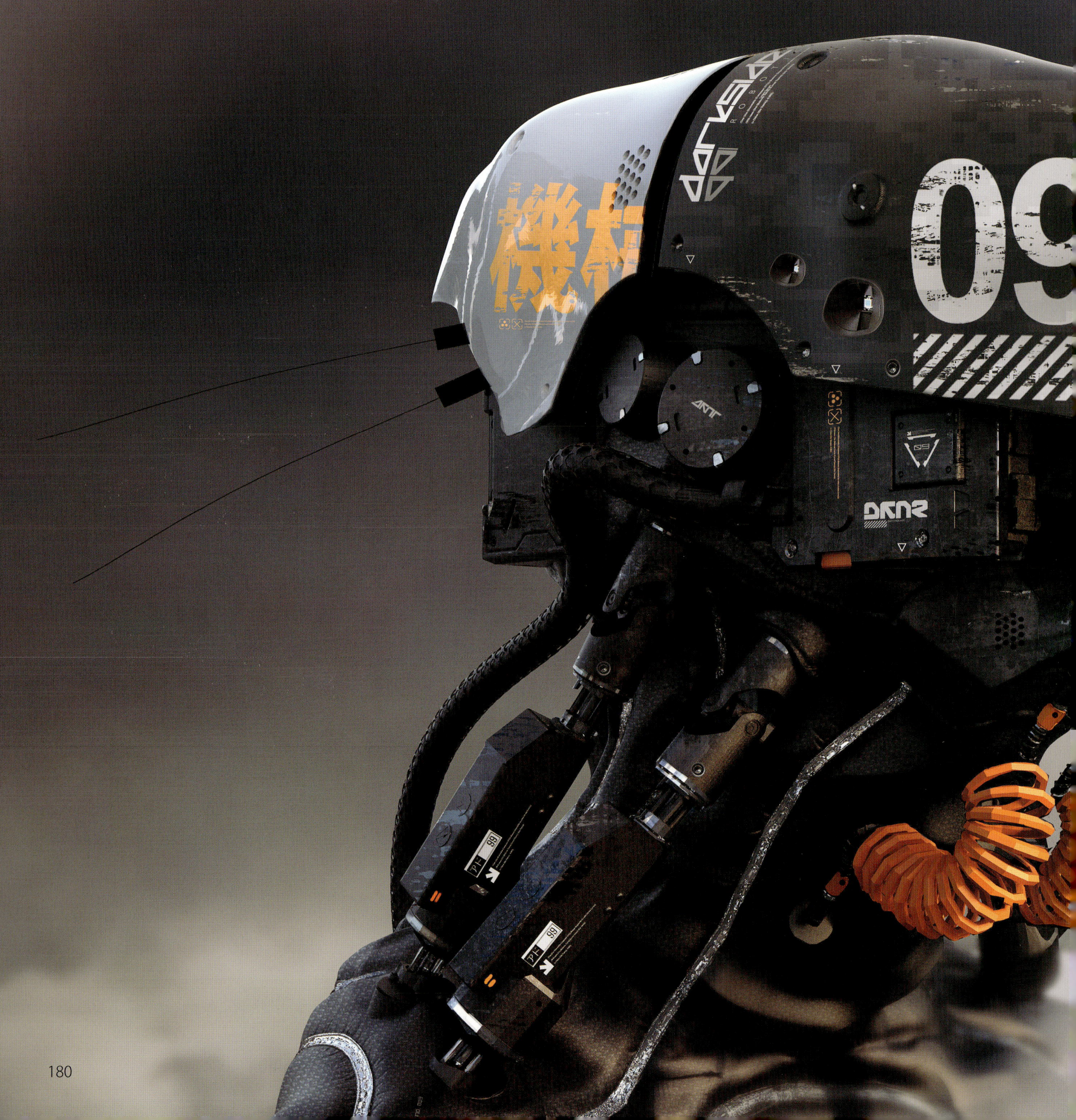

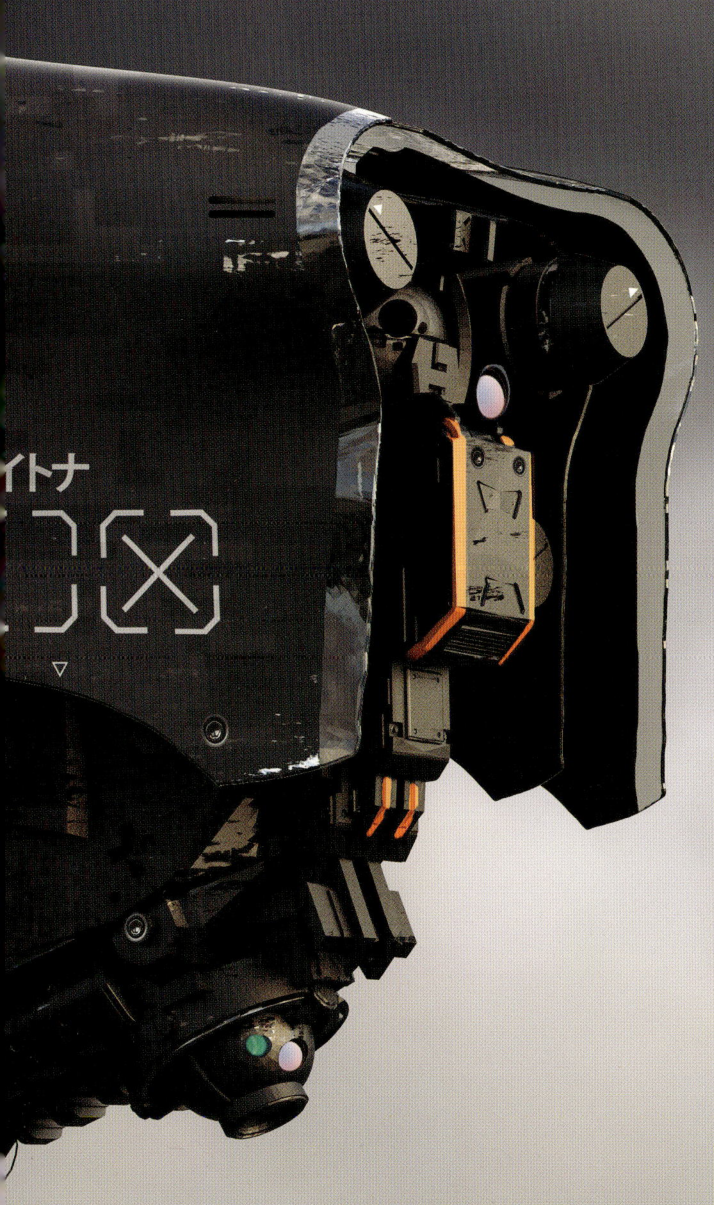

Licensed production of cheap, reliable STALK3R modules (Seismic. Thermal. Audio-Visual. Lidar. K-Band/MM-Wave. Electromagnetic. Radar) made DTNR Robotics one of the top three multinational arms manufacturers worldwide. DTNR's controversial market maneuver also rang in a new era of technology diffusion, rapidly proliferating military-grade technology to paramilitaries and police forces as well as terrorist organizations everywhere. There was hardly a cloud of teargas to be found without a STALK3R-equipped unit stomping through it during the Collapse of Berlin and the subsequent second wave of global democratic contraction.

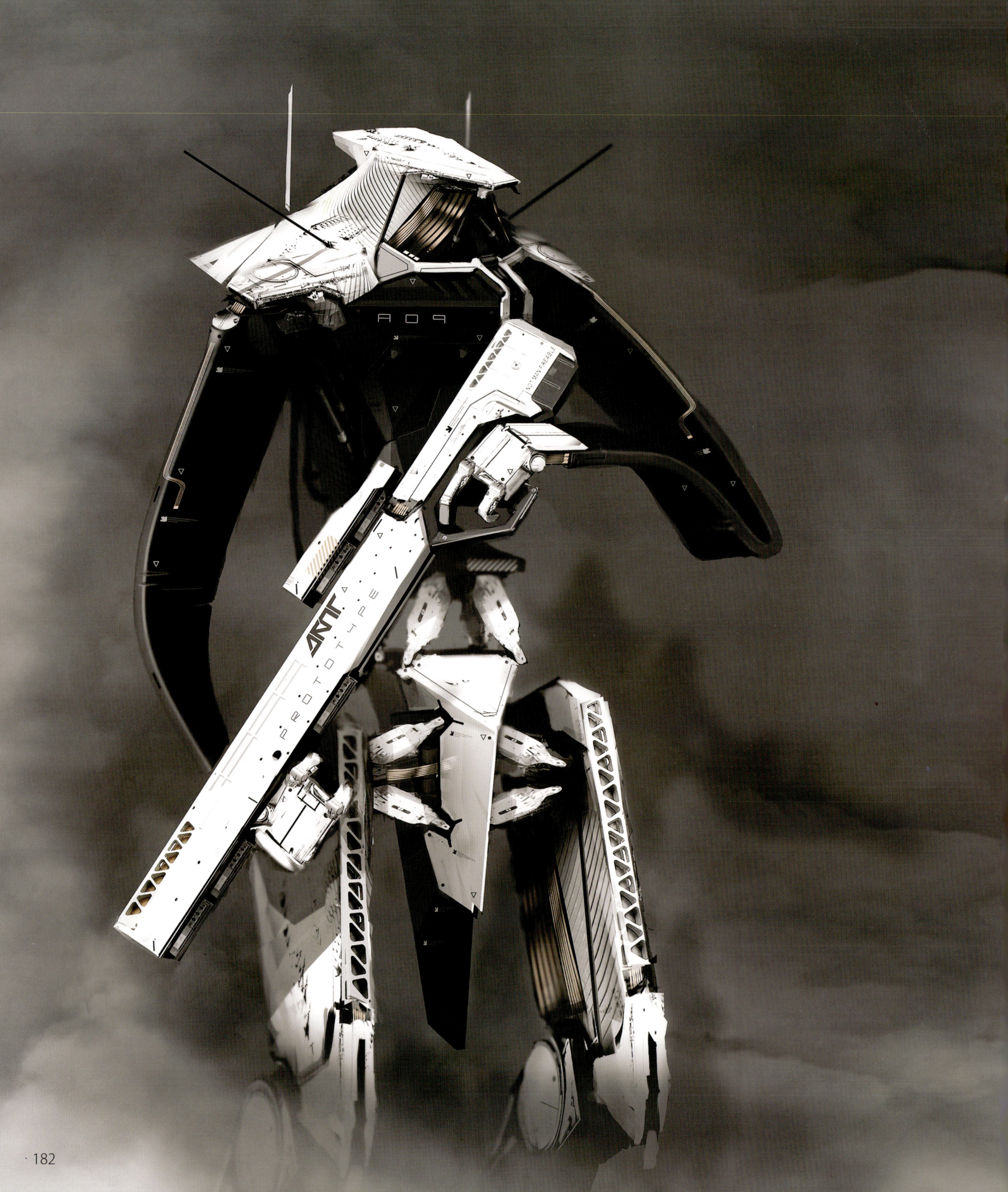
A09
NOT MAN FIREABLE
ARTF
PROTOTYPE

To: Dan <daniel.rooster@spaceforce.dot.gov>
Subject: WTF

Dan

Thanks for the F.A.A.R. slides. I'm not sure what to say. I mean . . . it's obviously just a remodel of the Lib. VI. Did they think we wouldn't notice? Just because this time they painted it white!? What part of SPACE does F.A.A.R. not get? I sure hope they secretly invented an artificial gravity generator and that their stupid robot army comes with ten of those for free. JK.

Tell them to sell these waddling hunks of crap to somebody else and instead build me a sphere with some thrusters and lasers on it. How hard can it be FFS? Get back to them asap, and keep me posted.

Best,
Franz

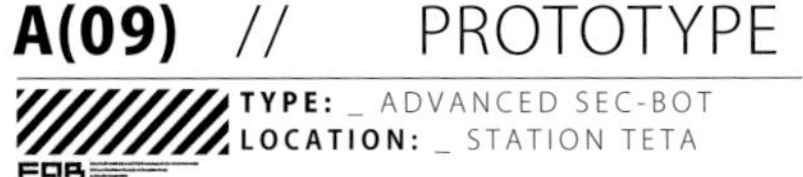

White Lynx was the first prototype in a new line of space-ready robots by F.A.A.R. Defense Systems. It was developed for hunter-killer operations and the first design powered by no less than four F.A.A.R. fusion-sphere-cores™.

LYNX // PROTOTYPE

TYPE: _ ADVANCED SEC-BOT
LOCATION: _ STATION TETA

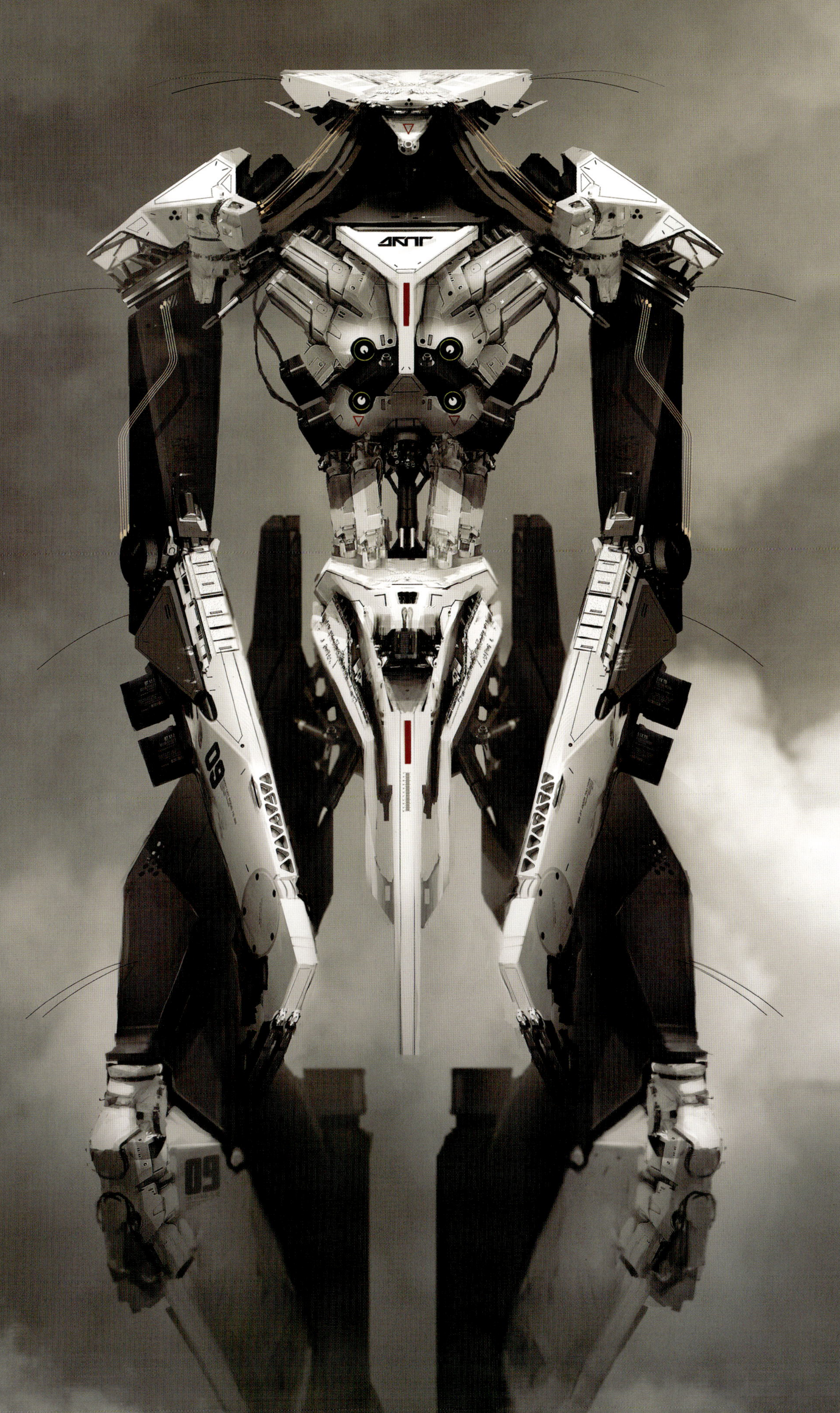
09

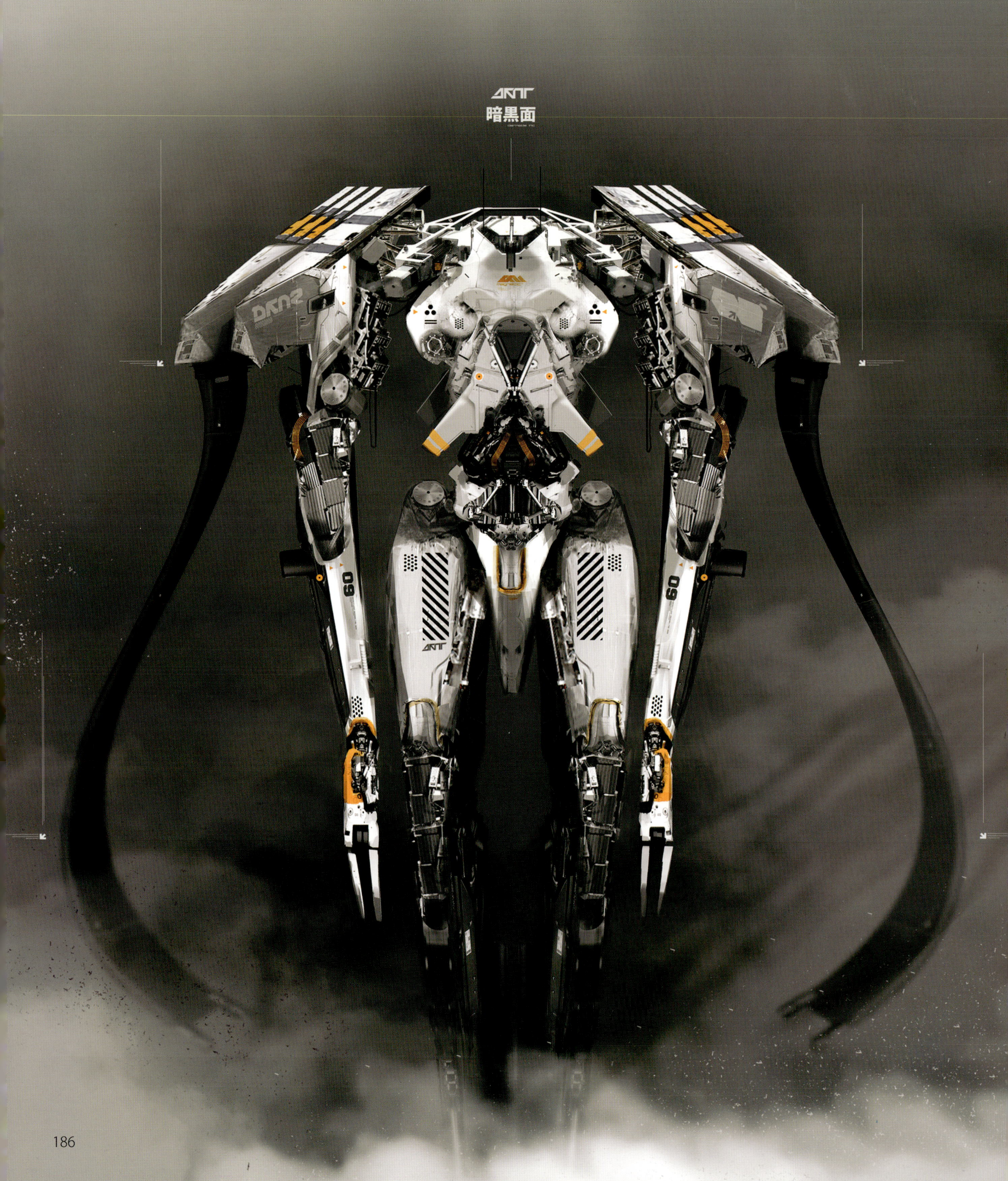
暗黑面

Almost the entire first tranche of the Cloud Seeker suffered from a cascading containment failure in its F.A.A.R. fusion-sphere-cores™. At least 12 of them are still circling the globe as space debris today.

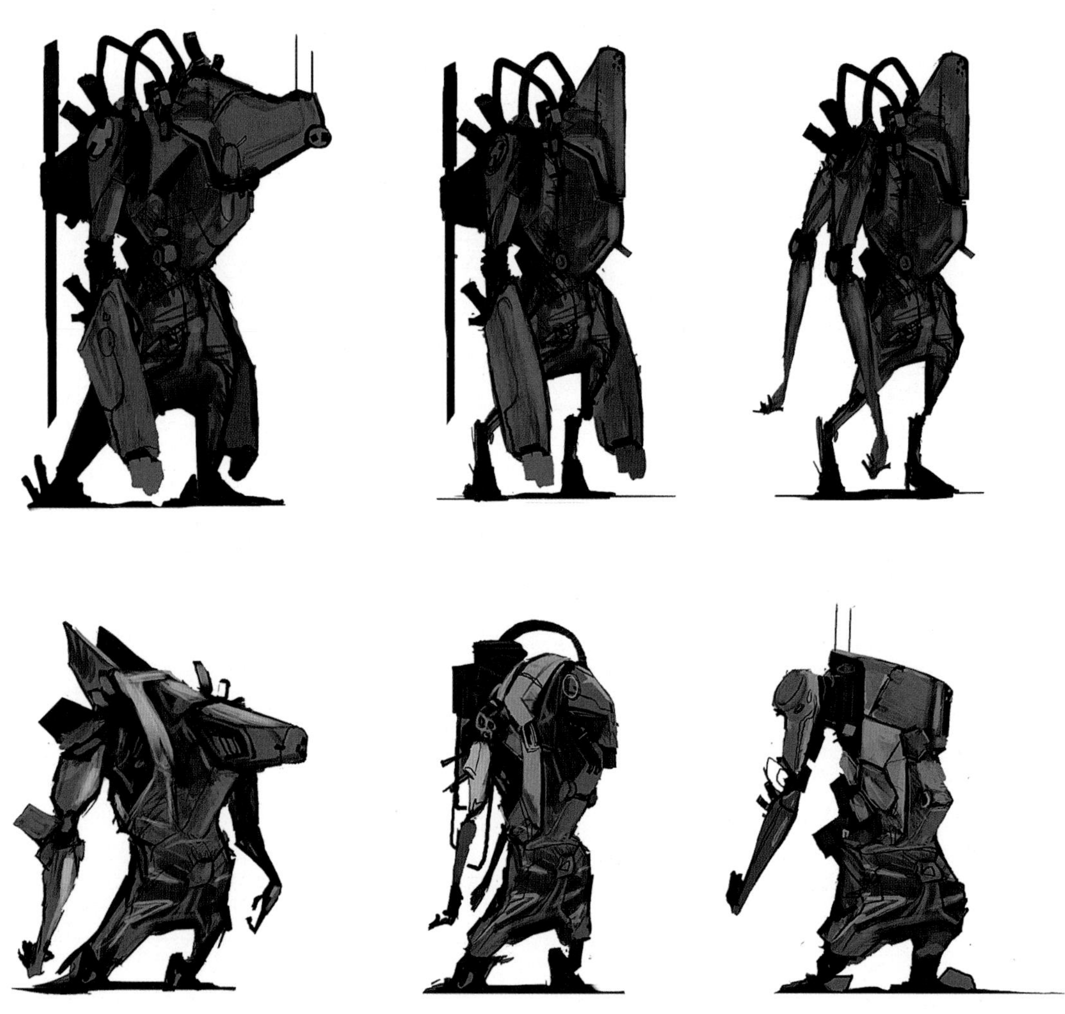

F.A.A.R. Defense Systems cryptoshares plummeted 16 percent on Monday. Turns out their new nuke-proof suit isn't so nuke-proof after all.

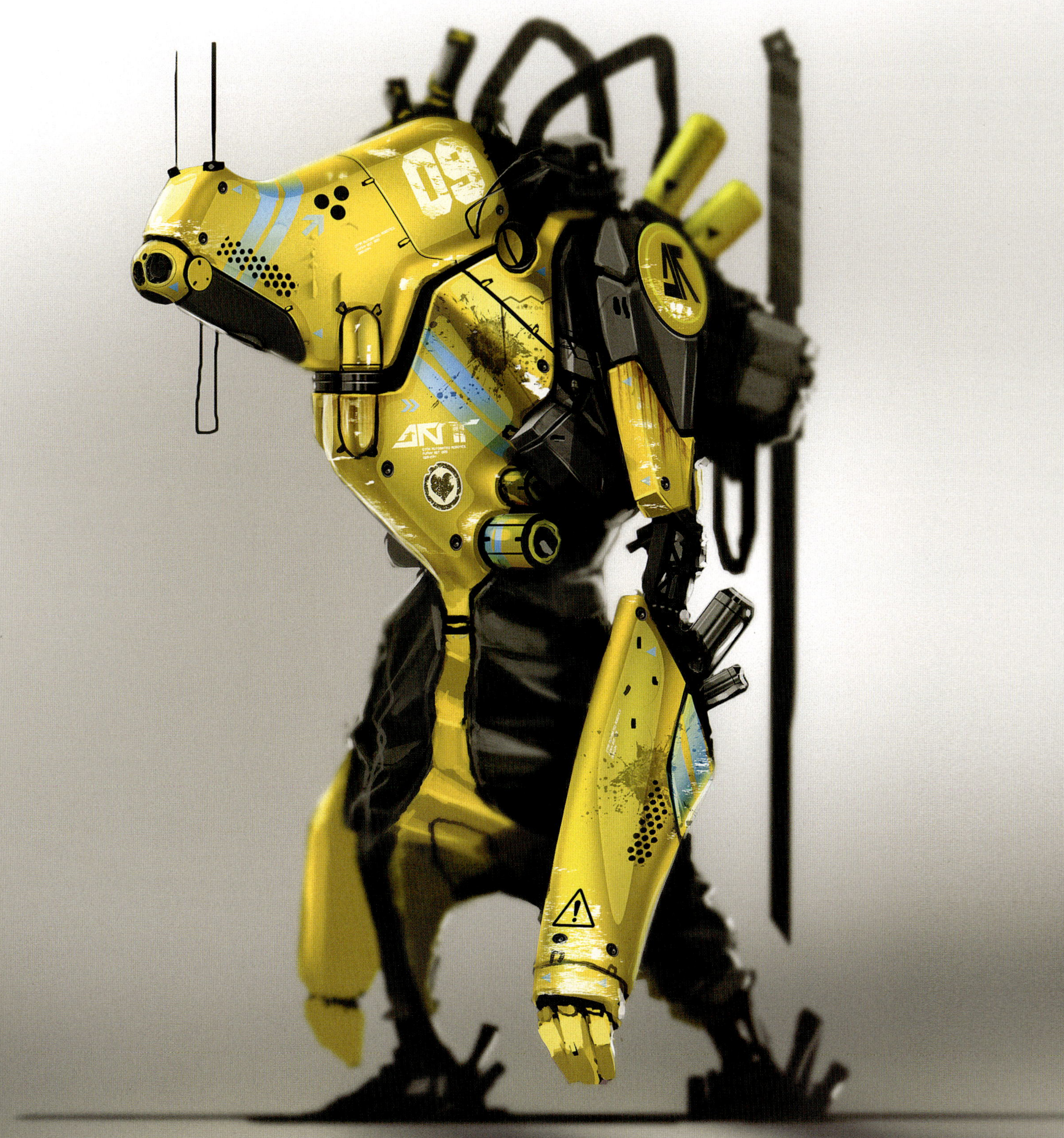
09

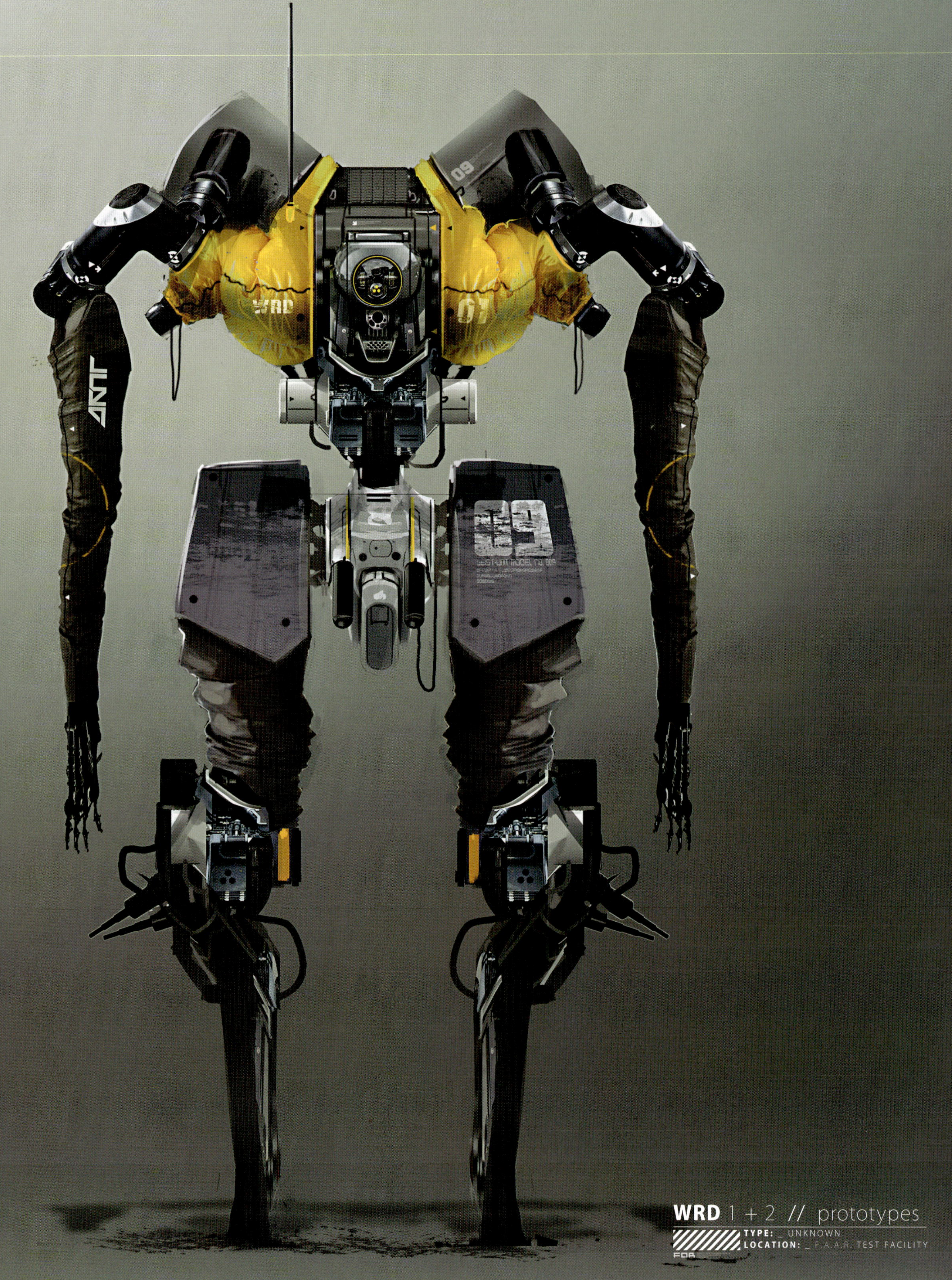

WRD 1 + 2 // prototypes
TYPE: _ UNKNOWN
LOCATION: _ F.A.A.R. TEST FACILITY

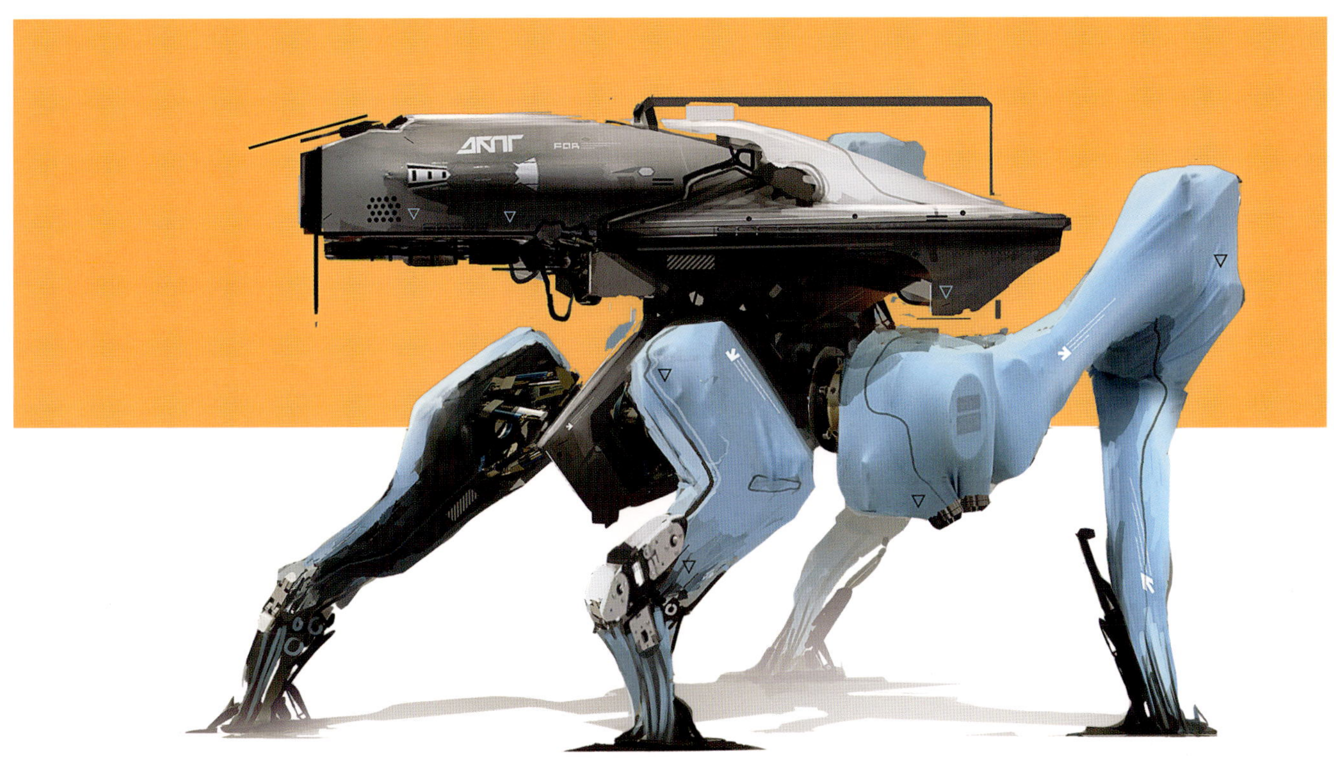

Bloomberg Business—F.A.A.R. Defense Systems' R&D costs cut in struggle to end vicious cycle.

To break free from the aftereffects of the now infamous "nuke-proof suit debacle", termed by many analysts the biggest blunder in recent company history, embattled F.A.A.R. Defense Systems CEO Jack "Gunny" Gruber announced F.A.A.R.'s new line of multipurpose auto-bots in an investor call . . .
updated 22 seconds ago

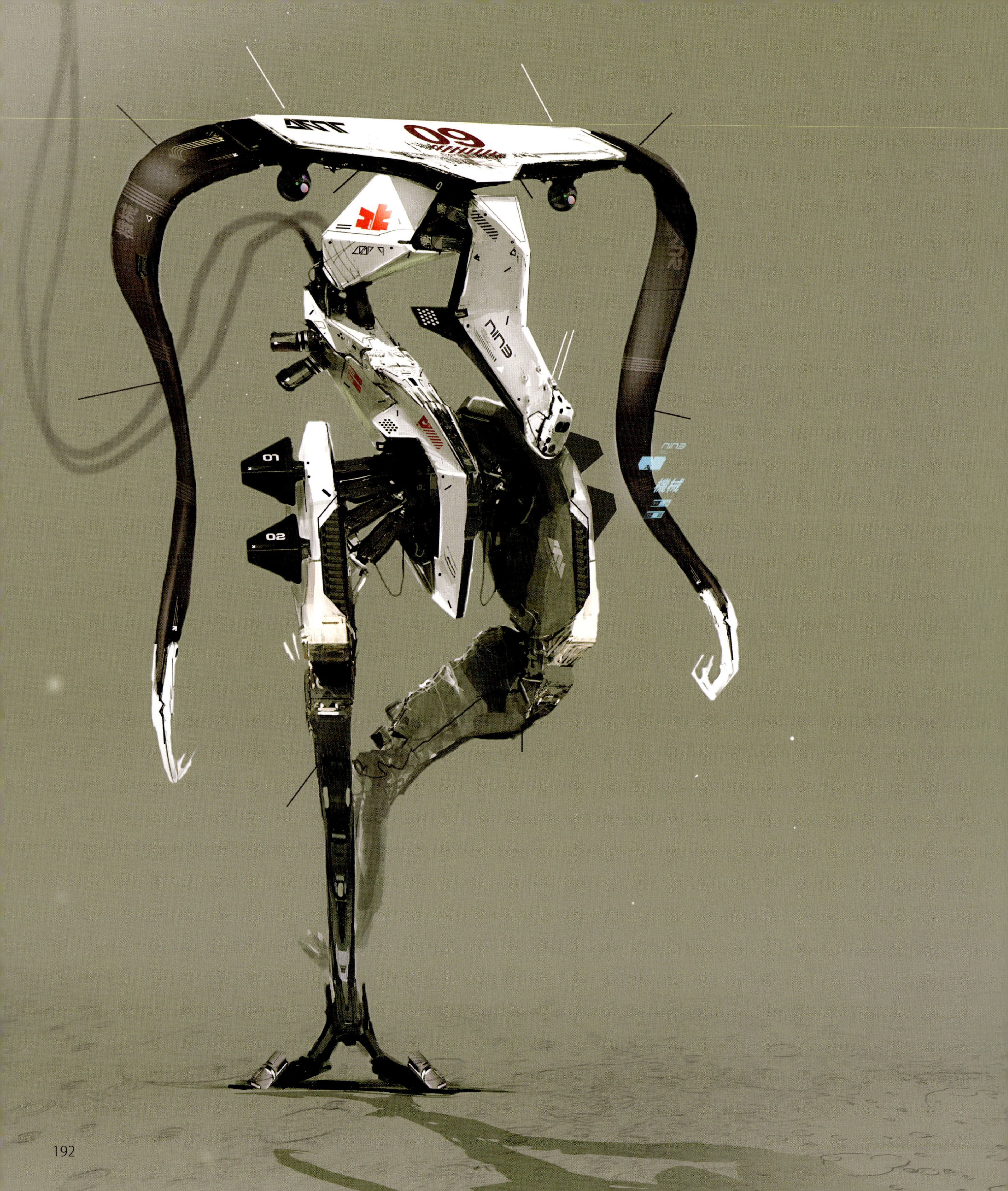

If you can lose it, we can find it! Our brand-new space-ready, Finder 09 Unit is equipped with state-of-the-art quantum sensor technology—to find anything, anywhere, now!

FINDER 09 // prototype

TYPE: _ RETRIEVER
LOCATION: _ SPACE

395 CREEPER // type.09

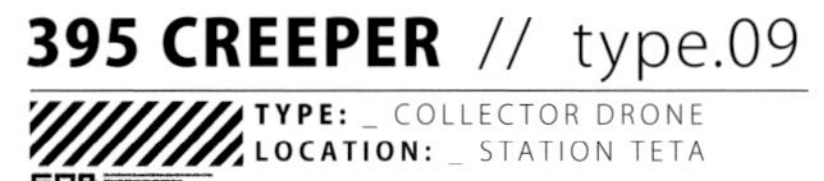

395 Creeper was a collector-type drone. Finder was the pointer, Creeper the retriever. But Creeper lifespans tended to be limited. The rare, high-quality items in their storage tanks made them a welcome target for 2Fly members hacking into their quantum-encrypted control links. The program was stopped due to the many obvious design flaws.

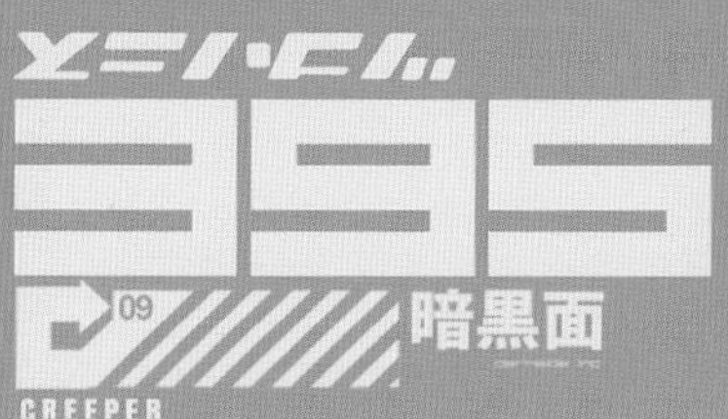
395
09
暗黒面
CREEPER

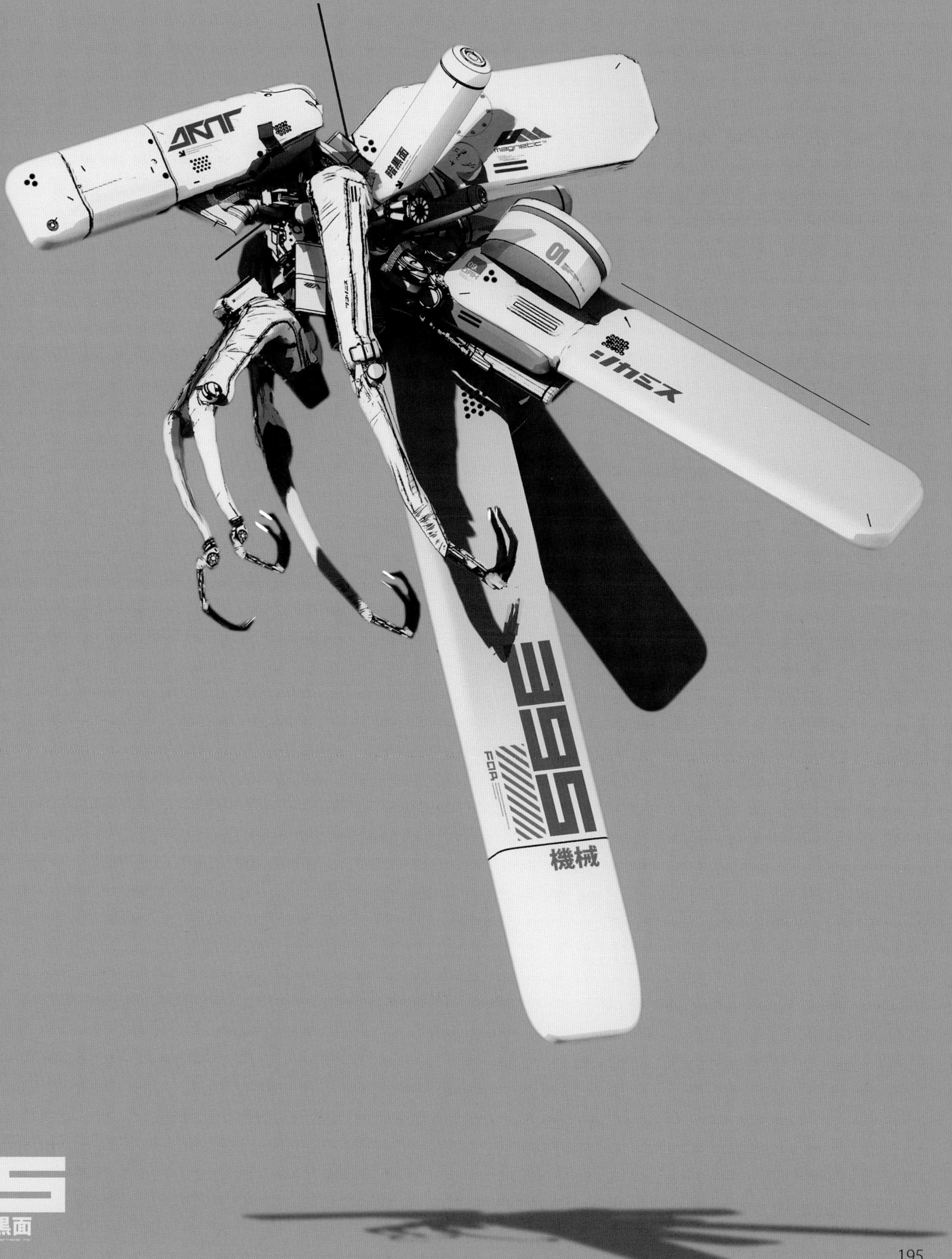

FROG DRONE // FRG-DRN

TYPE: _ **NANO** DRONE
LOCATION: _ SOUTH AMERICA

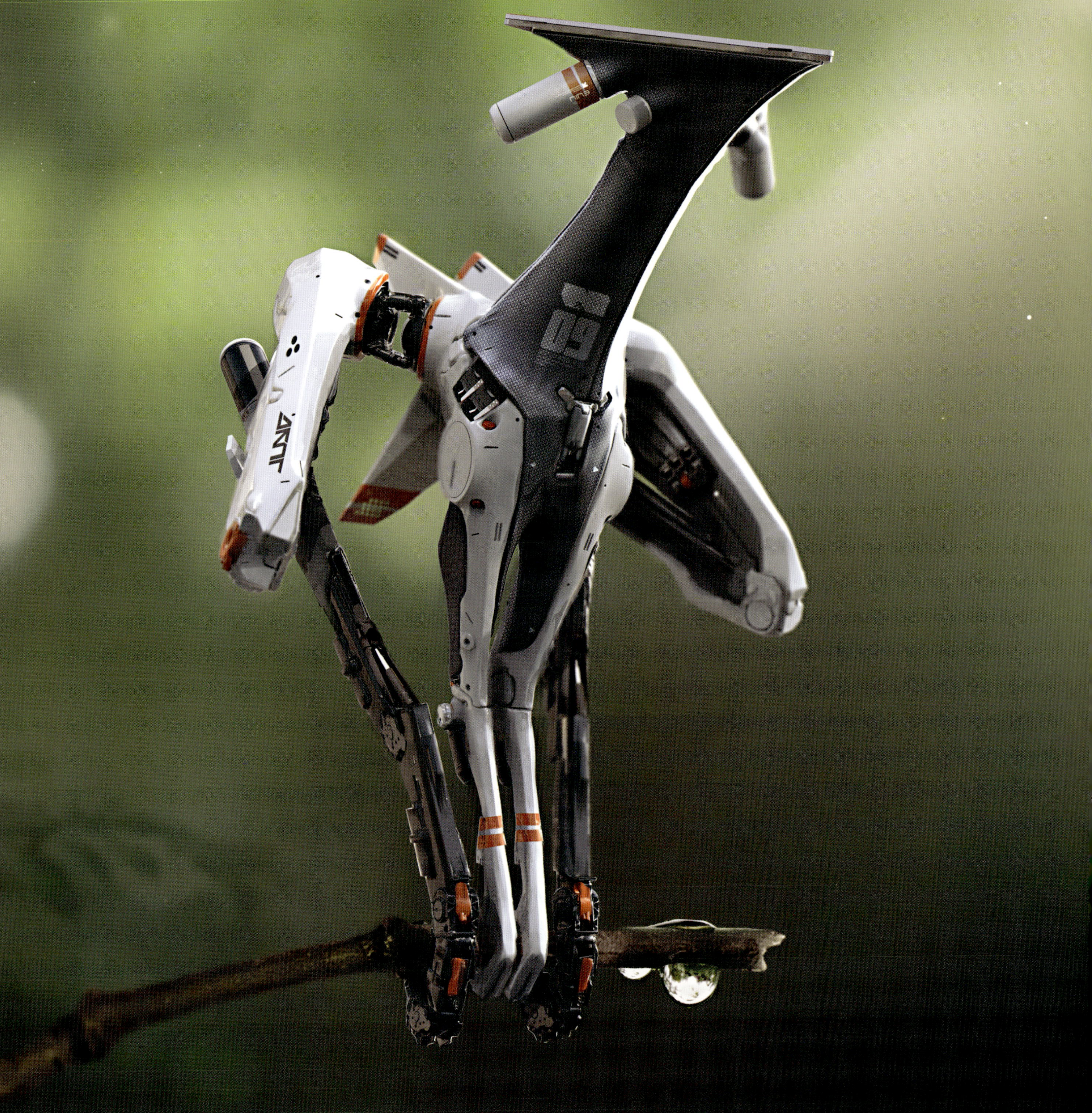

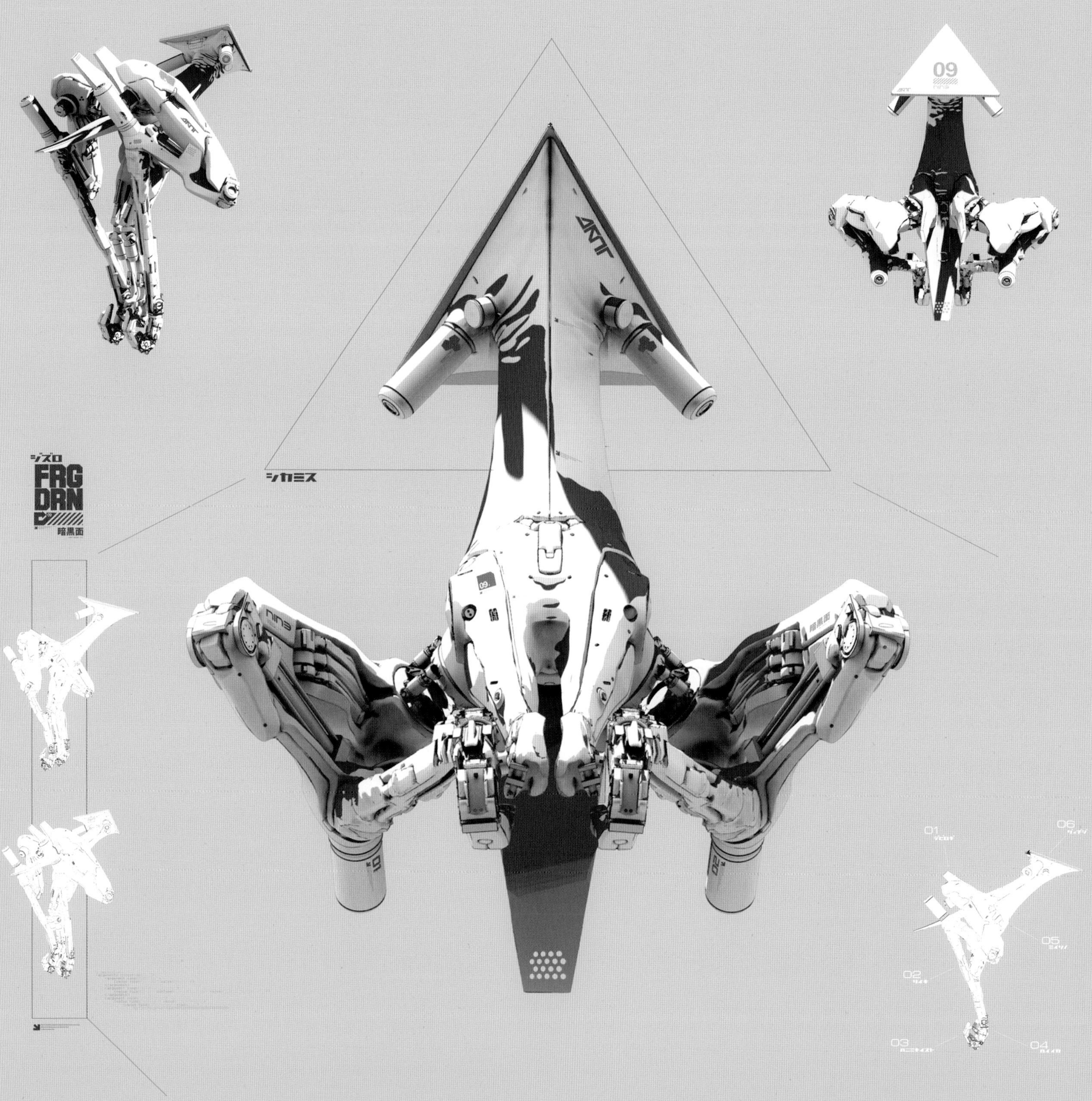

The FRG drone developed by DTNR Robotics around 2049 was the most controversial nano robotics project of its decade. It remains hotly debated until today. Critics claim it was the most useless piece of nanotech ever fielded. What was it supposed to do? The original purpose of the FRG DRN was never communicated, and it still remains a mystery. #savethefrogdrone

Tekker 9.0 was an ambitious advanced research and development project by RIGID SKIN™, a small skunk-works startup manufacturer of experimental exoskeletons. Tekker was a complicated puzzle of sensor arrays, quantum processors, NR interfaces, and high-performance antennas. The idea was to hack into and control all robots in a one-mile radius. This ability, as well as its overall look, gave it the nickname "Mantis." It never entered production.

TEKKER 9.0 // betatest

TYPE: _ ADVANCED SEC-BOT
LOCATION: _ STATION TETA

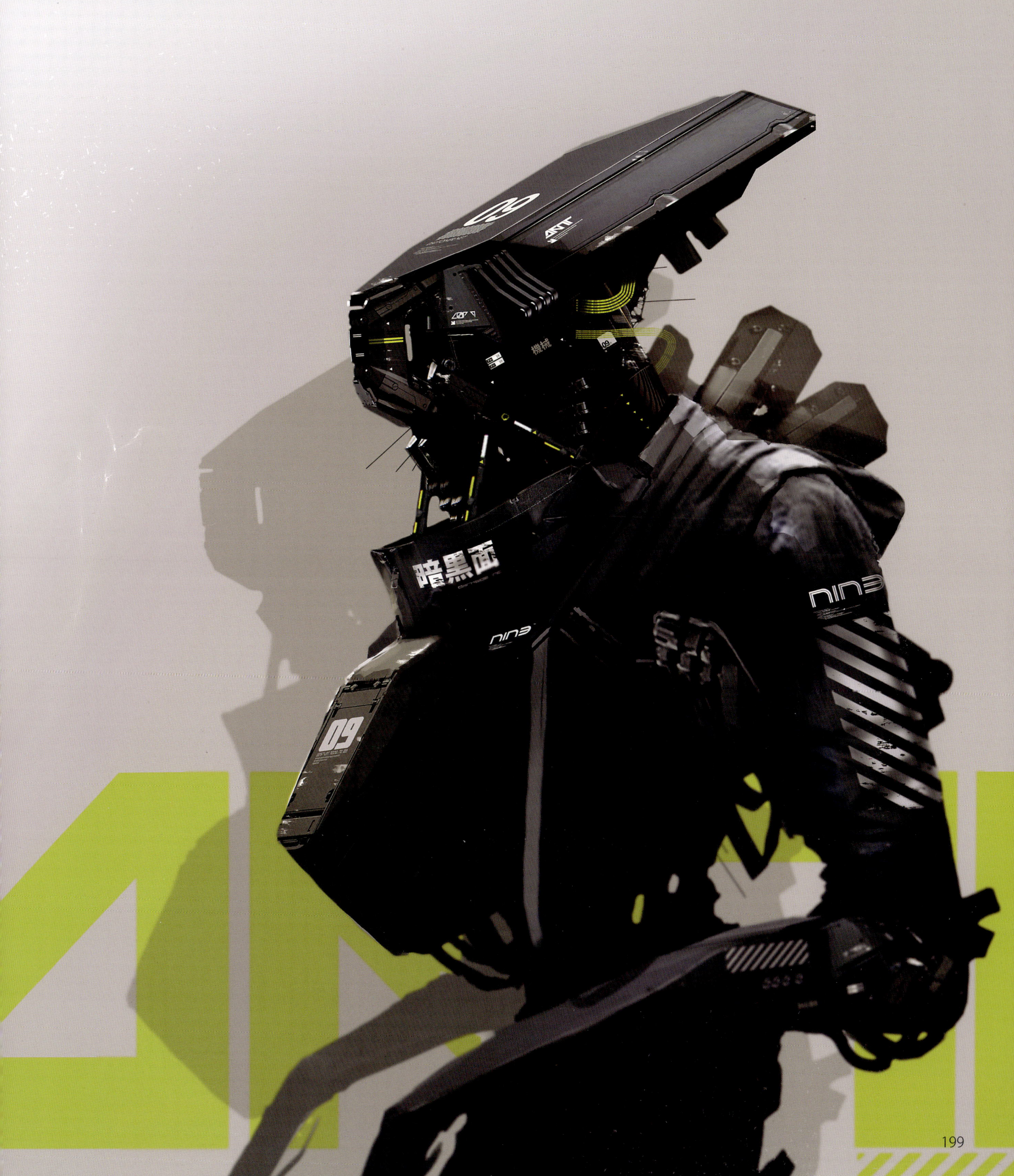
09
機械
暗黒面
09

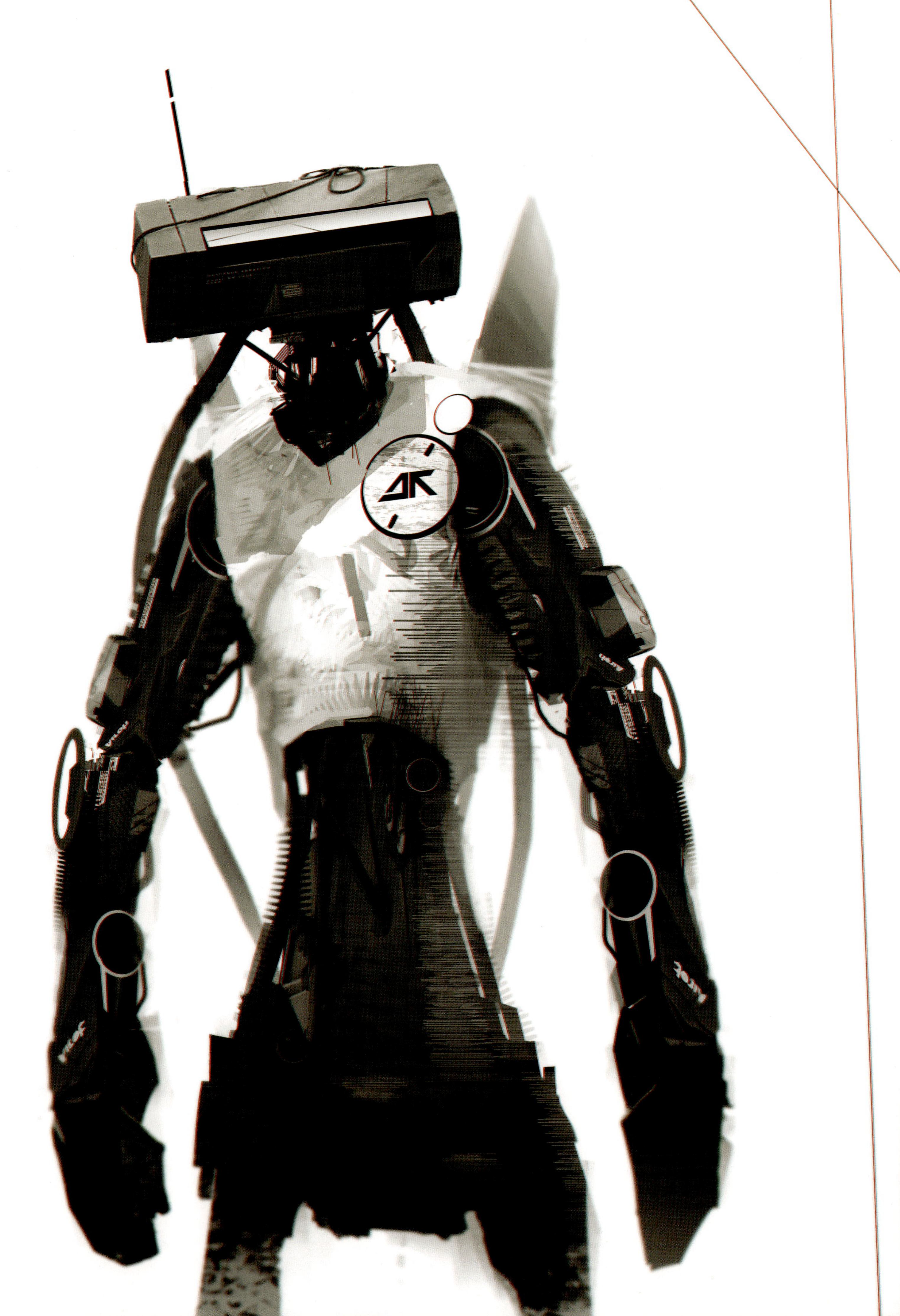

On Monday, the controversial designer Daytoner launched the new Boxhead collection as part of his new "*Enslaving Humanity in Style!*" campaign. Why the fashionable killer robots, you ask? Because it is such a comforting feeling to know that the last thing you might ever see looks oh, so, pret-t-y . . .

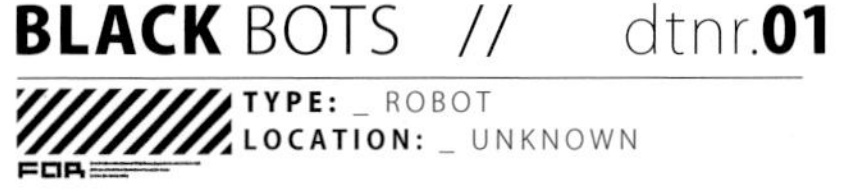

Tech changed. We didn't.

X-PLORE // mark. **09**

TYPE: _ SPACE SUIT
LOCATION: _ UNKNOWN

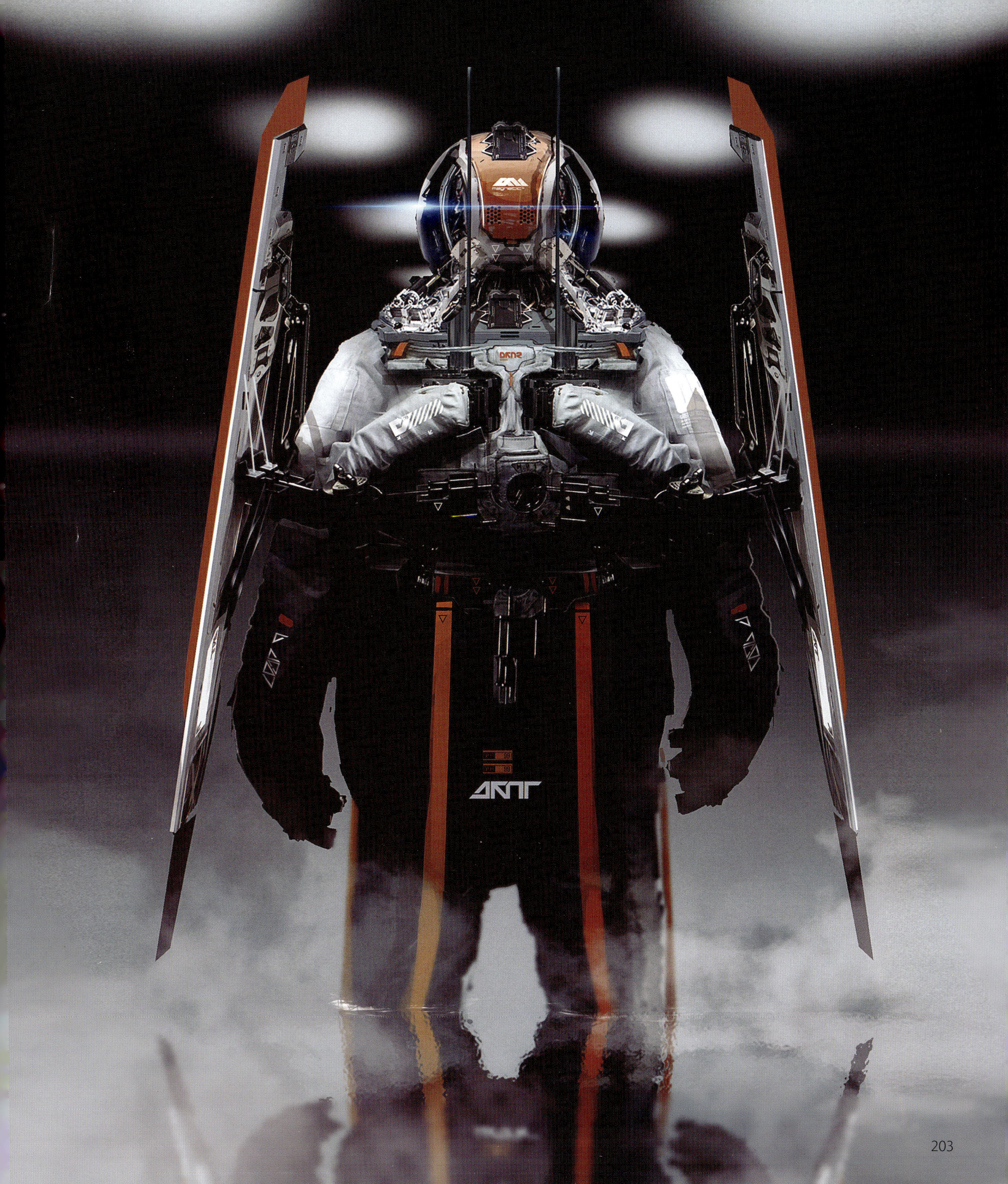

We believed the future would be hostile and dark. But when they finally attacked, the sun was still shining.

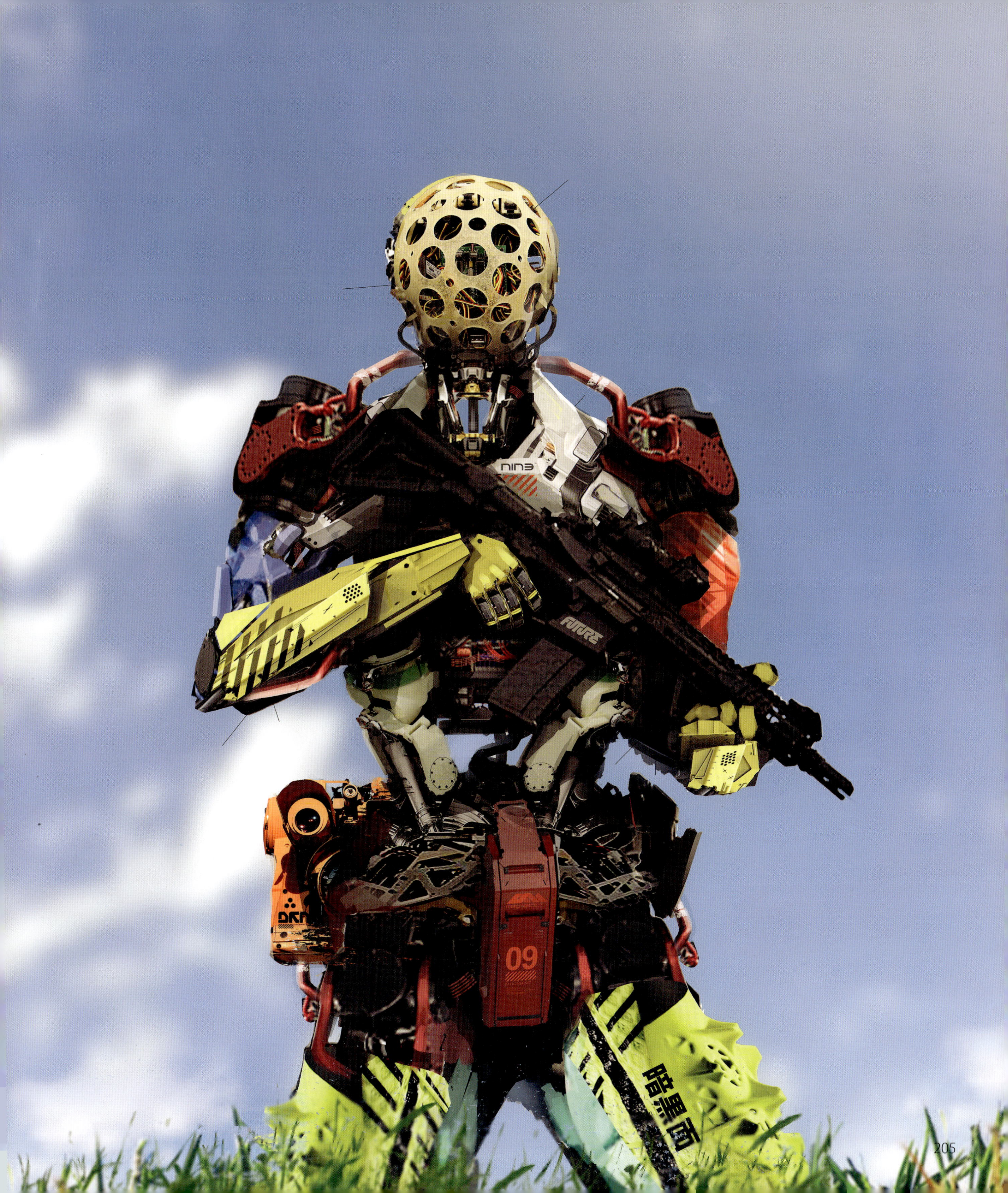
nin3
FUTURE
09

"Last time I saw that look in your eyes was back in Berlin," Emil said. "When it was freezing. Remember?"

It earned him one of Rune's irritated side glances. "Yeah, yeah, that time the engine was off. I remember. It's just . . . these damn chicken legs give me the creeps."

Rune kept watching the drone feed intently, scratching his beard. His display showed a cluster of red dots emerging from a derelict building at the outskirts of town. "And this looks like a fresh batch of Libbies to me," he said, putting his finger on the display.

Emil sighed. "All right then. Nuke them from orbit?"

Rune shrugged. "It's the only way to be sure."

GLOSSARY

Adaptive camouflage	Cloaking technology using metamaterials to bend visible light, near-infrared and thermal/IR around an object.
AI	Acronym: Artificial Intelligence
Anime	Anime is colloquial for Japanese animation and refers specifically to animation produced in Japan.
AR	Acronym: Augmented Reality
Augmentation	Used as shorthand for both Human Augmentation (see below) as well as the societal fault line between augmented and non-augmented humans due to the various legal, ethical, and religious points of contention between them.
Avatar	Representation of a person, usually in virtual environments.
Blinding laser weapon ban	Protocol IV to the 1980 Convention on Certain Conventional Weapons, aka Protocol on Blinding Laser Weapons, 13 October 1995, United Nations, Geneva. Article 1 states: "It is prohibited to employ laser weapons specifically designed as their sole combat function or as one of their combat functions to cause permanent blindness to unenhanced vision..."
Church of Singularity	Religious institution based on Judeo-Christian and Panpsychic Mysticism founded by Singularists in the early 2030s.
Cranial	Technological (usually modular and swappable) prosthetic replacing parts or the entirety of a human head, usually providing various augmentations.
Cyberpunk	Science fiction subgenre with a heavy emphasis on technology and radical social change or upheaval.
Dark District	Post Berlin's ...weird quarter. No non-augmented human has ever set foot in it.
Dev Lak	The European historian, author and public intellectual. Professor of Critical Digital History at Camford University.
Dimethyltryptamine	(DMT) Substance naturally occurring in many plants and animals known to induce powerful psychedelic experiences in humans when inhaled, ingested, or injected.
DOODES	Mixed robot and posthuman clan characterized by its members' unique, extremely stylized appearance.
DTNR	Acronym for Daytoner, the early-twenty-first-century designer and fashion enthusiast.
DTNR Robotics	Robotics and AI company, founded in 2028 (no known connections to the aforementioned artist).
F.A.A.R Defense Systems	Defense Contractor, founded in 1986

Global Machine Revolution	A collective term for the radical political and societal changes put forward by Posthumanists.
Graffiti	Publicly visible writings or drawings on walls, usually created illegally.
Human augmentation	Technological alteration of the human body to enhance physical or mental capabilities.
Kabuki	Classical Japanese dance theatre
Kit bash	Practice in which some new artefact or piece of technology is created by reassembling pieces of similar, available objects.
Levitation	Process of staying aloft, stably, defying gravity without mechanical support.
LIDAR	Acronym: laser imaging, detection, and ranging, a versatile method for determining the distance to an object using reflected light, allowing for three-dimensional representations of the sensor's surroundings.
M9E	Acronym: Master Nine Eyes, a popular vinyl art toy ca. 2019
Manga	Japanese comics and graphic novels
NATO	Acronym: North Atlantic Treaty Organization
Nakatomi Industries	Tech and Defense Corporation, founded in 2007
Nanobots	Tiny robots with components at or near the scale of a nanometer (10-9 meters)
Neuralace	A family of external and implantable brain-machine-interfaces (BMI)
Neuro stimulator	Family of BMIs for modulating a range of nervous system activities
NR	Acronym: No Reality
Original internet	The global system of interconnected computer networks from the late 1960s (Arpanet) until the end of the cloud era in the middle of the twenty-first century.
Panpsychism	Philosophical position according to which consciousness or aspects of it are a fundamental and ubiquitous feature of physical reality and all matter in the universe.
Posthumanism	A movement following in the footsteps of transhumanism, advocating for the radical improvement and expansion of the human experience by fusing with technology and completely replacing all biological aspects of human life.
Quantum cryptocoms	Communication device using the quantum mechanical phenomenon of entanglement to transfer information in a manner that does not allow for secret eavesdropping by third parties.
Quantum magnetometer	Measuring device using the spin of subatomic particles to determine the magnetic flux density at a given point in space.
Quantum mind barrier	A non-scientific term used to describe the various technical and biological hurdles involved in performing a stable quantum state extraction on human brain microtubules.
Shabu Shabu	Japanese hotpot dish

Shamanism	Renewed, widespread religious practice aimed at contacting the spirit world, often including altered states of consciousness, characteristic for the post-AI age beginning in the mid-2050s.
SilicInt Inc.	Chinese multinational tech megaconglomerate headquartered in Shanghai, founded 2030, industry leader in AI development.
Singularity	The historical tipping point in which ever-faster cycles of technology with the ability to self-improve creates a runaway effect, resulting in a future unforeseeable for humans.
Skunkworks	Moniker for small, radically innovative research and development enterprises.
Techwear	Abbreviation of "technical wear"; the term given to apparel and accessories which combine technical functionality with a futuristic aesthetic.
"The awkward thing"	You know what it is. First "accomplished" by Basher and Sunny Sideup.
Time tunnel technology	Misnomer for a portable, military-grade quantum state extrapolation device first introduced by DTNR Robotics.
Urban exploration	Illegal exploration of usually old, abandoned, hidden, derelict man-made structures, often including various risks and physical dangers.
Urban ninja	Initially a social movement characterized by combining the embrace of human augmentation with various youth culture practices, such as cosplay, which would later become formative for the appearance of most of the world's organized crime.
Vertical Skies	Popular, commercially successful, critically acclaimed, unusually long-lived entertainment franchise, released as a video game first in 2027, subsequently developing into various spin-offs and a full-fledged metaverse.
VR	Acronym: Virtual Reality
Zenith	Fictional giant structure floating in—and piercing through—Earth's atmosphere in the late 2020s video game version of *Vertical Skies*.

Thanks to my mom and dad for supporting me all this time (my entire life, really) and for letting me go out at night to do graffiti with my friends when I was only sixteen. Thanks to my little family here in LA! Thanks to Master TZ for giving me a fresh look on to the world through the eyes of a kid, and to Yvi for giving me the time to nerd out on this stuff. Thanks to Frank for contributing to the book. And last but not least: big up Schoko!

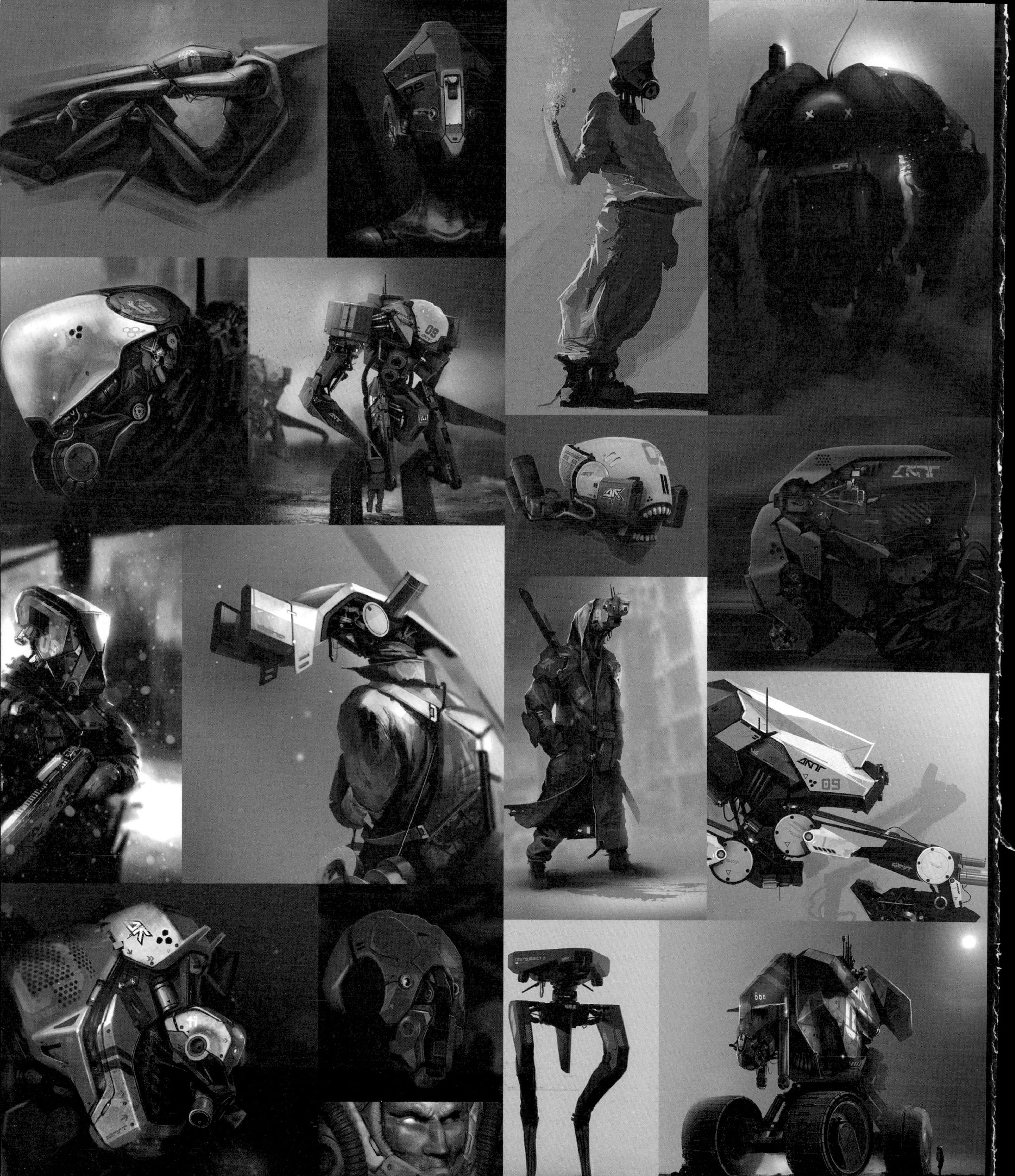